A Queer Sort of Materialism

For Ronn —
    With much appreciation
    and love.
        Dim

TRIANGULATIONS
Lesbian/Gay/Queer ▲ Theater/Drama/Performance

Titles in the series:

Tony Kushner in Conversation
  edited by Robert Vorlicky

*Passing Performances: Queer Readings of Leading Players
in American Theater History*
  edited by Robert A. Schanke and Kim Marra

*When Romeo Was a Woman: Charlotte Cushman
and Her Circle of Female Spectators*
  by Lisa Merrill

Camp: Queer Aesthetics and the Performing Subject
  edited by Fabio Cleto

Staging Desire: Queer Readings of American Theater History
  edited by Kim Marra and Robert A. Schanke

A Problem Like Maria: Gender and Sexuality in the American Musical
  by Stacy Wolf

A Queer Sort of Materialism: Recontextualizing American Theater
  by David Savran

A Queer Sort of Materialism

recontextualizing american theater

David Savran

the university of michigan press

Ann Arbor

Copyright © by the University of Michigan 2003
All rights reserved
Published in the United States of America by
The University of Michigan Press
Manufactured in the United States of America
♾ Printed on acid-free paper

2006   2005   2004   2003   4   3   2   1

*A CIP catalog record for this book is available from the
British Library.*

Library of Congress Cataloging-in-Publication Data

Savran, David, 1950–
    A queer sort of materialism : recontextualizing American theater /
David Savran.
        p.   cm. — Triangulations
    Includes bibliographical references and index.
    ISBN 0-472-09836-5 (acid-free paper) — ISBN 0-472-06836-9 (pbk. :
acid-free paper)
    1. Gay theater—United States.   2. American drama—20th
century—History and criticism.   3. Gay men's writings, American.   4.
Homosexuality in literature.   5. Sex role in literature.   I. Title.
II. Series.
PN2270.G39 S28 2003
791'.086'640973—dc21   2002153618

To Scott

You're romance,
You're the steppes of Russia,
You're the pants on a Roxy usher.
   —Cole Porter

Preface

Sitting on the beach at Fire Island with my boyfriend, Scott, feeling the hot sand between my toes, listening to the gently breaking waves, I watched the men pass by. They were tanned, buff, liposucted, and rich, while I was an unrepentant academic with a taste for theater, historical materialism, and windswept utopias. Gazing at nature and artifice so cunningly intertwined, I thought about the meaning of the spectacle passing in front of me. Fire Island may be one of the most uncloseted spots on earth, the scent of sex and money hanging heavily in the sultry air. But the Speedo-clad Apollos are hardly the only things that suggest that there is far more on this fragile sandbar than greets the uninitiated eye. For like all playgrounds, Fire Island is a place of relentless dissimulation in which what you see is never quite what you get. On this most ravishingly material—and materialistic—of islands, nakedness paradoxically covers up the difference between rich and poor, property owner and time-sharer, David Geffen and the day-tripper at the water's edge.

Later that same afternoon, as Scott and I joined the parade walking up and down the beach, we talked about the difficulty of reading the signs. And I confessed, not for the first time, that I felt rather out of place. Here I am, a man committed to Marxist scholarship, in this place of sensual overload. Not that Marxism requires an abnegation of the senses. On the contrary. But it has long been linked to dry, intellectualized tongue-wagging and finger-pointing. If, however, you sit down and actually read Marx—something even I was not about to do on the beach—you will see that he was obsessed with the texture and materiality of everyday life; with the richness of the sensuous world; and with real, active human subjects, producing and reproducing willy-nilly. I thought about how my scholarship has similarly been obsessed with materiality, with the materiality of desiring bodies and the materiality of culture. I asked Scott to indulge my academic fantasy for a moment and told him I wished I could bring my recent essays together in a volume that focused on these two kinds of materiality, the sexual and the cultural—which are in fact one kind of materiality. That is the book you are holding in your hands.

Although resorts are designed to make us forget the workaday world from which we have momentarily escaped, my brief sojourn on Fire Island reminded me yet again of the very different worlds I inhabit and the very different kinds of persons with whom I routinely speak. My desire to converse so liberally is certainly linked to my vocation as a theater scholar. For theater is an activity in which many Americans delight (not least among them my friends) because they can take it more seriously than most forms of mass culture. So many theatergoers, especially in New York, have fashioned themselves highly professionalized spectators. Most of the men on the beach, for example, would have been quite willing to offer an informed opinion of the new Terrence McNally play or the latest soft-core revue titled something like *Cute Boys in Their Underpants Sing Your Favorite Showtunes.* Moving back and forth between communal dinners in our Fire Island time-share and the academic world in which I spend so much of my time, I am always conscious of the need to address different audiences. And I feel this need ever more urgently because I am committed to progressive scholarship.

In Jill Dolan's study of the American academic domain, *Geographies of Learning,* she analyzes the position of intellectuals and argues that progressive scholars must be prepared to participate in many different kinds of conversations. Because we academics all move among many communities, it is not enough to address our students and professional associates in the relatively esoteric language we employ in scholarly articles and seminars. Rather, Dolan forcefully advocates: "Respect and engage the new theoretical vocabularies while taking [care to] translate them for less specialized audiences. Practice code switching and stay aware of the multiple contexts into which we speak." She suggests, in other words, that we address multiple constituencies using their vernaculars, that we publish both "in university presses and trade presses," and that we try even to master the art of the sound bite.[1]

Because I share her convictions, I have deliberately put together a book that speaks many languages. *A Queer Sort of Materialism* thereby testifies shamelessly to my attempts over the years to address multiple au-

diences—my friends on the beach as well as my colleagues. Two of the essays began as talks, two as scholarly articles, three as journalistic pieces,
and two were written specifically for this volume. Although most of them
now speak with an academic inflection, the pieces on Tennessee Williams, Paula Vogel, and gay cinema represent an elaboration of summer-
time conversations I had over lobster and corn on the cob. Although I deliberately write for different sets of readers, the distinction between my
more academic and more casual modes is complicated and confounded
by the fact that I have long taken pleasure in consciously mixing levels of
discourse as a way of defamiliarizing both the scholarly and the vernacular. Because I am committed to many different kinds of mixing, I believe
it immensely productive, for example, to examine the popular next to the
elite, the sacred next to the profane, and the aesthetic next to the economic. In fact, I find these juxtapositions indispensable to a historical-
materialist project of radically contextualizing different forms of cultural
production. To (re)construct the context of a play or performance, I am
obliged to defamiliarize it, to analyze its historical location, and to map
the different cultural fields in which it takes positions.

This book, however, represents more than an exercise in contextualization. It is also about the politics of pleasure, and I hope that it will provide readers with a degree of that most precious of sensations. If, to borrow a metaphor from Brecht, it does indeed represent a culinary, or
pleasure-giving, exercise, then the essays herein must be said to comprise
something of a buffet.[2] Because they were written over a period of ten
years, they testify to my attempt to cook up many different kinds of
dishes. But they also document a shift in the contents of my *batterie de
cuisine*, from the instruments used to analyze sexuality to those of a more
sociological bent. (Thus the earliest essay in this collection, "The Sadomasochist in the Closet," focuses squarely on gender and sexuality, while
a more recent piece, "Middlebrow Anxiety," virtually forsakes sex for a sociology of theatrical forms.) This change was induced in part by an experience I had several years before that day on Fire Island. As I was writing the essay on *Angels in America* that is included in this volume, and as
I was analyzing the relationship between the play's triumph on Broadway
and its inadvertent defense of liberal pluralism, I found myself increasingly fascinated by theoretical work on cultural fields and hierarchies,
especially that of Pierre Bourdieu. For it became clear to me that the

play's content is the result more of its location in the cultural hierarchy than of Tony Kushner's ideological predispositions. Although I had long accepted the intentional fallacy, I began to realize more and more that, to quote Bourdieu, the positions that producers occupy "within the field of production and circulation of symbolic goods" are in large part responsible for "determining their ideology and their practice."[3] My confidence (first inspired by Brecht) in the singular importance of an economic analysis of culture and society was, in short, reinforced.

Because the context for each essay in this volume is different, the frames of analysis change. My subjects range from Rodgers and Hammerstein to Paula Vogel, from *Suddenly Last Summer* to *Iron John,* and from Freud to the *New York Times.* The historical correlations I draw, meanwhile, range from the construction of masculinities to the economics of the performing arts, and from the imperatives of geopolitics to the structure of cultural hierarchies. Yet these essays are not a collection of random meditations. In all of them I attempt to analyze how different forms of abjection are produced. Most frequently, abjection is a result of processes of normalization, for orthodoxy defines itself only by constructing a heretical Other. In most of the texts I examine, abjection is cordoned off and associated with subjects who usually subsist on the margins of dominant social formations and whose presence in plays and other cultural forms is always vexed. These are the troublemakers—the ghost, closeted lesbian, masochist, drag king, anticolonialist, or angry white male—who, because they are both present and absent, are never offered to the unobstructed gaze of the spectator. They are the forces that disrupt—respectively, *Angels in America, In the Summer House,* "Desire and the Black Masseur," *How I Learned to Drive, Wedding on the Eiffel Tower,* and *Iron John*—the figures who I argue function as deconstructive tropes, always threatening to undo the very binary oppositions they secure.

When I first fantasized about this book on the beach at Fire Island, I knew that the coherence of the essays collected in these pages would depend not on common subject matter but on the historical-materialist method I employ. Yes, all focus on post–World War II texts. Yes, all attempt to illuminate facets of American society and culture. But they do not set forth a cohesive argument. Rather, they represent studies in different modes of contextualization. In particular, they search the social and cultural margins for those unusually revealing contexts that tend to be repressed, forgotten, or cancelled out. To do so, they no more travel the straight and narrow than Scott and I did on our walk along the water's edge. For the experience of moving among vastly different communities always reminds me that tracking context is an unmethodical method, a mode of chasing down the similar and dissimilar, visible and invisible, past and present. If this book is read as an exercise in materialist analysis, it would suggest that materialism is always (to borrow a phrase that Marx uses in a different context) "a very queer thing."[4] "Queer" in the most literal sense: "strange, odd, peculiar, eccentric, in appearance or character" (*OED*). Meandering through cultural texts, I hope to re-create the sense of strangeness, fascination, and disorientation I felt that luminous afternoon perched between the sand dunes and the sea.

Acknowledgments

Because the essays in this book were written over a span of ten years, there are many people I would like to thank. First, my tireless research assistants: Laura Braslow, Ed Brockenbrough, Mark Fitzgerald, Jesse Goldstein, Rhett Landrum, Sianne Ngai, and Jesse Wennik. Second, I want to express my appreciation to my friends and colleagues, who have given me invaluable feedback on these essays and with whom I have had many rich and productive conversations: Marvin Carlson, Gay Gibson Cima, Elin Diamond, Jill Dolan, David Hult, Jennifer Jones, Tamar Katz, Neil Lazarus, Judy Milhaus, Framji Minwalla, Andrea Most, Matt Rebhorn, Janelle Reinelt, Joe Roach, John Rouse, Susie Schmeiser, Pamela Sheingorn, Ronn Smith, Alisa Solomon, Paula Vogel, and Stacy Wolf. Third, I would like to thank Marcia LaBrenz for her excellent copyediting. Fourth, I want to single out and especially thank Rose Subotnik, with whom I twice had the privilege of teaching a class on American musical theater and from whom I have learned so much about that most distinctively American form of theater. Fifth, I owe a great debt to LeAnn Fields, who, by encouraging me to put this book together, has allowed me to think about the development of my own scholarship since 1990 and to explore the relationship between gender studies and historical materialism. Finally, I want to thank Scott Teagarden for his love and generosity and his ability to extract countless hidden gems from movies and plays. Who else would have noticed that Gore Vidal's frightful cameo in *Gattaca* was no accident? Or that the wedding scene with two brides from *In the Summer House* bears an uncanny resemblance to that in another, somewhat more frivolous 1953 text, *Gentlemen Prefer Blondes*?

Earlier and abbreviated versions of some of the essays in this book have been previously published. Parts of "Middlebrow Anxiety" appeared as "*Rent*'s Due: Multiculturalism and the Spectacle of Difference," *The Journal of American Theatre and Drama* 14, no. 1 (2002); and as "Middlebrow Anxiety," *American Theatre* (October 1999). An earlier version of "The Queerest Art" was published as "Queer Theater and the Disarticulation of Identity," in *The Queerest Art*, ed. Alisa Solomon and Framji Minwalla (New York: New York University Press, 2002). An earlier version of "The Haunted Stages of Modernity" was published in *Modern Drama* 43, no. 4 (2000). "Ambivalence, Utopia, and a Queer Sort of Materialism: How *Angels in America* Reconstructs the Nation" was first published in *Theatre Journal* 47, no. 2 (May 1995). An earlier version of "The Sadomasochist in the Closet: Sam Shepard, Robert Bly, and the New White Masculinity" was published as "The Sadomasochist in the Closet," *Contemporary Theatre Review* 8, part 3 (1998). A portion of "In and Out" was first published as "Closet Dramas," *Brown Daily Herald*, February 6, 1998.

Contents

Part I: Historical Pageants

Part II: Closet Dramas

Part I: Historical Pageants

Chapter One

Middlebrow ${A}$nxiety

The self-appointed arbiters of taste during the 1950s were obsessed with cultural hierarchies. Given their insatiable appetite for categorization, they no longer judged the opposition between highbrow and lowbrow sufficient to account for the unprecedented variety of cultural productions made in the United States, from teen movies to abstract expressionism, from bebop to *Queen for a Day,* from "Hound Dog" to *The Sound of Music.* The terms *highbrow* and *lowbrow* were widely popularized, despite the fact that, as Michael Kammen points out, they "derived from the mid-Victorian fascination with cranial capacity, a curiously racist outlook that equated one [term] with high intelligence and the other with very limited mental abilities."[1] Although the nineteenth-century phrenology that coined the words had long been discredited, the racist implications of these categories were less forgotten than disavowed in a society that was just beginning a long and violent process of desegregation. Nevertheless, the binary opposition produced by these terms could provide no more than a crude map of the patterns of cultural consumption during the post–World War II boom years, years that institutionalized bowling leagues and paid vacations and brought television, long-playing records, and paperback books into almost every American home.

To complicate the opposition between highbrow and lowbrow, the arbiters of taste started increasingly to use the term *middlebrow,* an elastic category into which a great many cultural productions could conveniently fall. Although the word dates from the 1920s, "it did not," as Janice Radway notes, "become a prominent part of the cultural mapping until significantly later."[2] By February 1949, middlebrow's moment had arrived. Russell Lynes penned a gently satirical essay for *Harper's* entitled "Highbrow, Lowbrow, Middlebrow" that caused quite a stir. *Life* magazine homed in on the story, "summarizing Lynes's bemused conclusions about American taste" and publishing a "two-page 'chart' [by Tom Funk] that classified and exemplified the public's taste levels in everything from clothes, entertainment, and drinks to reading, phonograph records, and games." *Life*'s article became so popular that pigeonholing one's brow level became "for many months" a "favorite parlor game."[3] Despite his essay's title, Lynes in fact produces four categories by dividing middlebrow into "upper" and "lower," the former peopled by "the principal purveyors of highbrow ideas," "cultural do-gooders" like publishers and art dealers, and the latter by "the principal consumers of what the upper middlebrows pass along to them."[4] Given his bemused tone, he is remarkably tolerant of differences in taste, unlike most of the critics who later weighed in on the subject—including Dwight Macdonald, Clement Greenberg, and Leslie Fiedler—who were far more condemnatory, far more concerned to position themselves in the highbrow category.

Although these cultural critics (all of them associated with *Partisan Review* or other so-called little magazines) were at best distrustful, at worst contemptuous, of lowbrow, they reserved a special animus for the middlebrow culture from which they were so eager to distance themselves. As Andrew Ross emphasizes, the Cold War "age of consensus, which established liberal pluralism as the ideal model of a fully democratic, classless society . . . depended, to a degree hitherto uncalled for, on the cultural authority of intellectuals," most of them leftists formerly associated with the Popular Front who were trying to navigate between the Scylla of anti-Stalinism and the Charybdis of McCarthyism. All felt a palpable distress over "terms like 'class' and 'mass,' so redolent of that vestigial marxist culture," and endeavored to contain "intellectual radicalism and cultural populism alike."[5] Their obsession with taste thus represents an attempt to purge the social body of dangerous, seditious, and degrading cultural commodities and to educate and uplift. And they did so by championing a distortingly aestheticized rendering of the work of the high priests of the modernist avant-garde (Eliot, Joyce, Pi-

casso, Stravinsky, and Frank Lloyd Wright), all of whom, Dwight Macdonald—incorrectly—alleges, "turned their backs on the marketplace,
preferring to work for a small audience that . . . was sophisticated
enough to understand them."[6]

The cachet of highbrow culture was dependent on its purported refusal of commodity status and its ability to function as a signifier of cultural purity, consecration, and asceticism during a period marked by the
widespread and unprecedented availability of luxury goods, both utili-
tarian and decorative. For the hierarchization of taste did not correspond with social class. Lowbrow taste was almost always associated
with a fraction—or perhaps I should say a fantasy—of the working
class, the primitivized "masses" who were usually seen as dupes, or potential dupes, for those most un-American of ideologies, communism
and fascism. But "most highbrows," according to Lynes, were members
of "the ill-paid professions, notably the academic."[7] The highbrow thus
represents what Pierre Bourdieu would call a "dominated fraction of the
dominant class," a highly educated and professionalized bourgeois(e)
exiled, because of income level, from the upper classes.[8] And the highbrow's contradictory class positionality and dedication to a then old-
fashioned avant-gardism distinguished this aristocrat of taste from the
upper-class, genteel tastemakers of the late nineteenth century who, according to Joan Shelley Rubin, "assigned to the 'best men' (like themselves) the task of freeing society at large from superstition, conformity,
mediocrity, and debilitating economic competition."[9] As Ross notes, the
later Cold War highbrows, along with those arbiters of taste who were
their apologists, represented, in contrast, "archaic hangovers of earlier
modes of production" who were "still 'living off the capital' of the avant-
garde," basing their cultural authority "upon borrowed and accumulated
foreign (European) prestige." In a society undergoing swift and trauma-
tizing changes and eager both to reinforce class boundaries and yet to
deny their inflexibility, the appeal to the phrenological scale of brow
level "legitimizes social inequalities because it presents social differences
between people as if they were differences of nature," which is to say, biological rather than cultural.[10] And in a country that had long disavowed the irreducibility of class struggle, "making hierarchical distinctions about culture," as John Seabrook notes, "was the only acceptable
way for people to talk openly about class."[11]

If, in Lynes's estimation, the "highbrow's friend is the lowbrow," because the former "enjoys and respects the lowbrow's art—jazz for instance," then his or her "real enemy is the middlebrow," a social-climbing parvenu trying to "pre-empt . . . the highbrow's function" and "blur the lines between the serious and the frivolous." Unlike the lowbrow, who is positioned on the side of nature, the body, enjoyment, and "immediate pleasure or grief," the middlebrow is the unapologetic consumer and cultural middleman, a "pretentious and frivolous man or woman who uses culture to satisfy social or business ambitions."[12] Lynes then approvingly quotes Clement Greenberg's accusation that "middlebrow culture attacks distinctions as such and insinuates itself everywhere." Like the portrayals of communism or homosexuality limned by Senator McCarthy and his associates, middlebrow culture represents a contagious social pathology, "infecting the healthy, corrupting the honest, and stultifying the wise." Because "insidiousness is of its essence, . . . its avenues of penetration have become infinitely more difficult to detect and block."[13]

All the attacks on middlebrow culture imagine it to be a feminized and/or homosexualized product (and one must bear in mind here the almost continuous linkage during the twentieth century between gender deviance and sexual deviance in a wide variety of discourses). The term was first popularized, after all, during the 1920s, shortly after women were granted the right to vote and were beginning to pursue, as Radway notes, a measure of sexual liberation "as dancing flappers and vamps." Surveying these political and social changes in connection to the rise of the Book-of-the-Month Club, she argues that "middlebrow culture belongs at the chiasma of several intersecting histories, that is, where the history of the rapidly restructuring economy intersects with the history of cultural production and with the history of women's changing social status and position." Throughout this period, the middlebrow reader "was typically gendered as female," associated with mass-produced and -distributed goods and considered part of "an undifferentiated mass of passive 'consumers.'"[14] Thus the editor of the *Bookman* in 1926 warned of the rising "danger" of "regimentation," which he declared "as dangerous as Bolshevism."[15] By so collapsing "machine culture itself and the rise of the masses" into the figure of the woman reader, the "critics of the book clubs" betrayed their fear of "engulfment, ingestion, and absorption less by the spreading ooze of middlebrow culture than by the effeminate masses that middlebrow culture materialized in its scandalous marketing."[16]

The attacks on middlebrow culture during the 1950s performed a function uncomfortably similar to those of the 1920s. For the post–World War II era saw a concerted attempt, after the considerable successes of the labor movement during the Great Depression, to control and cripple the masses—that is, organized labor. Congress passed the Taft-Hartley Act in 1947, one of the most repressive labor laws in U.S. history, which granted the president "the right to obtain injunctions forcing strikers to return to work"; banned "contributions from union dues to political candidates"; gave "states the power to pass 'right-to-work' laws, outlawing the closed shop"; and required "union officials to sign non-Communist affidavits."[17] The postwar tastemakers, however, associated organized labor less with lowbrow than with middlebrow culture. According to Lynes, "the middlebrows" represent "the dominant group in our society—a dreadful mass of insensible backslappers, . . . the willing victims of slogans and the whims of the bosses, both political and economic." And although this portrayal fixates on an implicitly male union member or "organization man," Lynes immediately switches gender as he elaborates on this image. For the middlebrow world through which this man passes is unrelentingly feminized insofar as he is imagined to be an obedient stooge and victim. His world is that of "'the typical American family'—happy little women, happy little children, all spotless or sticky in the jam pot, framed against dimity curtains in the windows or decalcomania flowers on the cupboard doors." Focusing on the lower middlebrows in particular, Lynes observes that they

> decorate their homes under the careful guidance of *Good Housekeeping* and the *Ladies' Home Journal* . . . and are subject to fads in furniture. . . . In matters of taste, the lower-middlebrow world is largely dominated by women. . . . Except in the selection of his personal apparel and the car, it is almost *infra dig* for a man to have taste; it is not considered quite manly for the male to express opinions about things which come under the category of "artistic."[18]

The lower-middlebrow worldview is thus defined not in the occupational or professional realms but in the private sphere, through feminized domestic labor and the pursuits that occupy a man during his leisure hours. And as becomes visible in unmistakably middlebrow cultural productions (like Arthur Miller's *Death of a Salesman*), fears about standardization, commodity culture, victimization, organized labor, and "mass man" are routinely displaced onto women and the domestic sphere.

Unlike the discourse of taste during the 1920s, that of the 1950s routinely imagines the feminization of the middlebrow to be accompanied by suggestions of sexual deviance. This is in part the result of the routine conflation of effeminacy with male homosexuality during the period. But writers like Dwight Macdonald take this association well beyond the routine. Masscult ("mass culture") is bad enough; it is "an instrument of domination" that is exercised on that "collective monstrosity, 'the masses,' 'the public.'"[19] But middlebrow culture, for Macdonald as for Greenberg before him, is first and foremost a depravity that is clearly sexualized in Macdonald's lurid prose:

> In these more advanced times, the danger to High Culture is not so much from Masscult as from a peculiar hybrid bred from the latter's unnatural intercourse with the former. A whole middle culture has come into existence and it threatens to absorb both of its parents. This intermediate form—let us call it Midcult—has the essential qualities of Masscult—the formula, the built-in reaction, the lack of any standard except popularity—but it decently covers them with a cultural figleaf.[20]

For Macdonald and all the midcentury theorists of taste, middlebrow culture represents first and foremost a scandalous interpenetration of high and low. Combining opposites, it blurs boundaries or—worse yet—obliterates them entirely. A virulent form of cultural miscegenation, it brings together those things (and presumably persons) that should be kept separate. Yet Macdonald sexualizes middlebrow more explicitly than most of his contemporaries. For him, it is a vexing, obscene, and contradictory phenomenon. On the one hand, it represents the product of a perverse, heterosexual—and arguably, miscegenated—coupling that produces a "bastard" child.[21] According to this logic (and the long association of mass culture with both femininity and African American traditions), Masscult is figured as a kind of loose woman, a Delilah or Jezebel, who seduces and pollutes High Culture in order to produce a dangerous, cross-race, illegitimate upstart who threatens, Oedipus-like, to destroy its progenitors. Moreover, the "essential qualities" of this bastard offspring are figured as being so obscene—and genital-like—that they must be covered by a "figleaf." On the other hand, the "unnatural intercourse" that produces Midcult also bears the unmistakable signs of a homosexual seduction. This is in part the result of Cold War culture's habit of telescoping, as Elaine Tyler May notes, the various "degenerative seductions" that preyed upon a man and that could occupy the category of the unnatural: "pornography, prostitution, 'loose women,' or homosexuals." More important, however, is the fact that Midcult, like the homosexual or communist of Cold War fantasies, attempts to pass for something else. As May emphasizes, both figures were imagined as being subversive infiltrators whose power came from their ability to dissimulate: "Like communists who would presumably infiltrate and destroy society, sexual 'perverts' could spread their poison simply by association."[22] Boring from within, insinuating and subverting, Midcult "pretends to respect the standards of High Culture while in fact it waters them down and vulgarizes them."[23] Exploiting "the discoveries of the avant-garde," it surreptitiously turns them into "*kitsch* for the elite."[24] If, according to a Senate report, it takes only "one homosexual" to "pollute a Government office," it takes only one Midcultist to destroy legitimate cultural values.[25]

Although Macdonald's attack on culture is more panic-stricken than most, all the pronouncements on taste, like so many Cold War discourses on politics and sexuality, seem motivated by fear—fear of communism, fascism, standardization, "mass man," unrestrained sexuality, miscegenation, loose women, "artistic" men, sexual perverts. But social power derives less from the stigmatizing force of these categories than from the ability to fashion them in the first place. Anticommunism and homophobia were such effective tools during the 1950s because they kept the already anticommunist and heterosexual majorities in line. The policing of political affiliations, sexual practices—and, I would add, levels of taste—thus functioned as an extremely efficient and far-reaching mode of containment during a period of controlled panic over perceived threats to U.S. economic, political, and cultural hegemony. For all the Brahmin-like assurance that writers like Macdonald and Greenberg seem to project, their discourses are in fact shot through with a profound sense of dis-ease. And I want to argue that the principal affect associated with middlebrow—understood as a mode of cultural production, a level of taste, and a critical apparatus—is anxiety. Middlebrow cultural producers, consumers, and critics alike are always looking over their shoulders; always fearful of encroachments from above or below; always uneasy about their own class positionality and their own tastes; always trying to negotiate between creativity and the exigencies of the marketplace, between politics and aesthetics, between an art that requires studied investment and the desire for untrammeled pleasures.

The linkages among middlebrow culture, anxiety, and Cold War America are by no means illogical. For despite all the attempts (in Hollywood and elsewhere) during the 1950s to portray the United States as a consumerist utopia, many deeply intransigent social problems, inequities, and oppressive social conditions were either ignored or naturalized. Simultaneously, as if taking their cues from these disavowals, many of the leading figures in the social and biological sciences became preoccupied with anxiety, which, not surprisingly, they suddenly saw everywhere. It was, after all, as W. H. Auden put it, the "Age of Anxiety." In 1950, Rollo May published *The Meaning of Anxiety,* in which, drawing on Freud's theory of anxiety being the result of unconscious conflicts and desires, he carefully distinguishes anxiety from fear. The latter represents a response to "the presence of a *known* danger," a response whose "strength" is "more or less proportionate to the degree of danger."[26] But "anxiety is unspecific, vague, 'objectless'"; attacks "the 'core' or 'essence' of the personality"; and is characterized by "diffuse, painful, and persistent feelings of uncertainty and helplessness."[27] According to May:

> *Anxiety is the apprehension cued off by a threat to some value that the individual holds essential to his existence as a personality.* The threat may be to physical life (the threat of death), or to psychological existence (the loss of freedom). Or the threat may be to some other value one identifies with one's existence (patriotism, the love of another person, "success," etc.).

The key to anxiety, and the reason why it is so difficult to treat, is that it "indicates the presence of a problem that needs to be solved but cannot be solved because the person who has the problem is unaware of its nature."[28] It is, in short, an unconscious response to unconscious fears. Despite the widespread acceptance of this theory during the postwar era, the pharmaceutical companies were eager to cash in on the anxiety craze, and these years bore witness to the marketing of new classes of psychoactive drugs formulated specifically to deal with anxiety: Miltown in 1950, Thorazine in 1954, and Librium in 1958.

One need not look very far to find the unacknowledged sources of the anxiety that so disturbed the Cold War arbiters of taste. Many of the not-so-secret concerns that I have cataloged about the social, political, and economic well-being of the nation had significant (and sometimes unanticipated) consequences for all U.S. citizens. And similarly, fears about potentially dangerous political or sexual associations could easily prey on anyone's mind. (How secure, for example, can any heterosexual identity be when all persons, if Freud is to be believed, are not only "capable of making a homosexual object choice" but "have in fact made one in their unconscious"?)[29] But for the tastemakers of the 1950s and early 1960s, anxiety over the hegemony of middlebrow culture was based on the fear of their own increasing obsolescence in a culture that had less and less time for their pronouncements from on high. Ross is certainly correct to argue that the production of the category "middlebrow" was of such great use to the arbiters of taste because it is most "responsive and sensitive to the marks of difference." It thus requires the most sophisticated and subtle of palates to distinguish between levels of middlebrow. The tastemakers may have been afraid of the unnatural intercourse of high and low, but they were even more anxious about a changing culture in which "the channels of power through which" they exercised "intellectual authority" were becoming increasingly obsolete. For "cultural power does not inhere in the contents of categories of taste. On the contrary, it is exercised through the capacity to draw the line between and around categories of taste; it is the power to define."[30] What most terrified the tastemakers was, to borrow Rollo May's phrase, the increasing "threat of meaninglessness"—both their own and that of the highbrow culture before whose throne they prostrated themselves.[31]

The anxiety that circulates so palpably through the texts of the tastemakers is then clearly a response to the fact that the 1950s and early 1960s—the period during which so many critics and consumers alike were obsessed with pigeonholing taste—represent the very end of the era during which a hierarchy of taste was a useful and accurate guide to the disposition of economic, educational, and cultural capital in the United States. Or as Kammen puts it, "From the 1870s until the 1960s, a great many Americans did in fact believe that cultural stratification existed and they responded accordingly."[32] But that widespread belief began to wane during the 1960s. With the rebirth of political and social radicalism; with the rise of feminism and various cultural nationalisms; with the explosion of youth culture; with the demise of abstract expressionism and the triumph of pop art; with the advent of art rock, fusion, minimalism, and other populist alternatives to academic serialism; with the decline of the International Style; and with the wholesale politicization of culture, the Cold War consensus came to an end. In its place a new culture has emerged—many call it postmodernist—that pointedly challenges the opposition between elite and mass culture as well as the hierarchy of taste that was consolidated at the end of the nineteenth century. Formerly lowbrow forms started to deploy various avant-gardist techniques (fragmentation, montage, dissonance, chance) to an unprecedented degree while retaining their mass appeal. Lowbrow or middlebrow genres like film, theater, and popular fiction embraced increasingly esoteric content (under the influence of European existentialism) or formerly taboo subjects (like sex, drugs, and madness). And due to the work of Andy Warhol (among many others), painting—which had long been considered a bastion of highbrow culture—celebrated the commodity status of the work of art in a way that would have shocked the modernist highbrow, for whom the commodity remained something of an embarrassment. Reacting against the inflexibility of the cultural hierarchy, emergent artists delighted in extending the range of art; in juxtaposing the exalted and abject, the sacred and profane, the orthodox and heretical; in being vernacular and relevant; and in rudely transgressing the canons of taste. Since the 1960s, new styles, forms, and genres have proliferated; new hierarchies and subcultures have continued to emerge with ever greater rapidity. The rules, in short, have changed radically since *Life* magazine could publish a neat compartmentalization of taste.

With the triumph of unfettered capitalism during the last decade of the twentieth century, and the commodity's penetration (in the United States, at least) into virtually every area of social life, the cultural hierarchy may have become even more disorderly, but it has by no means disappeared. This is the era when, in John Seabrook's words, "paintings by van Gogh and Monet are the headliners at the Bellagio Hotel while the Cirque du Soleil borrows freely from performance art in creating the Las Vegan spectacle inside."[33] Hollywood films and blockbuster museum shows become mere adjuncts to merchandising extravaganzas, while the borders between avant-garde and kitsch, art and advertising, politics and celebrity, have become virtually nonexistent. New media fill the marketplace, like the Internet, DVD, and magalog (part magazine, part catalog). As Kurt Andersen explains, "In this age of hypercapitalism and thus also hypermarketing, all the old lines between editorial content and advertising—like those lines between high art and pop culture, and between news and entertainment—are blurring and breaking down."[34] MTV has succeeded in undermining "the old barrier between . . . mainstream and underground, mass and cult, it and you," and in allowing "the avant-garde [to] become mainstream" overnight.[35] This is the moment (which Seabrook calls Nobrow) when the "old distinction between the elite culture of the aristocrats and the commercial culture of the masses was torn down, and in its place was erected a hierarchy of hotness. Nobrow is not a culture without hierarchy, of course, but in Nobrow commercial culture is a potential source of status, rather than the thing the elite define themselves against."[36]

The emergence of a culture of hotness and a seemingly endless array of commodities signals an unprecedented decentralization of the cultural marketplace. Yet this decentralization is ironically the product of an unprecedented concentration of media production companies: a new cartel, "a global oligopoly" of "the entertainment industry," in which "eight transnational corporations" (down from about fifty in 1983) have come to dominate "the global media market."[37] In this age of globalized monopoly capitalism, there is a strict division of consumption between the affluent First World and the Third, whose workers are becoming increasingly proletarianized and have direct access to far fewer hot commodities. But in much of the First World, particularly the United States, hypermarketing services an identity politics in which taste, Seabrook argues, is linked not to quality but to a personal, subculturally defined identity (closely tied to occupation, age, race, social class, and place of residence) that is acquired through the commodity form. To purchase a music video, a book, a pair of sneakers, or tickets to a play is to make an "investment in these relationship economies . . . in the stock market of public opinion." But because "no value endures," one must always "take care to surf ahead" to the next hot marker of subcultural identity.[38] Although Seabrook's theorization of Nobrow is persuasive, his title is somewhat misleading insofar as the new culture of hotness does not so much abolish the hierarchy of taste as reformulate it. If the old hierarchy was, like the stock prices of yore, revenue based and relatively slow to change, the new one is almost entirely speculative and subject to rapid and unforeseeable oscillations as the value of commodities precipitously (and seemingly illogically) rises and falls. If the old was vertical, the new seems "to exist in three or more dimensions," a hypertextual hierarchy in which the click of a mouse opens up new vistas of fashions and commodities, all the while increasing the insatiable desire for the next big thing.[39]

Theater as Middlebrow Culture

Long before the culture of hotness, when hierarchies of taste were relatively stable, theater was an important marker on the cultural map. Without exception, the tastemakers of the 1950s, like Lynes, considered it a lower- or upper-middlebrow art. The *Life* magazine chart puts it in the upper-middlebrow category (where it is designated by actors decked out in Shakespearean garb), while the pile of records in the upper-middlebrow's collection includes Cole Porter's *Kiss Me, Kate* sandwiched between Chopin and Sibelius.[40] Macdonald, meanwhile, finds theater a particularly striking example of middlebrow culture's perversions. For him, the legitimate theater is truly a bastard art. Two of the four Pulitzer Prize–winning texts he analyzes happen to be plays, Thornton Wilder's *Our Town* and Archibald MacLeish's *J.B.* And he seems to harbor a particular animus toward Rodgers and Hammerstein, who, he alleges, foisted off on an innocent public "the folk-fakery of *Oklahoma!* and the orotund sentimentalities of *South Pacific*."[41] Although theater for him by no means has a monopoly on Midcult, it is arguably the most emblematic

Midcult genre because it is the one in which art and commerce are most complexly and irreducibly interwoven. Although Macdonald does admire "old plays" by the likes of Chekhov, Shaw, Ibsen, O'Neill, Brecht, Beckett, and Shakespeare, and approves "a vigorous off-broadway theater," he notes that "except for *The Connection* [!] and *The Zoo Story,* [theater] has had almost nothing of significance by hitherto unknown playwrights." An old-fashioned avant-gardist to the end, Macdonald produces a masculinist, Eurocentric canon that enshrines orthodox iconoclasm. But even the presence of these esteemed plays cannot relieve theater audiences of their distinctively Midcultish conformism and their cowed submission to highbrow tastemakers: "We have . . . become skilled at consuming High Culture when it has been stamped PRIME QUALITY by proper authorities, but we lack the kind of sophisticated audience that supported the achievements of the classic avant-garde, an audience that can appreciate and discriminate on its own."[42] So even highbrow plays fall as pearls before Midcultish swine. Moreover, the very structure of theater's system of production, distribution, and consumption—as well as its heavy reliance on the "proper" authority of daily critics—would seem to guarantee its middlebrow status in perpetuity.

The postwar arbiters of taste were by no means the only cultural critics to pigeonhole theater as a middlebrow form. Indeed, for virtually the entire twentieth century, theater occupied what I would describe as an intermediate position in U.S. culture, recycling and recombining elements of, on the one hand, public amusements like cinema, minstrel shows, and vaudeville and, on the other, serious art. Neither high nor low—or rather, *both high and low at the same time*—theater has consistently evinced those characteristics that have historically been branded as middlebrow: the promiscuous mixture of commerce and art, entertainment and politics, the banal and the auratic, profane and sacred, spectacular and personal, erotic and intellectual. Even with the breakdown of the old hierarchy and the development of a new culture of hotness, theater remains the emblematic middlebrow genre. For if popular culture is defined—albeit crudely—by a rough equivalence between economic and cultural capital, and elite culture by an inverse relationship between the two (what Bourdieu calls "a generalized game of 'loser wins'"), then middlebrow culture must evince an unstable, unpredictable, and anxious relationship between the commercial and the artistic.[43] Certainly in the United States there have been a small number of theatrical enterprises performed for highly professionalized audiences that could qualify as elite, stretching from the work of the so-called little theaters of the first decades of the twentieth century to the performances that filled experimental stages from the 1950s through the 1970s. But with the institutionalization of what used to be called the avant-garde by the early 1980s, there is very little theater left in the United States that amasses the kind of cultural cachet or enjoys the prestige of what passes for elite culture. Work by the likes of Richard Maxwell and the Wooster Group that continues to be performed in tiny venues perhaps qualifies, but certainly not the mammoth productions that fill the Brooklyn Academy of Music during the ludicrously misnamed Next Wave Festival. Moreover, with the increasing dependence since the 1970s of the major nonprofit theaters on profit-making ventures (beginning with *A Chorus Line* in 1976), and the growing number of collaborations between nonprofit and commercial producers, the line between art and commerce has become all the more indistinct.

Elite culture, meanwhile (which includes a very small number of theatrical enterprises), has, it seems to me, been effectively bifurcated since the 1970s. On the one hand, it persists in large nonprofit institutions like opera and ballet companies, symphony orchestras, and art museums (although even here the lines become indistinct when museums sponsor blockbuster shows of Monet or Norman Rockwell and opera companies perform *West Side Story*). On the other hand, elite cultural capital also accrues to the consecrated avant-garde (New York's fashionable Chelsea galleries, the plays of Richard Foreman, Merce Cunningham performances) or to exhibitions and performances of what is coded as an indigenous, anticonsumerist (and usually non-American) folk culture (such as Japanese No theater, traditional South Asian music, or certain varieties of American primitive art). The former kind of elite culture is supported by big money and prestigious foundations and caters to the champagne and caviar crowd. The latter trades on its purported authenticity and its continuing resistance, to some extent at least, to commodity culture. Both, however, imagine high art as being either sacred and wrapped in mystique or a modern substitute for the sacred in an age when religion has lost its purchase.

My interest in theorizing American theater as a middlebrow art is not the result of a sudden taxonomic delirium brought on by having spent too many chilly hours in the Lincoln Center Library. For any hierarchization of culture is at best a suspect and self-serving enterprise. As Radway, Ross, and Rubin have demonstrated, the symbolic power of middlebrow has derived historically less from its innate characteristics than from the determination of the arbiters of taste to use the category to secure their own intellectual authority. Hence all the anxiety that swirls around the concept of middlebrow, which, after all, has consistently been deployed as a term of opprobrium. Nonetheless, it seems to me that the category is useful for theorizing the predicament of theater in the United States since the late 1920s—its ebbing popularity, its steady decline as a vital force on the American cultural scene, its disreputable and precarious position in many universities, its marginalization in English departments, its exclusion from the fashionable field of cultural studies, and its increasing superannuation and subordination in elite graduate programs in relation to performance studies. Theater is so irredeemably middlebrow that even Radway, Ross, and Rubin ignore it.

If one identifies the most salient characteristic of middlebrow to be the unstable, unpredictable, and anxious relationship between art and commerce, the category can provide a key to understanding the histories of American theater and dramatic writing in part because it allows one to recognize them as sites of constant, sometimes fierce, and often futile struggle for different forms of capital. Bourdieu argues that middlebrow culture represents a reaction against the aestheticism that was consolidated at the end of the nineteenth century. As he notes, the "aesthetic disposition . . . tends to bracket off the nature and function of the object represented and to exclude any 'naive' reaction[,] . . . along with all purely ethical responses, in order to concentrate solely upon the mode of representation, the style, perceived and appreciated by comparison with other styles."[44] Middlebrow, in contrast, "undermine[s] the notion of aesthetic autonomy," as Marianne Conroy observes, by "bid[ding] to be at once politically effective, morally responsible, commercially successful, and culturally respectable."[45] Theorizing middlebrow as the impossible conjunction of these different enterprises, one can analyze the different forces at work in the construction of a canon of American drama, whether that canon is defined by the syllabi of university drama courses, the plays regularly revived on American stages, or a list of

Pulitzer Prize–winning plays. It helps one to understand the curious resilience and vitality of the antitheatrical prejudice during a period when theater has for the most part lost its claim to moral outrage. It also forces one to be a comparativist, always keeping in mind the evolving relationship between theater and other forms of cultural production. Most important, the theorization of middlebrow as a site of struggle allows one to recognize that the multifarious makers of theater are by no means free and independent agents. On the contrary, they are the servants of a system of production (what Brecht calls an apparatus) that will always make extravagantly contradictory demands they can never completely fulfill. As a result, the content, style, and forms of American theater must be understood as a compromise, not in the sense of a middle ground, but as active and evolving conflict and negotiation. Moreover, what we call "drama" can be theorized only by reference to the positionalities of the agents who make it in response to these impossible demands, to theater's relationship with other cultural forms, to an audience whose tastes and expectations can never be completely known in advance, and to the variable amounts of capital—economic, cultural, social, and symbolic—at risk in any performance.

Despite the recent and conspicuous success of the most mass-produced and widely syndicated of theatrical spectacles—say, *Beauty and the Beast* or *Riverdance*—theater is not and has never been a form of mass culture. (And here I take issue with Philip Auslander less because I think his deconstruction of the opposition between liveness and mediatization is wrong—I don't—than because, unlike him, I am more interested in the sociology than the ontology of performance.)[46] First, live performance will always retain a certain auratic quality, even when the performers are condemned to try to imitate animated versions of their characters or disappear into a pseudo-Irish folk version of the Ziegfeld Follies. Second, no two productions or performances of the same text can be identical. Even plays like *The Heidi Chronicles* or *Angels in America* that seem to have been franchised to every resident theater company in the United States will often be produced in radically different ways according to the tastes and abilities of directors and actors. Bus-and-truck companies will always be subtly—or strikingly—different from each other and from the New York prototype. And, as every actor or experienced theatergoer knows, even the same production changes from night to night, due in part to the changing composition of the audience. Third, even with recent technological innovations, including computerized lighting and almost ubiquitous amplification, theater remains, in Jack Poggi's phrase, a "'handmade' product" in relation to film and television.[47] It simply cannot be mass-produced and -distributed in the way that films, videotapes, and DVDs are.

Although not a form of mass culture, theater in the twentieth century never enjoyed, as Paul DiMaggio argues, a secure place among elite, sacred forms, those that could be neatly "separated . . . from profane performance and exhibition."[48] In the early years of the century, Oscar Hammerstein described this hieratic quality—which theater lacked but "grand opera" allegedly possessed—as "the most elevating influence upon modern society, after religion." Lifting "one out of the sordid affairs of life," it represents "the awakening of the soul to the sublime and the divine."[49] Theater, in contrast, remained entirely commercial and, in DiMaggio's phrase, "not easily etherialized." Only with the development of the "art theater, or little theater," movement around 1910 did young, idealistic playwrights, directors, and actors attempt to produce "'serious drama' for . . . a high-status public" in the hope of "chang[ing] the theater and, in some instances, the world."[50] As Sheldon Cheney observed about one of these companies, the Chicago Little Theatre "gained a reputation for a restricted appeal. It became known as a theatre for a specialized audience, if not for a cult, and this militated against its wider acceptance . . . and cut off needed income."[51] These little theaters, both amateur and professional, quickly proliferated, and at their peak, in 1929, "there were over one thousand noncommercial stages throughout the United States."[52] And despite the fact that few of the noncommercial professional companies survived the Depression, the "art theaters of New York, the amateur playhouses around the country, and their academic allies succeeded in developing a legitimating ideology and a canon" whose contour, in fact, is remarkably similar to that described a few decades later by Dwight Macdonald.[53]

The little-theater movement was instrumental in elevating theater in the cultural hierarchy and positioning it between, on the one hand, mass-cultural forms like cinema and radio and, on the other hand, elite forms like "trustee-governed art museums and symphony orchestras," which "by 1930 . . . were common in cities across the United States."[54]

Relegated to an intermediate position in U.S. culture, theater was—and, I would argue, remains—not a single medium but a clearly stratified grouping of several different kinds of live performance, with its audiences distinctly "segmented by class, . . . rank," and race. During the first quarter of the century, burlesque belonged "at the bottom," as it

> appealed to audiences of working-class men and was shunned by women and the well born. Variety entertainment, originally also a male preserve, was differentiated into vulgar and "progressive" vaudeville . . . by expunging "blue" humor . . . and hiring high-priced and fashionable talent from the legitimate (i.e., dramatic) stage.[55]

Above vaudeville, the commercial, legitimate theater was, in turn, divided between "'low-brow' or 'popular-priced' theaters in most large cities," which catered to lower-middle-class audiences with plays that were a few years old, and "'first-class' theaters," which presented star-studded, elaborate productions of new plays and classics.[56] At the very top of the hierarchy (but still not quite a part of elite culture) were the newly professionalized and not-so-little theaters like the Provincetown Players, the Washington Square Players, and (at least in its early years) the Theatre Guild.[57] And as Poggi emphasizes, even within individual theaters, "there were clear-cut social lines[,] . . . evidence of which is still visible in the architecture of some of the older playhouses, with their boxes for the elite and their galleries . . . for the mob."[58] With the exception of theaters built specifically for African American patrons, almost every playhouse was segregated, with African Americans having to "undergo the humiliating experience of entering the theater by a back entrance and taking seats in the upper galleries."[59]

The first three decades of the twentieth century, during which the legitimate theater was consolidated as a middlebrow art, also—and ominously—marked a serious decline in its popularity. The number of theater companies on tour fell from over three hundred at the turn of the century to about twenty during the first years of the Depression.[60] And although the number of new productions and theater weeks (weeks a theater is occupied by a production) in New York climbed steadily until 1927 (from 96 in 1900–1901 to 264 in 1927–28), theater thereafter began a precipitous retreat that has continued to this day. Cultural historians agree that the advent of the talkie sounded the death knell to theater as a broadly popular form. But even before the widespread distribution of films with synchronized sound in the late 1920s, Hollywood succeeded in luring large numbers of new, mainly immigrant spectators to the movies and simultaneously stealing "the working-class audience from the legitimate stage" by providing them with "comfortable seats, thick rugs, elegant lounges[,] . . . all the trappings of wealth that had previously belonged to a select few in the orchestra of a legitimate theatre— and all for twenty-five cents."[61] Theater galleries were rarely filled after 1912, as the audience was increasingly divided by class in an institutional framework that, Poggi suggests, "became somewhat *less* democratic . . . after the triumph of the movies."[62] Moreover, for virtually the entire twentieth century, theater tickets were considerably more expensive than tickets to other popular entertainments. During the 1920s, "the average price differential" between the legitimate stage and the movies "was five to one."[63] And for the whole of the century, the ratio ranged between five-to-one and ten-to-one, depending on the particular venue. Even before the advent of the talkie, in 1925, "the average weekly attendance at movies . . . was at least fifty-six times the maximum possible weekly attendance at legitimate plays."[64] As theater's popularity was declining, the range of options it offered was becoming more and more circumscribed. A steep rise in theater ticket prices during the 1920s led to "the increasing division into 'hits' and 'flops'" as spectators became "more selective about their playgoing"—another pattern that has continued to the present day.[65]

   Statistics tell only a part of the story, but they do clearly suggest that the cultural positioning of theater—and the kind of struggles that take place within the field—have been remarkably consistent since the 1920s, when its lower- to upper-middlebrow position became consolidated. And although the Depression saw a general contraction of the theater, it also bore witness to several attempts to raise the brow level of the stage through, for example, the stylistically experimental and politically progressive yet populist work of the Federal Theatre Project and the more elitist presentations of the Group Theatre and the Theater Guild. But in the years following World War II, theater's middlebrow status was rapidly confirmed by the Pulitzer Prize–winning (and now canonical) plays of Williams, Miller, Inge, and Rodgers and Hammerstein and by theater's opposition to a new medium, television. As Conroy emphasizes, this positioning was reinforced by the growing hegemony of method acting, which "threatened the orthodox categorical distinctions between popular and prestigious forms on which the entire notion of a national culture depended" by combining "high cultural purpose with a popular commercial ethos."[66] With the growth of regional and other nonprofit theaters during the 1960s and 1970s, theater became more decentralized and theater budgets far more dependent on government funding and corporate, foundation, and private giving. This had the effect of pushing the nonprofit theater ineluctably toward the upper-middlebrow end of the spectrum. As this was happening, working-class audiences were continuing to desert the theater either for television or for other more accessible, cheap, and exciting forms of entertainment. According to one survey from the mid-1960s, "blue-collar workers make up less than 3 per cent of the legitimate-theater audience, though they represent nearly 60 per cent of the urban population."[67] Although cultural hierarchies have grown less and less distinct since the 1960s, these habits have become even more ingrained. Theater audiences in the United States are now composed almost exclusively of "middle-aged, high income, high education, professional, managerial and white-collar groups."[68] Educational level is a particularly important gauge of cultural literacy, and, as of 1992, college-educated theatergoers outnumbered those with a high-school education or less by a factor of six to one.[69]

Theater fare has also changed with the growth of the nonprofit theater and the aging of the theater audience. The 1970s saw a considerable gulf develop between the kind of play—or, more likely, musical—produced on Broadway and the kind originating in nonprofit arenas. This division has evolved in a contradictory way. Despite the success of regional and other nonprofit theaters, the bus-and-truck business has more than doubled since the mid-1980s, and "in recent years, musical reproductions (touring versions of current or recent Broadway hits) or restorations (adaptations of past Broadway hits) have accounted for more than 80% of total commercial theater ticket sales."[70] Serious, upper-middlebrow drama, meanwhile, is now entirely the preserve of the nonprofit theater. During the 1990s every Pulitzer Prize–winning play was first produced in a nonprofit arena. Yet even as this schism is widening, the commercial theater is coming to depend more and more

on its nonprofit, erstwhile competitors. With the conspicuous exception of the Disney and Cameron Mackintosh musicals, most Broadway
productions are now the result of a collaboration between commercial
and nonprofit producing organizations. Audiences, meanwhile, whether
lured by a road show or a regional theater, remain overwhelmingly
middle- to upper-middle-class. Even the largest and most prestigious
nonprofit theaters (like the Manhattan Theatre Club) do not attract the
same A-list donors who are so eager to sponsor sumptuous buffets for
opera companies and art museums.

So despite a significant disruption and weakening of the cultural hierarchy in the United States since the 1960s, theater, it seems to me, is becoming more determinedly middlebrow. And if that category has a
slightly old-fashioned ring to it, perhaps it is appropriate for an art that
remains similarly old-fashioned, if not exactly stuck in the 1950s. Moreover, short of a radical economic restructuring, there is little chance that
it will become any more accessible, either financially or aesthetically, to
members of the working classes. In recent years the increase in average
theater ticket prices has far outpaced inflation, jumping from about seven
dollars in 1970 to forty-eight dollars in 1996.[71] And while theater audiences are less likely to be discouraged by rising ticket prices in the short
term, their steady increase bodes ill for theater's long-term popularity.[72]
For the laws of economics suggest that theater admission prices will not
decline in the foreseeable future. That would be possible only during a
period of deflation or as a result of increased productivity. But increased
productivity is unlikely as long as theater remains a "handmade" art. For
as William J. Baumol and William G. Bowen point out (in their now-
classic analysis), "ouput per man-hour" in the U.S. economy "doubled
approximately every 29 years" for most of the twentieth century. But because theater remains a business in which the "performers' labors themselves constitute the end product which the audience purchases," "productivity" remains "relatively immutable."[73] During the first three
decades of the twentieth century, theater production costs rose much
faster than inflation—a pattern that has continued to this day.[74] And bar-
ring large subsidies, this increase must be passed on to consumers. For
theater is quite unlike forms of mass culture—such as film, television,
and music videos—that, because they are highly dependent on technology, have "made possible a revolutionary change in the mechanics of

presentation." As these forms have become more sophisticated and efficient, "the cost of providing a given hour of entertainment to each member of the audience has dropped precipitously."[75] But theater is an industry that cannot benefit from technological advancements or from "significant increases in output per man-hour" to anywhere near the same degree as mass-cultural forms. It therefore will "inevitably experience a growing gap between income and expenditure, even if there is no inflation."[76] And although high ticket prices are by no means the only, or even the most important, barrier separating theater from mass culture, this does suggest that the class composition of theater audiences is unlikely to change.

This rather bleak prognosis is symptomatic of the fact that the legitimate theater, whether commercial or nonprofit, has since the end of the nineteenth century been run by businesspersons worshiping at the altars of two hostile gods, the god of commerce and the god of art. Charles Frohman, a respected producer, made this clear more than a century ago, using words that could have been spoken by virtually any American producer or artistic director of the past hundred years:

> My work is to produce plays that succeed, so that I can produce plays that will not succeed. . . .
> What I would really like to do is to produce a wonderful something to which I would only go myself. . . . But I can't do that. The next best thing is to produce something for the few critical people. That is what I'm trying for. I have to work through the commercial—it is the white heat through which the artistic in me has come.[77]

For Frohman, theater's ideal remains a "wonderful something" to which he is unable to give a name, a transcendent performance that might, like Hammerstein's grand opera, awaken "the soul to the sublime and the divine." But this represents an impossible ideal. Instead, he chooses another impossibility, working "through" the "white heat" of the commercial to reach "the artistic." Yet it is precisely this contradictory logic that describes the predicament of a theater that, for intractable economic and social reasons, seems doomed to "a continuing state of financial crisis" and a middlebrow purgatory.[78] Rather than cringe at this category, perhaps we should try to use it to pry open the economic and social relations that produce—and are produced by—what we call American theater.

The Pulitzer Prize and American Musical Theater

Dwight Macdonald's singling out of Pulitzer Prize–winning texts as prime examples of Midcult was not an arbitrary choice. The prizes in the arts have long been regarded as a reward for what can at best be considered a kind of upper middlebrow excellence. When the prize for drama was first given in 1918, to Jesse Lynch Williams's now-forgotten play, *Why Marry?*, it was explicitly charged with uplifting the stage in what was, after all, the heyday of vaudeville, the Ziegfeld Follies, silent film, and other even less reputable public amusements. Indeed, the drama award was the only one in the arts to mandate that the winning text should instill "educational value and power" and so improve the genre in question, "raising the standard of good morals, good taste, and good manners."[79] The clause about "raising the standard" was dropped from the description in 1929 thanks to the already elevated work of Eugene O'Neill and other serious and "substantial" playwrights.[80] For they had succeeded in changing "the style of American drama," as John Hohenberg reports, "from song and dance confections and poor imitations of Scribe to realistic and outspoken efforts to reflect American life on the stage with honesty."[81] ("Honest," "serious," and "authentic" are the adjectives that are endlessly reiterated in paeans to middlebrow culture.) In other words, theater's middlebrow status had stabilized. But the "'uplift' clause" remained on the books until the controversy over *Who's Afraid of Virginia Woolf?* in 1964, after which it too was dropped.[82]

Because the Pulitzer jury in drama is composed mostly of theater reviewers (along with a few academic critics), the winning plays are almost invariably, as Thomas Adler reports, "the same ones that have gone on to become commercial and popular successes as a result of initially favorable reviews." The drama award thus functions primarily to reaffirm the critics' authority by turning their reviews into self-fulfilling prophesies and to reward those plays that have most fortuitously balanced "educational value" against commercial viability. Adler argues that, as a result, "the Pulitzer plays provide a far more reliable accounting of the nature and development of serious American drama than the equivalent novels do of classic American fiction."[83] If Adler is correct, it is only because the canon of "distinguished" plays (in the words of the charge to the Pulitzer jury beginning in 1964) has been defined precisely by the combination of seriousness and popular success that has been considered distinctively middlebrow.[84] For the prize by definition excludes determinedly avant-gardist work as surely as it does shameless crowd pleasers devoid of "educational value." And indeed, although many widely respected, taught, and revived plays never received the prize, about half of the Pulitzer plays remain more or less canonical.

Among the Pulitzer Prize–winning plays, the musicals comprise a particularly vexing category, one in which the mixture of high and low is most perceptible and, for many, unsettling. Only seven pieces of musical theater have won the award, one per decade beginning in the 1930s: *Of Thee I Sing* (1931–32), *South Pacific* (1949–50), *Fiorello!* (1959–60), *How to Succeed in Business Without Really Trying* (1961–62), *A Chorus Line* (1975–76), *Sunday in the Park with George* (1984–85), and *Rent* (1995– 96). Given the opprobrium that has long attached to American musical theater (as evidenced by Macdonald's contempt), it is little wonder that musicals have accounted for less than 10 percent of the awards. When the jury honored the Gershwins' musical about a presidential sex scandal and impeachment, *Of Thee I Sing,* it felt obliged to adopt a defensive posture: "This award may seem unusual, but the play is unusual. Not only is it coherent and well-knit enough to class as a play, aside from the music, but it is a biting and true satire on American politics." It is telling that although the librettists and lyricist were singled out, George Gershwin was ignored in the citation despite the fact that the score is one of his most sophisticated, borrowing liberally, if satirically, from the conventions of operetta and opera and clearly anticipating *Porgy and Bess.* But the music was deemed an "aside," a dangerous supplement that made the work distinctive but did not contribute substantially to its "admirable" qualities.[85] While most critics applauded the selection, Brooks Atkinson in the *New York Times* (long the most powerful definer and champion of upper-middlebrow taste) predictably excoriated the committee for "turn[ing] its back on the drama" and for having stripped the prize of "a great deal of its value."[86]

Although the other prize-winning musicals proved less controversial, these plays provide a particularly important and vivid example of the conflicting motives and species of capital that have structured the American theater since the 1930s. For musical theater is more than a special case. It also epitomizes many of the struggles that have long haunted the American stage, in particular, the opposition between crass commercialism and "distinguished" art. Each prize-winning musical, moreover, clearly emblematizes many distinctive formal and stylistic features of the commercial theater of its particular decade. Yet the musical has long been ignored, marginalized, or cordoned off in scholarly work on American theater, just as it has traditionally been positioned "outside the mainstream of American music history."[87] To all but legions of enthusiastic theatergoers, musicals remain, in Gerald Mast's pithy account, "essentially frivolous and silly diversions: lousy drama and lousy music."[88] Because they represent the most suspect of all so-called legitimate theatrical forms, they are the most skillful, I believe, at arousing the critical disdain and anxiety so strongly linked to middlebrow culture. Yet seven have garnered glowing notices, have enjoyed long and successful runs (with the exception of the relatively avant-gardist *Sunday in the Park with George*), and have been awarded the most prestigious prize for American drama. And while all do what musicals have always done best—produce pleasure that is all the more irresistible for its studied ingenuousness—they also and variously address issues that the arbiters of taste (and the Pulitzer juries) have regarded as substantial: politics, racism, the mass production of corporate entrepreneurship, stardom, the making of art, homosexuality, and AIDS.

Among the seven musicals, I want to concentrate on two, *South Pacific* and *Rent*. The former is the only Rodgers and Hammerstein musical to be awarded the Pulitzer Prize and remains, in Stanley Green's estimation, their "most universally admired achievement."[89] It is also almost shockingly symptomatic of the contradictions structuring not only theater but also American culture during the height of the post–World War II economic boom. The latter, meanwhile, succeeded in reviving both the American musical and the rock opera at a time when both had been left for dead. Its critical acclaim and great popularity (especially with younger audiences) mark it as a telling index of a society in which cultural hierarchies have been all but overthrown, abjection has been increasingly fetishized and commodified, and hotness reigns. Despite their obvious differences, however, both plays recycle musical and dramatic tropes associated with opera and combine them with the pop vernaculars of their day. And both are in part precisely about that mixing. Both feature cross-race romances in which persons of color are exoticized and sexualized. (Both thus rehearse an unnatural intercourse of persons as well as musical and dramatic styles.) Both are centrally concerned with the dynamics of the marketplace and the Americanizing effects of entrepreneurship. Both oppose what is coded as an authentic folk culture to a distinctively American brand of commercialism. Both are war stories, one pitting its heroes against the Japanese, the other against poverty, exploitation, heroin, and AIDS. Both feature the death of a protagonist. And both were sensationally successful when they opened on Broadway, spinning off wildly popular recordings and chalking up legendary runs.

Rodgers and Hammerstein's fourth stage musical, *South Pacific* had the largest advance sales of any Broadway musical up to that time. With a near-perfect example of the so-called integrated musical they perfected, it is little wonder that the team insisted on coproducing (with Joshua Logan and Leland Hayward) and retaining a 51 percent controlling interest in the show. Not only were Rodgers and Hammerstein the leading brand name in the Broadway musical by 1949, but James Michener's *Tales of the South Pacific* had the year before won the Pulitzer Prize for fiction. So no one was surprised when the musical garnered almost unanimous rave reviews, became "the 'hottest' ticket that Broadway had ever known," and went on to become the then second-longest-running musical (surpassed only by *Oklahoma!*).[90] And its "original cast album," as Andrea Most notes, "popularized the 33 1/3 RPM format for LPs, selling one million copies and holding the number one position on the charts for sixty-nine weeks."[91] Even Brooks Atkinson came around, citing the work as a "magnificent," "rhapsodically enjoyable," and "thoroughly composed musical drama."[92] Other critics singled it out for being "novel in text and treatment" and "rich in dramatic substance."[93] Although only implied in most reviews, the critics seemed impressed, in David Ewen's words, by the writers' "courage" in making "a middle-aged, gray haired man the hero of a musical." But "even greater independence of thought and action was required to make the secondary love plot . . . a plea for racial tolerance," complete with a song ("You've Got to Be Carefully Taught") that, according to one commentator, "attacks the issue with a vehemence never before . . . seen on the stage."[94] And while the combination of an explicitly antiracist politics (a mere one year after Truman had desegregated the military) with a nakedly racist exoticism may make for uncomfortable listening in this era of identity politics, *South Pacific* is celebrated in most critical accounts of musical theater as, in Philip Beidler's words, a "cherished legend" that makes "a courageous statement against racial bigotry in general and institutional racism in the postwar United States in particular."[95] Although this mythologization vastly oversimplifies and whitewashes the musical's racial politics, it is also responsible for reconstructing *South Pacific* as a middlebrow masterpiece: a politicized, and hence serious, example of a frivolous theatrical form.

Although hailed as Rodgers and Hammerstein's most accomplished *Gesamtkunstwerk, South Pacific* is in fact a perfect illustration of the sleight of hand responsible for producing the illusion of the so-called integrated musical. For none of their other works is as much the jerry-built collage that *South Pacific* is. Beidler's list of its components ranges neatly from highbrow to lowbrow: the "grandeur of opera; the seriousness of 'legitimate' theater; the comedic possibilities of the variety show and vaudeville; the emotionality of melodrama."[96] And it is hardly coincidental that the hero, Emile de Becque, happens to be French (although played originally by Ezio Pinza, a leading Italian operatic basso), since the musical is suffused by a French-inspired orientalism that gives it much of its highbrow appeal, including its echoes of the orientalist operas of Delibes and Saint-Saëns, the modernist exoticism of Debussy and Ravel, and the sexualized yet innocent South Seas women popularized by Gauguin. Uncharacteristically for Rodgers and Hammerstein, however, the main plot is somewhat less highbrow in tone and structure than the subplot, despite its more Europeanized music. (In almost all their other musicals, a more vaudevillian subplot is subordinate in terms of both narrative structure and brow level.)[97] For while the main plot pits an American innocent, Nellie Forbush, against a cosmopolitan, rich, miscegenating, and once-homicidal European, the subplot could have come out of any number of nineteenth-century French operas that feature a white hero who ventures "into mysterious, dark-skinned, colonised territory represented by alluring dancing girls and [a] deeply affectionate, sensitive" native temptress, "incurring" the "wrath of [a] brutal, intransigent tribal chieftain," who, in this case, happens to be her mother, Bloody Mary.[98] And as in almost every orientalist narrative, Western, liberal, humanist values finally triumph over oriental despotism, despite—or perhaps because of—Lieutenant Cable's death. Sacrificed both to the American war effort and to the then-unforgiving laws of cross-race desire, Cable can resolve an otherwise unresolvable plotline only by dying.

South Pacific's unnatural intercourse of high and low is imagined first and foremost in racial terms—as fear of miscegenation—in both main and secondary plots. In the main plot, Nellie recoils in terror when she discovers that the man she loves "lived with a Polynesian woman" and fathered two children with her.[99] As Beidler emphasizes, de Becque is sullied by his miscegenation, but not irretrievably. He may have "gone Asiatic but, because he is an occidental, he can come back across the line."[100] In the more tragically highbrow subplot, racial boundaries are more stubbornly drawn, in part because of Cable's upper-class, Princeton, mainline pedigree. He and Liat celebrate a sublime eroticism and delight in their "Happy Talk" despite the fact that Liat is, in Most's trenchant words, condemned "to silence, a sentence in the musical theatre akin to death."[101] Then the cruel Bloody Mary destroys their idyll with a promise that inadvertently becomes a threat: "You have special good babies" (339). At that moment, a "Happy Talk" fanfare bursts out in the brass over rolled tympani and resolves into an ominous minor chord, signaling both Cable's racist panic and his reversal of fortune. (Because the U.S. Supreme Court did not rule anti-miscegenation laws unconstitutional until 1967, cross-race sexual relations in the late 1940s remained a criminalized and perilous practice in many parts of the United States, especially the South, where *South Pacific* was routinely assailed for its alleged anti-Americanism.)[102] The musical's liberal polemicizing, however, demands a different resolution, and Cable later recants his own panicked renunciation. For its argument—which is more accurately characterized as anti-anti-miscegenation than pro-miscegenation—is predicated upon a universalized heterosexuality in which sexual difference is mapped onto racial difference, naturalizing, or at least depathologizing, the unnatural intercourse of white and colored. *South Pacific* undeniably trades in colonialist representations of the native Other, but it is also deeply committed to the idea of a redemptive "romantic love" that, in Bruce Mc-Conachie's words, is "the natural expression of an inner self beneath an outer facade of cultural and racial difference."[103]

The trope of miscegenation works in deeply contradictory ways, however, producing panic but also utopian figurations and fantasies. Bali Ha'i, in particular, the site of miscegenated eroticism, is an explicitly fantasmatic locale, an Imaginary paradise (in Lacanian terms) in which "you" may discover and realize "Your own special hopes, / Your own special dreams" (294). The locale of pleasure and excess, the island is an unmistakably feminized landscape (with its "two volcanoes" [294]) that calls out to Cable through Bloody Mary's voice. Its siren song is *South Pacific*'s persistent, if only unconsciously heard ostinato, beginning the overture and haunting much of the play's almost operatic—or, more accurately, cinematic—underscoring. For "Bali Ha'i" is a song that carefully works its subliminal seduction, relying heavily, as Rose Subotnik notes, on pentatonic and whole-tone scales, preferring a slithery chromaticism to Western-style propulsiveness and producing a sense of oriental languor and stasis.[104] Because Bali Ha'i is an "off-limits" tropical paradise, it abounds in luxurious goods that, because they are coded as the authentic, handmade products of an artisanal, primitivized, and still-ritual culture, presumably escape the curse of the commodity form: "shrunken heads, bracelets, old ivory" (287). On the one hand, the premodern Bali Ha'i is clearly counterposed against the flamboyantly entrepreneurial capitalism of "Luther Billis Enterprises," whose assembly lines launder clothes for "special rates" and mass-produce grass skirts (284). But the multiple narratives of *South Pacific* are unable to sustain this opposition between the artisanal (let us call it highbrow) and the mass-produced (let us call it lowbrow). For Bloody Mary's ability to traffic in both economies betrays the always already commodified nature of the ritual objects and pastoral pleasures of Bali Ha'i. And Cable's erotic idyll with Liat can do no more than momentarily disguise the fact that she too is an object (like the boar's tooth) traded by her mother, who, as agent of an orientalist traffic in women, is sure to occupy a masculinized subject position and stand in for the Law of the Father. By offering to labor for her daughter's pleasure, Bloody Mary erases the differences between ritual charms and commodities: she volunteers to cash in her always marketable artifacts so that Cable and Liat can "walk through woods, swim in sea, sing, dance, talk happy" (337). But even her dream of an Imaginary "Happy Talk" must be predicated on Cable's willingness to "buy" the dream and the girl (337). In other words, even the allegedly authentic work of art is revealed to be a consumable object that accrues mystical powers only insofar as it is able to conceal its commodity status. And all the while that *South Pacific* both exploits and debunks Bali Ha'i as a feminized, oriental paradise, it also reveals it as a place where a man can purchase what he wants. For seen from the postwar perspective, Bali Ha'i is clearly a newly packaged tourist destination for newly affluent Americans whom "World War II had turned . . . into globetrotters" and who were keen to exploit their new purchasing power on a global scale and trade in their capital for exotic experiences and fetish objects.[105]

South Pacific is not usually classified as a play-within-a-play, despite the Thanksgiving Follies drag show. But like so many of the most celebrated musicals, it is in effect a backstage musical that stages and celebrates musical theater as a site of cultural mixing. The liberal, anti-antimiscegenation politics of *South Pacific* are thus played out not only on the level of content but also in the very form of the musical, which promiscuously mixes high drama with low and uses several quite distinct musical styles. At one extreme are the most highbrow styles, invariably associated with European art music: the *La Mer*–inspired orchestral interludes for Emile and Nellie; their accompanied recitatives; Emile's quasi-operatic perorations; and the Frenchified orientalist music of Bali Ha'i. At the other extreme are the unabashedly vernacular forms, which are coded as paradigmatically American: the almost Sousa-like march, "There Is Nothin' like a Dame" (replete with its colloquially dropped final consonant); the vaudevillian "Honey Bun"; the white blues of "I'm Gonna Wash that Man right outa My Hair"; and that inimitable anthem to the American heartland, shameless heterosexuality, and the delicious cliché, "A Wonderful Guy."

"I'm Gonna Wash that Man right outa My Hair" may be the only song in *South Pacific* that explicitly alludes to African American musical forms, but it cannot erase the fact that musical theater remains the most miscegenated of theatrical forms. The song rearranges the blues structure, twice repeating the first line (instead of the more conventional single repeat), shifting back and forth between major and minor modes, and incorpo-

rating the so-called blue notes (in this case, flatted sevenths) so characteristic of both blues and jazz. Even the lyrics evoke the independent-
minded female blues singer of the 1920s and 1930s who takes a positive
enjoyment in ridding herself of her no-good man. In the context of *South
Pacific*, "I'm Gonna Wash that Man right outa My Hair" instantiates the
syncretism that characterizes both the American popular song and the
American musical as they were institutionalized during the 1920s. For
both derive from the intercourse between high and low, European American and African American forms. The popular song fuses ragtime, jazz,
blues, the sentimental ballad, folk and minstrel songs, the operatic aria,
and the European art song; the musical represents an amalgam of minstrelsy, vaudeville, comedy, opera, operetta, and melodrama.

As Gerald Early notes, "Blacks may very well have created most American forms of music and dance, but they certainly could not popularize
them." It took Paul Whiteman's 1924 Aeolian Hall concert (which
marked the premiere of Gershwin's *Rhapsody in Blue*) to put an elevated,
"bowdlerized" version of "black, lower-class music" on the cultural map,
thereby remodeling and reinventing "white bourgeois American music
and white bourgeois tastes." The demand for a bowdlerized version of
jazz is symptomatic of a profound uneasiness that many European Americans felt about certain forms of black music that they considered too
sexualized, primitivized, and frankly lowbrow. It is also a sign of the fact
that the black jazz musician (like the native of Bali Ha'i) retained a special place in the cultural imaginary as "a magical primitive . . . producing
art without a text," while his or her music supposedly "touch[ed] a more
authentic, more primal core of creative consciousness." The allure of this
primitivism is in part responsible for the repeated and ongoing expropriation of African American musical forms, going all the way back to the
beginnings of minstrelsy in the early nineteenth century. Yet Early is correct when he notes that it is also quite precisely this "racial syncretism
that gives American popular music its distinctiveness and its power."[106]
During the 1920s, in the works of Hammerstein and Kern (especially
Show Boat), the Gershwins, Berlin, Rodgers and Hart, and many others,
Broadway and Tin Pan Alley successfully mixed high and low and standardized its product, as Jeffrey Melnick notes, by "collat[ing] many styles
into a recognizable musical language which could then be commodified
and distributed nationally."[107]

Although it is sometimes difficult to distinguish between African American jazz of the 1920s and early 1930s and the product of a mostly white Tin Pan Alley, the styles of black music and white music steadily diverged between the mid-1930s and the mid-1950s as bebop was born, the big bands proliferated, and popular songs became more sentimental. And while many of the early standards produced by Broadway composers are strongly inflected by the chromatic melodies, harmonies, and swing of jazz, the so-called integrated musical virtually disavowed African American musical forms (or they became cordoned off in so-called black musicals). *Oklahoma!* and *Carousel,* by way of example, forge a musical and dramatic language far more obviously indebted to opera and operetta than jazz. But as "You've Got to Be Carefully Taught" makes painfully clear, cross-race complications in places like Bali Ha'i inevitably derive much of their resonance and force from analogies with racism and race relations back home. As a result, a so-called integrated musical like *South Pacific*—which could more accurately be described as a segregated musical—carefully displaces anxieties about the expropriation of African American, artisanal forms onto the happy natives of Bali Ha'i, who are all too willing to commercialize their charms. For *South Pacific* all too equivocally celebrates the return of the repressed: the triumph of a primitivized, folk culture whose allure will long outlast the intrusion of those American G.I.s, who remain, however, the ones with the capital to commodify and distribute the precious, homemade artifacts they buy for a song. And it celebrates the musical form itself as the site and the occasion for a shameless, miscegenating romance between the handmade and the mass-produced; the high and the low; the American and the European; the cultured white and the vibrant, seductive primitive.

Paying the Rent

If *South Pacific* is the result of an unnatural intercourse between white and colored, then *Rent* is the bastard child of an even more perverse coupling of high and low, art and commerce, straight and queer, rich and poor. Unlike the scrupulously plotted Rodgers and Hammerstein music drama, Jonathan Larson's multicultural rock opera is a deliberately disheveled affair. *Rent* takes a promiscuous pleasure in mixing musical, poetic, and dramatic styles and in bringing together all those persons that give social conservatives the heebie-jeebies: "faggots, lezzies, dykes, cross dressers," junkies, anarchists, the homeless, people with AIDS, and artists of all stripes.[108] Moreover, its translation of *La Bohème* into a kind of "Lower East Side Story" mixes high and low more aggressively than any other play of the 1990s, turning the frail Mimi into an S/M-club stripper and junkie, the musician Schaunard into a transvestite who dies of AIDS, roasted chestnuts into heroin and Ecstasy, and "Musetta's Waltz" into a few feverish guitar licks. Unlike Puccini's opera, which does not take on explicitly political issues, Larson's first act ends with a celebration of "going against the grain"; of "Revolution, . . . / Forcing changes, risk, and danger"; of "Tear[ing] down the wall" (1:23). As Ben Brantley notes, however, this radical posture cannot disguise the fact that "'Rent' is ultimately as sentimental as 'Carousel' or 'South Pacific'" and that the cast members (as well as the characters) "beam with the good will and against-the-odds optimism that is at the heart of the American musical."[109]

In development for over five years, *Rent* opened at the 150-seat New York Theatre Workshop (NYTW) in February 1996, two weeks after the sudden—and sensationally reported—death of its author, and at once became, in Peter Marks's words, "the story of the theater season, a surprise triumph in an industry short on sensations."[110] The small, nonprofit theater, along with three commercial producers who had been involved with the production for over a year, reopened the play on Broadway in April to "a tornado of hype" and generally ecstatic reviews, bagging the triple crown: the Pulitzer Prize, the Tony Award, and the New York Drama Critics' Circle Award.[111] Four months later, the two-CD recording "entered the Billboard Top 200 album chart at number 19, the highest Broadway cast album debut in more than a decade," and "went gold" by the "end of the year."[112] The musical spawned a *Newsweek* cover story, a Bloomingdale's boutique, and a double-decker-bus New York Apple Tour of the East Village. As was repeatedly pointed out, "the easy intercourse (social even more than sexual) among characters with variegated and flamboyant predilections" clearly struck a nerve in the cultural body politic, making the musical the most successful American play of the 1990s.[113] *Rent,* in short, held out the promise of bringing the theater back to life by attracting "a new" and much younger "audience to Broadway and thereby stak[ing] a claim to [Broadway] for a new generation."[114]

Rent's success is the product of what has been portrayed as a harmonious cohabitation of the nonprofit and commercial theaters, the kind of cohabitation that has become all the more important as the nonprofits' costs have risen and they have been forced increasingly to try to support their seasons with income derived from a Broadway transfer. New York Theatre Workshop was particularly well positioned to bring a "radical chic" musical to Broadway, in part because it has been one of the most adventurous and at times experimental of the off-Broadway theater companies, premiering work by Caryl Churchill, Tony Kushner, and other writers who are regarded as edgy and politically progressive.[115] Moreover, its East Fourth Street home placed it in the very heart of the East Village scene that was being represented on stage. Because the scale of the production was far larger than that of most NYTW shows, however, three commercial producers came on board in late 1994 (Jeffrey Seller, Kevin McCollum, and Allan S. Gordon), when the play was still in workshop. Jim Nicola, NYTW's artistic director, spelled out his anxiety over the arrangement: "We were a little nervous, as we always are when we take money from a commercial producer." But because the theater's board of directors refused to put up the money, Nicola accepted the support of "dream partners" who "wrote the checks and . . . were quiet."[116] The producers' own recollections, however, are somewhat at odds with Nicola's. Gordon insists that they were actively involved, "hands-on" producers who funneled extensive notes to the production team through the artistic director. Describing the tightrope they attempted to walk, Gordon's words represent a pedestrian paraphrase of those uttered by Charles Frohman a hundred years before: "We are trying to create the very best product, but we're also looking to present it in such a way that it's profitable, without sacrificing artistic merit." This 1990s commercial-nonprofit hybrid thereby reinforced theater's middlebrow status by devoting itself to the familiar task of balancing the "meaningful" with the "profitable."[117] And there is no question that *Rent* succeeded during the 1990s in achieving an unparalleled level of both critical acclaim and profitability.

Like *South Pacific* before it, *Rent* is the product of the unnatural intercourse of elite and popular cultures. And despite the fact that its appeal across generations and classes is predicated on the deterioration of the cultural hierarchy that was firmly in place fifty years before, *Rent* still stakes a claim to certain styles and cultural tropes associated with what little remains of high culture. On the one hand, the piece appropriates the plot and characters of what continues to epitomize old-fashioned high culture: opera. On the other hand, it also cops a hipper-than-thou attitude, recycling the forms, technologies, and conventions of new media and performance; taking up for its guiding philosophy a kind of watered-down, generic existentialism ("There is no future / There is no past / I live this moment / As my last" [1:15]); and exploiting the chic of "anything taboo," particularly when it is embodied by a sexual avant-garde that comes in all colors and flavors (1:23). At the same time, *Rent* is unabashedly populist in its use of a musical style best described as 1980s commercial, corporate rock with touches of rhythm and blues, house music, techno, and club. Unlike *South Pacific,* which borrows musical styles conscious of their histories and associations, *Rent* uses a more disorderly and at times arbitrary melange of styles. But there is no question that its particular mixture of high and low, of avant-gardist and vernacular, is in large part responsible for its great appeal to a youth culture Bruce Weber dubs the "hopefully hip."[118]

Rent's unique positioning in the cultural field—its difference from, on the one hand, more conventional Broadway musicals of the period (like *Ragtime* or *Footloose*) and, on the other, serious Hollywood appeals to youth culture (like *Shakespeare's Romeo + Juliet* or *Clueless*)—lies in its claim to a kind of gritty authenticity. For the piece unquestionably looks back to and tries to revive the project of the first avant-garde—the bohemians of Puccini's era—so intent on defying both aestheticism and the commodification of the artwork by "reintegrat[ing] art," as Peter Bürger famously explains, "in the praxis of life."[119] *La Bohème,* for this reason, provides an especially apt scaffold for Larson's neo-avant-gardist design. Yet at the same time, *Rent* is very obviously a product of a society in which all cultural productions are widely acknowledged to be always already commodified. Like its 1969—and even then neo-avant-gardist—predecessor, *Hair, Rent* is clearly aware of its status as art object, but quite unlike the far more political *Hair, Rent* uses a calculated reflexivity to pass itself off as a relatively elitist, theory-conscious, postmodernist representation. The actors conspicuously sport headset microphones and, as in most musicals, perform unabashedly for the theater audience. The staging tends toward the emblematic and presentational. Mark, a documentary filmmaker who is in fact filming a part of the action that he screens in the second act (shades of MTV's pioneering series *Real World*), is foregrounded as the play's *raisonneur* and "witness" (2:11). And the musical clearly spotlights Maureen's performance art at a pivotal moment in the unfolding of the plot. It is, after all, the spark for the riot and the text that Mimi recalls when she magically comes back from the "tunnel" of death (2:17). Like a self-consciously Baudrillardian simulacrum, *Rent* flaunts its status as endlessly self-reflexive re-presentation.

Rent's awareness of itself as text is not, however, the relatively guilt-free and delighted celebration that characterizes so much art classified as postmodernist. Rather, its self-awareness is the cause of considerable pain and anxiety because it is continually linked—both in the musical itself and in the discourse surrounding the production—to the problematics of selling out. This anxiety clearly distinguishes it from the mass culture that surrounds it, in which, Seabrook points out, "concepts like 'going commercial' and 'selling out' became empty phrases."[120] Mark's only real inner conflict is his ambivalence about selling his footage of the riot to and working for Alexi Darling, who, like an information-age Mephistopheles, tempts him to "sell us your soul" (2:8). In the end he refuses to work for her, despite his admission (in one of Larson's many flat-footed lyrics), "So I own not a notion / I escape and ape content" (2:13). Maureen is chided by Joanne for wanting an agent— "That's selling out" (2:4)—while Benny is ridiculed by all for his attempt to unite art and commerce and for having lost "the ideals he once pursued" (1:11). Most tellingly, Mark is denounced by the Blanket Person he attempts to film for being a "bleeding heart cameraman . . . / Just trying to use me to kill his guilt" (1:17).

Rent's considerable fear for its own representational strategies is echoed by members of the production team. Indeed, the only issue that aroused more anxiety for them than the collaboration between the non-profit and the commercial arenas was the play's purported authenticity. They were especially eager that *Rent* not be seen to exploit and commodify the experiences of persons who, by any measure, must be numbered among the abject. They were very nervous, for example, that the musical present an "honest" picture of the homeless rather than an "insulting" "chorus of cute homeless people."[121] Michael Greif, the director, was particularly concerned that *Rent* maintain the precarious balance that has long characterized middlebrow: "I think the issue has always been preserving authenticity and preserving real integrity in the way we present these characters, and also presenting them in ways that make them very identifiable and sympathetic and human."[122] He goes on to explain that his casting choices were decisive in constructing the mystique of authenticity that makes *Rent* unique among contemporary musicals:

> I thought that we really needed some sort of kooky, authentic folks to pull it off, to teach me and Jonathan things. I wanted to see how the real thing responded to the material. And we learned that those authentic presences really, really, really made it exciting. The audience could tell the difference between someone who'd lived in that world and someone who hadn't. One of the reasons we all loved Daphne [Rubin-Vega] so much is that she found a way to seem like she really lived in that world—not in the world of musical theater, but in the world of *Rent*.[123]

On the one hand, Greif's concept requires "kooky, authentic folks," these "authentic presences" whose uniqueness is founded on their experience living in "that world." For like the identity politics to which it is obviously indentured, his discourse fetishizes personal experience as the defining characteristic of "the real thing." Despite the irreducibly personal, unique, and incommunicable quality of experience, Greif fantasizes that this "thing" possesses an almost magical power to bring "the material" to life, to give it that unmistakable aura of authenticity that is antithetical to "the world of musical theater" but that presumably characterizes the urban folk culture of the East Village. He imagines that *Rent* must be the result of a necrophiliac intercourse between "the real thing" and "the material," between the agents of pure experience and that dead simulacrum that is the text. But "the real thing" by definition defies representation—it does not show itself, it merely is. So to re-present it is always already to have turned it into something else: a play, an image, a fake, the "virtual life" that Maureen finds so repugnant (1:22). The impossibility of pure presence does not stop Greif from using an exorbitance of "reallys" to try to coax it into existence, but it does guarantee that the musical can be no more than a failed representation of that which by definition can never be represented. And it doesn't take a deconstructionist to spot a three-dollar bill. Howard Kissel described the play as being "full of phoniness."[124]

In order to bring the text of *Rent* to life, Greif and the producers made several important decisions. Although the cast of the first NYTW reading had been "nearly all-white," it became "increasingly racially diverse" as the play neared production.[125] Greif may not admit it, but his singling out of Rubin-Vega betrays an unspoken assumption on the part of the production team that persons of color—who play five of the eight major roles—give the musical the aura of "kooky" authenticity it so desperately needs. For like *South Pacific, Rent* uses persons of color to turn what would otherwise be just another Broadway commodity into "the real thing." And while there is no question that *Rent* remains, in Jesse L. Martin's words, a "minority heaven" in a musical theater that offers few roles to persons of color except in so-called black musicals, it also clearly needs persons of color to give it the "exoticness" that Greif finds so alluring.[126] On the one hand, it is arguably salutary for Broadway to provide a home for a long-running musical with a largely nonwhite cast that is not in fact about race. On the other hand, *Rent* (unlike *South Pacific*) completely sidesteps issues of racial discrimination, using its persons of color to provide a middle-class, "not exactly rainbow-colored" audience with an exotic, multicultural experience guaranteed to make it feel liberal and hip.[127] And while it clearly attempts to break with certain forms of racial stereotyping (by casting Benny, for example, the "yuppie scum," as an African American), it also manages all too neatly to portray the two Latina characters, Mimi and Angel, as updated tragic mulattas (2:12). And in the case of Angel, his tragic and exotic status is made all the more vivid by his positioning between races and, as a drag queen, between genders as well.[128] Moreover, although it was written during a period when hip-hop had become the most popular music in the United States, *Rent* remains as white as *South Pacific* in its musical pedigree and, with the exception of Angel's house-music-inspired "Today 4 U," virtually ignores the unprecedented richness of both African American and Latino musical forms.

Rent's exploitation of racial minorities is echoed by its exploitation of sexual minorities. Five of the eight leads are coded as queer: two lesbians; two gay men; and, in the case of Mimi, a sex worker in an S/M club. The representations may not be obviously homophobic but they function, even more distinctly than the portrayals of racial minorities—because more premeditatedly—as the sign of upper-middlebrow chic, giving the musical an air of danger and daring and clearly distinguishing it from Hollywood films and other mass-cultural representations. Celebrating what Michael Greif calls "queer life"—along with "bisexuals, trisexuals," and other perverts—the musical takes a positive delight in letting the characters sing out in chorus the glory of "sodomy" and "S & M" (1:23).[129] Nonetheless, the central romantic couple in the piece remains heterosexual, as does Mark, the *raisonneur*.

Perhaps the most disturbing change that Larson effects in his rewriting of *La Bohème* is his transformation of the economic plight in which the characters find themselves. As Howard Kissel emphasizes: "Puccini's bohemians are genuinely destitute. Several of Larson's have wealthy parents eager to help them out."[130] Most are well educated and have marketable skills. But almost as if Larson were adopting the rhetoric of the religious right that regards homosexuality as a choice, his musical takes up the kind of lifestyle politics that became so popularized during the 1990s (as a substitute for class politics) and that regards one's associations, pleasures, and purchases as volitional. Roger may be despondent at the beginning of the musical, but he considers his "life" and that of his cohort to be something "that we've chosen" (1:4). And later Mimi assures him when inviting him out to a club, "We don't need any money / I always get in for free" (1:14). For these new bohemians are all committed to a kind of guerrilla warfare against bourgeois culture. All the leading characters (except Benny) can retain and fortify their outlaw status only by foregoing economic success (that is why Mark must refuse Alexi Darling's offer). And although HIV status is not (to Larson's credit) regarded as volitional, most of the protagonists are in the enviable position of being able to exploit poverty for the cultural chic it supplies them.

A kind of conspicuous impoverishment thus becomes, as Kissel notes, "a merchandising handle," both in the play itself and in its promotion and marketing. After its brief but sensational run at NYTW, its designers commandeered the Nederlander Theatre, which had long been dark, and, in John Simon's words, "tarted [it] up inside and out with countercultural, grunge chic" to look like an East Village dive.[131] Brantley correctly identifies this makeover as producing "the stuff of theater-as-theme park" and providing some carefully staged and controlled sex and grittiness in a renovated, sanitized, desexed, tourist-friendly, Disneyized Times Square—courtesy of then Mayor Giuliani.[132] And this version of environmental theater for an unapologetically consumerist and voyeuristic audience has become an increasingly prevalent phenomenon as Broadway has become more and more expensive and as the movies (with which Broadway must compete) have developed ever more sophisticated technologies to envelop the spectator in digitalized sound and light. The immersion ritual that *Rent* subjects spectators to can also be seen as an updated version of the so-called poverty balls of the Gilded Age that gave the wealthy the opportunity to indulge their appetite for abjection for a few hours by masquerading as the poor. One San Francisco hotel gives theater lovers a chance to relive such a poverty ball for days at a time. The Hotel Triton offers a "Room for *Rent*," designed by the play's assistant set designer, that features all of *Rent*'s "'tacky chic'" furnishings and set pieces as well as a "private bar" that sells "CD's, temporary tattoos, stationery, and T-shirts." Meanwhile, the closet—and where would a *Rent*-head be without one?—is stocked with "three costumes from the show" that allow the eager fan to try on one of the roles in the privacy of his or her hotel suite or simply prance about in "Angel's Santa suit" or "Roger's shirt."[133] And all for only $299 per night!

Rent's success testifies not only to the disruption of cultural hierarchies but also to the utter commodification of what used to be called the counterculture. It unquestionably looks back to and places itself in the tradition of the youth culture of the 1950s and 1960s, attempting in "La Vie Boheme" to appropriate the oppositional posture and the belatedly highbrow appeal of the original White Negroes and hipsters, figures like "Ginsberg, Dylan, Cunningham and Cage Lenny Bruce" (1:23). By aligning itself with the White Negroism of the 1950s, *Rent* updates the anarcho-libertarian politics of the so-called rebel without a cause. And while this 1950s rebel was contemptuous of the increasingly standardized and commodified postwar society, his or her desire for change was routinely channeled into nonpolitical—or, more commonly, antipolitical—

directions. *Rent,* meanwhile, for all its "anti-Establishment attitude," its lip service to "Revolution, justice, screaming for solutions, / Forcing changes," radically depoliticizes economic inequalities by imagining them as "chosen" (1:25).[134] In its consumerist utopia, all have access to the stuff of life and culture, "To hand-crafted beers made in local breweries / To yoga, to yogurt, to rice and beans and cheese / To leather, to dildos, to curry vindaloo" (1:23). For the "revolution" in *Rent* is clearly coded as an adolescent, Oedipal rebellion: "Hating convention, hating pretension, / Not to mention of course / Hating dear old mom and dad" (1:23). It's little wonder then that Maureen infantilizes herself in a performance piece that is allegedly a political protest. But it is never clear what exactly her paean to Elsie the cow is protesting. Gentrification? The eviction of the homeless? Dairy cooperatives? Bad art? Mom and Dad? Moreover, her transcendent "way out"—"Leap of faith"—epitomizes the quiescent, New Agey nonsolutions that during the 1990s came to substitute for political struggle (1:22). More than any other play of the decade, *Rent* is paradigmatic of a new era of hip consumerism in which buying is imagined as a subversive activity, Allen Ginsberg peddles for the Gap, and "hip" has become "the orthodoxy of Information Age capitalism."[135] It sadly testifies to the fact that the only apparent solution to the problems of a rotten world is to vacate the premises.

The true genius of *Rent* has been its marketing, which its producers describe as "a business revolution." (And indeed, that almost oxymoronic phrase is symptomatic of a culture in which the very concept of revolution—as exemplified by the American Revolution of 1994, Newt Gingrich's Contract with America—has been completely coopted by corporate interests.) They emphasize that they "were selling this concept called *Rent,*" in other words, selling less a musical play with a plot, characters, and score than a mystique, an aura, a mythology of an allegedly authentic urban folk culture that would appeal to "a young, hip, urban, bohemian sensibility."[136] But to do so, they needed "a distinctive marketing aesthetic." Unlike most other Broadway musicals that adopt logos that are iconic expressions of the narrative content of the show, *Rent*'s stencil-and-masking-tape logo is "based on the POST NO BILLS signs that are painted on construction-site walls" and evokes (variously) a guerrilla artwork-in-progress, a handmade yet mass-produced poster, a Robert

Rauschenberg knock-off, or an announcement of a hit-and-run politi-cal demonstration.[137] To this logo—which is nothing if not cool—the poster, program, and CD cover add distressed, slightly druggy, tinted photographs of the leading characters (four in close-up) that suggest the "warmth, tragedy, [and] laughter" that the designer, Drew Hodges, wanted to convey, as well as the characters' atomization and anomie.[138] Most important, the collage is eye-catching because of its many studied imperfections: the folds and tears in the photographs, the unaligned let-ters in the word "rent," and the violated borders of the photographs. For the design suggests nothing less than a series of stop-action frames of scarred young women and men living on borrowed time, an image cal-culated to appeal to rebellious adolescents convinced that they, too, are the isolated victims of a world—and parents—who cannot understand them.

The stark black-and-white billboard advertisement that long domi-nated Times Square is rather different from the poster. While it uses the stenciled title, it adds a manual typewriter font text—"TICKETS FOR RENT," a telephone number, and the name and address of the theater— that accentuates the contradictory, highbrow-meets-mass-culture quality of the poster design. It evokes the improvisatory, ephemeral, handmade yet mass-produced characteristics of a predigital era when writers (and activists) still used manual typewriters and oppositional social forma-tions had a precise meaning. Even more intriguingly, however, the bill-board represents a kind of visual pun that appears, if one merely glances at it, to advertise that the billboard itself is for hire. "Your ad here," it seems to be saying. In other words, it announces its own vacancy, the fact that it is an extremely profitable site at the crossroads of the world owned by invisible others but available to all with the money to lease it. Its very vacancy, moreover, signals that the billboard, like *Rent* itself, is a site on which one is free to project, a kind of blank screen just waiting for the fantasies of a public eager to buy some space and time.

Although the mystique of *Rent*'s logo clearly owes a good deal to the allusive logo developed for *Cats* some fifteen years before, the musical was fortunate to appear at a historical moment when the marketing of goods was undergoing a significant change. For the mid-1990s, as Naomi Klein demonstrates, bore witness to the swallowing of the prod-uct by the brand, the commodity by the image. Like Nike, Starbucks, and the Body Shop, *Rent* developed a distinctive logo and brand identity that allowed the producers to sell the show less as a play (with characters, plot, and music), or even as an experience, than as a kind of lifestyle philosophy: "No day but today," the ads proclaimed from seemingly every taxi and bus in New York. Like these other corporate success stories, *Rent* functions, in Klein's phrase, as a meaning broker that signifies and markets "experience," "lifestyle," and "corporate transcendence."[139] The show itself thus disappears into its logo and becomes much like its billboard, an "empty carrier . . . for the brand . . . [it] represent[s]."[140] Like *Star Wars* or *Forrest Gump,* it is transformed into a mere pretext for the merchandising of transcendence. For the *Rent* logo as meaning broker uses an obviously mass-produced image to point up by contrast the play's status as a live, ritual-like performance that will enable the consumer, like Maureen and her friends, to make a "leap of faith" (1:22).

No account of the selling of *Rent* can be complete without considering the other elements that comprise its social and economic context: the prolonged economic boom that particularly benefited the Broadway theatergoing classes; the gentrification of the East Village; the romance of miscegenated cultural forms; the commodification of queer culture; and the trickle-up effect of MTV-style editing, graphics, and rhythms into almost every form of culture. And because *Rent* is such an accurate barometer of present-day U.S. culture, it points up both the continuing middlebrow position of Broadway theater and the growing inadequacy of that category. *Rent* is derivative of so many different sources and mixes them so unpredictably that it is difficult to argue that it occupies any position that could be called median. Rather, it reveals the fact that so many U.S. cultural productions that aspire both to hotness (especially to the youth market) and to a measure of artistic seriousness require the simultaneous deployment of a standardized, easily recognizable formula and a mystique of authenticity (or realness). This new culture, which represents the persistence of what used to be called upper-middlebrow (and is clearly related to the idea of an elite folk culture), might now be renamed Hipbrow.[141] For it trades at once on anonymity and uniqueness, predictability and a radically chic pose. Hipbrow (like Seabrook's understanding of Nobrow) rewrites Walter Benjamin's theorization of art in the age of mechanical reproduction, for it is simultaneously mass-produced and auratic. The aura of old that used to attach to the unique art object has simply been remade for deconstructionist times when, we are assured, the "historical testimony" that "rests on authenticity" has been so completely shaken by a thoroughgoing and cynical relativism that the auratic itself becomes indistinguishable ontologically from the copy.[142] Authenticity is now imagined to be an effect produced by a particular kind of artistic self-consciousness, a knowing self-reflexiveness that results from both embracing and protesting the commodity form. In Hipbrow, in other words, the mass-produced becomes auratic when it advertises its own world-weariness and ennui, when it both succumbs to and tries to transcend the vertiginous play of doubles. On Broadway, this neoexistentialist brand of Hipbrow is in short supply, but it did attach to the revivals of *Chicago* and *Cabaret* and plays like *Art* and *Dirty Blonde,* all of which are very much about both liveness and the allure of the copy. If the Hipbrow appeal of *Rent,* with its empty gestures of rebellion, has indeed replaced a part of what used to pass for middlebrow, its hegemony is undoubtedly linked not only to the triumph of deconstruction but also to the near elimination of oppositional politics in the United States, a loss of faith in the idea of progress, and a profound disillusionment with government (as "master narrative") and all forms of social engineering and welfare. Disaffected with the possibility of political and social change, the new, young Hipbrows can do little more than echo Maureen—"Only thing to do is jump over the moon"—and retreat to a weary and cynical solipsism in their endless search for the transcendent commodity (1:22).

Policing the Cultural Hierarchy

Rent may testify to the invasion of Broadway by Hipbrow tastes, but it has hardly routed more traditional fare. At the beginning of the twenty-first century, Broadway remains the most doggedly middlebrow sector of the U.S. cultural economy and is occupied almost entirely by musicals and revivals, most of which do not aspire to the Hipbrow appeal of *Rent* (or to any residual avant-gardist chic) but are geared toward middle-class suburbanites and tourists. This is the theater that is squeezed between (and competes with), on the one hand, star-studded prestige films (like *The English Patient*) and, on the other, Disney World and the increasingly theme-park nature of expensive entertainments that attempt to provide the consumer with a total experience. Occasionally a *Bring In 'Da Noise / Bring In 'Da Funk*, a *Ragtime,* or a Sondheim musical is able to prosper, but these shows never enjoy the long runs of *Cats* or *Les Misérables.*

Even the *New York Times* admits that Broadway is no longer a forum for what Ben Brantley calls "serious commercial theater in New York."[143] That kind of theater (which has an unmistakably upper-middlebrow ring to it) is now located off-Broadway or off-off. Brantley notes (perhaps too nostalgically) that Broadway enjoyed a golden era between the 1920s and the 1950s, when its fare was "daring." And he is correct to observe that this period—which not coincidentally marked theater's sharp decline in popularity—saw the legitimate stage endeavor to separate itself from mass-cultural forms in part by cultivating "the power to shock." For Brantley, as for so many arbiters of what now pretends to upper-middlebrow taste, a "serious" theater is imagined as a site of authenticity and immediacy. It is opposed to the "synthetic and homogenized" products of mass culture and is instead "an essential part of the crude, sophisticated and sassy dialogue that made you feel more alive in Manhattan than anywhere else." A "serious" theater is teeming with unmediated presence and with plays that "actually speak to their audiences," quite unlike the "narcotic" effect of the Broadway megamusical. And Brantley is hardly alone in yearning for a more "daring" theater. On the other side of the trenches, Tony Taccone (artistic director of Berkeley Rep) also believes that "our culture is starving for authenticity," the recapturing of which he regards as the goal of theater's "potentially dangerous and subversive exploration."[144] Brantley, meanwhile, clearly finds the "gritty promise and sensuous danger" of the 1935 song "Lullaby of Broadway" far more to his liking—and far more descriptive of what Broadway theater should be—than the mass-cultural knock-offs that now fill the midtown theater district.[145]

As the chief theater critic for the *Times,* Brantley bears a heavy responsibility. For like the middle manager he is, he must juggle many different constituencies, including a wide range of theater professionals (like producers, who do so much of their advertising in the *Times*), his editors, and his readership, both in New York and nationally. In an era in which blockbuster musicals can earn two billion dollars or more, the stakes are very high indeed. Moreover, Brantley, like all the *Times* critics, is obliged to advocate for (under cover of simply reporting on) a particular kind of "serious" culture to which the newspaper has long been committed. The conventional wisdom that the *Times* drama critic is the most powerful man in the American theater—a woman has never held the job—is not altogether wrong. For although the critic is finally a mediator and recycler of opinion, he is able to exert an extraordinary amount of influence on New York theater and, by extension, on theater throughout the United States. Since the demise of the *New York Herald-Tribune* in 1967, New York has basically been a one-newspaper town when it comes to theater. Certain musicals (like *Sunset Boulevard* or *Jekyll and Hyde*) are review-proof, and a few other critics carry some weight, especially with audiences and plays that fall either above or below the upper-middlebrow category. But with "the decline of intelligent, provocative criticism at newspapers around the country," the *Times* remains by far the most important arbiter of taste in the American theater, delivering a thumbs-up or thumbs-down judgment that will ensure that a play *will* or, more likely, *will not* be seen on other stages. It thus serves to police the boundaries of the cultural hierarchy; to monitor and regulate the hotness of cultural commodities; and, less consistently, to reward its advertisers.[146] Moreover, despite the recent and relative decentralization of the nonprofit theater, its commercial cousin remains the most centralized and review-dependent of the culture industries. A bad review from the *New York Times* will not kill a film, television program, ballet company, or the career of a visual artist. But it will kill a show.

The *Times*'s arts policy is by default closely related to its editorial policies and goals. For the *Times*, as Edward Said observes, "aspires (and is generally considered) to be the national newspaper of record." Carrying "a sober authority," the Gray Lady has remained the preeminent liberal newspaper in the United States since the 1960s, regularly endorsing Democratic candidates and liberal social policies and trotting out William Safire and A. M. Rosenthal as almost token conservatives on the op-ed page.[147] At the same time, U.S. political culture has veered sharply to the right, and the *Times* has consistently underreported that shift as well as the massive upward redistribution of wealth it has facilitated. During this period its arts policy (despite the considerable differences among its critics) could be categorized as being consistent with the paper's vision of a liberal, pluralistic, capitalist state, and it has sometimes given appreciative reviews to art whose politics its editorial writers would find distasteful. It provided ample coverage of the controversies of the late 1980s over government funding of allegedly obscene art and has sometimes supported artists on its editorial page during the ongoing culture wars. Since the disruption of the canons of taste during the 1970s, however, and the increasing confusion over what constitutes politically engaged art, the *Times* has become even more committed to promoting and, indeed, defining a kind of upper-middlebrow excellence in which formal mastery is combined with a soupçon of social engagement.

Ben Brantley's attempts to promote a "serious" theater are part of a long tradition at the *Times* and mimic those of his many predecessors, going back at least as far as Brooks Atkinson, who served as drama critic continuously from 1925 until 1960 (except during an overseas assignment during World War II). Atkinson's reviews in many ways hearken back to the genteel critics of the late nineteenth century, with their "emphasis on moral and aesthetic 'training'" and their determination to disseminate good taste.[148] His writing evinces a certain generous catholicity that inspires theater encyclopedias to judge it "gracious and gentlemanly" and his opinions "commonsense."[149] Like the middlebrow tastemakers of old, he felt that "the theatre should reach out and relate to the world outside." As Brantley acknowledges (in words he virtually echoes), Atkinson regarded the interwar years as a golden age when "American theatre was aggressive, intelligent, and dynamic, and it pioneered in many forms."[150] For Atkinson argued that the theater, which "not only reflected but also created public opinion," must, to be "dynamic," focus on "the causes, the political issues, [and] the human predicaments," from "fascism" to "political revolution," from the "dehumanization of industry" to "the segregation of Negro citizens."[151] During the period when the stage was first obliged to distinguish itself from mass culture, and the Hollywood film in particular, Atkinson was a pivotal figure in promoting a critical and liberal—rather than radical— drama that examined but did not challenge the fundamental disposition of power and capital in the United States and always finally honored, in his words, "the traditional optimism of America."[152]

Atkinson's successors at the *Times* have assiduously followed his lead. Frank Rich was particularly important in shaping American theater during his tenure as lead theater critic, from 1980 until 1994, in part because of his own highly opinionated style; in part because Broadway was then having to adjust to a serious decline in theater weeks, the rise of non-profit theater, and the disruption of the postwar cultural hierarchy; in part because this period witnessed a certain standardization of many of the innovations in writing and stagecraft initiated during the 1960s. Dubbed "the Butcher of Broadway" by his many adversaries, Rich is famously acerbic, attacking other critics and writing, as one thumbnail sketch has it, "for the literate reader with style and authority but with a hard intellectual edge and—in the estimation of the New York theatre community—little sympathy or affection for the theatre."[153] Equally contemptuous of both avant-gardism and rampant commercialization, political radicalism and political quiescence, he toed the middlebrow line and reinforced cultural boundaries with an unprecedented agressivity. Rich was promoted to the *Times* op-ed page in 1994, and indeed, his style is more appropriate for an opinion column since he regularly used his theater reviews as a kind of bully pulpit from which to hold forth on many issues that often had little to do with theater. It was from the safety of the op-ed page that he gave *Rent* its most ecstatic notice in the *Times,* opining (in a most Atkinsonian way) that the play "speaks for" a disaffected generation but still allows the characters to "revel in their joy."[154] Since his promotion, he has consolidated his position as the leading white, liberal social and cultural critic on the op-ed page, certain always to do the right thing and speak out against racism, homophobia, and all varieties of social conservativism.

In comparison with the imperious Rich, Brantley is a modest presence in the Arts section. Well versed in theatrical and cultural history, he promotes his own agenda, and his own tastes, far less aggressively than his predecessor. Despite his relaxed style, however, his carriage, like that of the other *Times* drama critics, consistently evinces the anxiety that has long characterized the arbiters of middlebrow culture. And given the virtual extinction of "serious" drama on Broadway, Brantley has had to venture further afield to find the kind of upper-middlebrow drama that the paper has long championed. In this context, the last full theater season of the twentieth century sparked something of an anxiety attack for the *Times* critics. The big news of the 1998–99 season—which was repeatedly being uncovered by the *Times*—was a British invasion of so-called straight plays. Like the American musical comedy, which was nearly asphyxiated to death by the British megamusical during the 1980s, new American drama was virtually banished from Broadway. Nine plays arrived in New York after a stop on London's West End. Even works by O'Neill and Williams were obliged to make the transatlantic crossing before being received on Broadway. Only one new American play, Warren Leight's *Side Man*, managed—barely—to sustain a Broadway run while the Pulitzer Prize–winning *Wit*, by Margaret Edson, thrived in an off-Broadway house. The contrast between these phenomena may well confirm the conviction of both commercial and nonprofit producers that Broadway theatergoers are far more likely to plunk down their seventy-five dollars to see a play if it has received the imprimatur of a British theater, especially one of the prestigious state theaters. It is also a sign that Broadway producers and critics have become more anxious than ever about new American drama.

Although the British invasion may suggest that the American theater retains a certain colonized mentality, I am more interested in analyzing why producers and critics worked so hard to bolster a belief in the superiority of the British theater. It would seem that in a time of unprecedented confusion in the United States between high and low, British (or Anglo-Irish) drama appeals to producers, theatergoers, and critics alike because it brings a whiff of elite culture, a touch of class, to American theater. Take, for example, the case of David Hare, who had three plays running on Broadway during that season (*Blue Room, Amy's View,* and *Via Dolorosa*). Hare's recent works are unmistakably literary, weighing in on political and social issues, formally adventurous without being avant-gardist, hewing to realistic styles while expanding their compass—all, in short, that the champions of upper-middlebrow could wish for. Yet Hare has achieved commercial success only by forsaking his class-based critique of British society, his formal experimentation, and the coruscatingly edgy style of earlier works like *Plenty* or *A Map of the World*. Studies in ambivalence, in not taking sides, his recent dramas are tailor-made for upper-middlebrow Broadway audiences, giving them the satisfaction of wrestling with difficult issues and so providing them with a self-congratulatory frisson of pleasure.

Yet this is precisely the kind of drama the *New York Times* seems intent on championing. In an almost embarrassingly revelatory conversation that appeared in the *Times* in 1999, the three lead theater critics, Ben

Brantley, Vincent Canby, and Peter Marks, agree that English theater is "visceral" and maintains a "vitality" that comes from its "connection . . . with its audiences." Because it maintains a "dialogue" with the public and produces a "buzz," English theater is the legitimate offspring of what the critics seem to regard as a natural and procreative intercourse. Its American counterpart, in contrast, is condemned to "trying to emulate the movies" and is thus positioned on the side of the simulacrum, the sterile copy that produces "no buzz" and leaves its audiences "anesthetized." While English audiences are stimulated by "politics and ideas," Americans "want the theater to be a geisha," a high-class and exotic woman-for-hire. Brantley's orientalist metaphor—shades of Bali Ha'i?—betrays an almost puritanical belief that American theater is too much of the flesh: "'If I'm spending this much money, you make me feel good. You give me a massage like I've never had before.'" In his fantasy, an implicitly male theatergoer demands to be serviced by a commercialized, prostitutional spectacle in which "the show *business* aspect" is dominant (emphasis added). The British audience, in contrast, is at home in a theater that in and of itself creates an "energy" and fills "a big space." These differences ensure that British drama is able to work "on all sorts of levels" and that British writers will produce universal works of art. After all, "Shakespeare is in their blood," and has he not long been regarded as the template for the natural, eternal genius? American drama, on the other hand (with the one "exception," the critics agree, of *Angels in America*), is "all about families, or about ethnic identity and gender identity." It's a "small medium" filled with "small plays" that focus on "relatively tiny concerns." So British theater stands on the side of the universal, vital, and artistic—and of the harmonious mixtures of body and mind, personal and political. American theater, on the other hand, stands on the side of the particular, anesthetic, commercial, fleshly, and perverse—and of an inconsequential identity politics.[155] Because the former does not, like its American cousin, strive to mimic mass culture, it works more successfully to reinforce what the *Times* would deem the proper cultural hierarchy. In other words, British theater (or at least that which the *Times* critics choose to see) knows its upper-middlebrow place. Its championing by these three critics, moreover, must not be seen as the product of their personal idiosyncrasies. On the contrary, the emphasis on moral uplift is a hallmark of the *New York Times*'s house style. In what other newspaper could a critic, without a trace of irony, ask the following question about the imminent demise of Broadway's longest-running musical: "Has the phenomenon of 'Cats' been a force for good in the world"?[156]

The distance that the *Times* would reinstall between theater and popular culture; its disdain for an identity-politics-driven drama and the vicissitudes of fashion; its refusal to recognize "politics and ideas" except when they're imported; and its longing for an uplifting, universal art end up privileging precisely the kind of well-crafted, Pulitzer Prize–winning, upper-middlebrow theater that was a staple of Broadway during what both Atkinson and Brantley describe as its golden age. It also ends up guaranteeing the irrelevance of the American theater to all but a few affluent, well-educated, liberal spectators. British theater can afford to be less commercial than American in large part because of the substantial government subsidies offered the prestigious state theaters (the source of most of the British imports on Broadway). And while government support of the arts has fallen since the advent of Thatcherism, the United States, in contrast, does not have a state theater or provide significant taxpayer-funded support for any of the arts. Combined government funding (federal, state, and city) for nonprofit theaters in the United States accounts for only 5 percent of their total income. And although corporations, foundations, and individuals pick up some of the slack, the average nonprofit theater must earn two-thirds of its income at the box office.[157] At the same time, theater administrators distressingly observe "negative trends" in donations plus an increase "in giving and support based on funder-driven concepts." These developments, combined with rising expenses and a slight decline in attendance, have made it even "more difficult" for nonprofit theaters "to take artistic risks or to present 'controversial' work."[158]

The Broadway theater, in contrast, at least as imagined by the *New York Times,* is a kind of mass-culture wannabe, maintaining a conflicted relationship with Hollywood, which it resents and from which it tries to distance itself, while envying its economic and cultural clout and imitating its product. The periodic incursions of British drama function in part as a remedy for Broadway's recurrent middlebrow anxiety attacks by elevating its stature (at least as far as the *Times* is concerned), giving it a certain elite appeal, and staving off the culture of hotness. For at the risk of indulging in the kind of identity politicking that the *Times* finds so déclassé, I am obliged to point out that all except one of the 1998–99 season's imports happen to be the products of the same straight, white men who have long held a monopoly on what passes for the universal (the exception is Williams's *Not About Nightingales*). The invasion thereby implicitly guarantees that the work by and about persons of color, women, lesbians, and gay men will be performed well away from the new, improved, spic 'n' span, tourist-friendly Times Square (of which, not coincidentally, the *New York Times* owns a big chunk). Theater producers, in other words, have in effect colluded with the critics to keep the Great White Way white—except, of course, for the occasional August Wilson play or African American musical. It is especially telling in this regard that the 1999 Tony Awards committee ruled the black vaudeville revue *Rolling on the T.O.B.A.* ineligible for a Tony despite the fact that it played in the same theater that housed *Cabaret* the year before, when it won four Tony Awards. Citing *Cabaret*'s "long history of Broadway productions," the committee tacitly reconfirmed precisely the pattern of slighting black performance that *Rolling on the T.O.B.A.* so angrily protests.[159]

In 1998–99, Broadway enjoyed its then most lucrative season. But its success was due in part to its exclusion of work that producers and critics regard as unsuitable for an increasingly corporatized commercial theater and an increasingly gentrified city. The British invasion thus neatly and anachronistically reinforces the old cultural hierarchy that had been institutionalized in the theater between the world wars by helping to maintain Broadway's distance from Hollywood, on the one hand, and from more risky off-Broadway drama, on the other. It works to balance lower-middlebrow fare (which has always had a place on Broadway) with "serious" drama. It helps to assuage critics' anxieties about the commercial theater's seemingly inexorable slide into mass culture. It reassures spectators out for "an experience" that their most dearly held assumptions and prejudices will not be seriously challenged.[160] It helps keep the straight play, well, straight. It guarantees that a truly "visceral" American theater that mixes high and low cultural forms far more provocatively than David Hare's *Blue Room* will flourish only on the margins of what all the world regards as America's center stage.

Given the economic situation of both the commercial and nonprofit theaters, and the contradictory demands this makes of producers, theater professionals, audiences, and critics alike, it is unlikely that the American theater will see significant growth or change in the foreseeable future. Producers will continue to try to make money and art at the same time, while critics will continue to put the squeeze on them. Audiences will go to the theater expecting a performance that is more exciting and "visceral" than what they find at the movies but that speaks the same language. And theater professionals, especially in nonprofit arenas, will continue to work, alas, for such "woefully low" salaries that they become "the field's greatest philanthropists."[161] Despite this dreary forecast, there are some positive signs: the continuing efflorescence of innovative theater, usually located far from Broadway's precincts, that delights in all forms of unnatural intercourse; and the development of a new generation of musicals, post–Rodgers and Hammerstein, post–Lloyd Webber, post-Sondheim, post-Larson. Many are collaborations between commercial and nonprofit theaters and represent, in Ira Weitzman's words, "a healthy mixture of established and emerging artists," both "more experimental composers" and "a groundswell of young people writing in a more pop vernacular."[162] So perhaps a revived musical theater that is both commercially viable and aesthetically and politically bold will find a way not of denying or renouncing theater's long-term middlebrow position in the cultural hierarchy but of exploiting it and discovering a new vibrancy in the unpredictable intercourse of high and low. The New York Times critics will continue to fret, wring their hands, and exhibit other symptoms of middlebrow anxiety. And they will continue to attack work, like the Michael John LaChiusa/George C. Wolfe The Wild Party, that too pointedly and angrily takes up the miscegenated history of the American musical theater. But rather than kill these innovative projects, perhaps each of them should just take a Valium, get a good night's rest, and call his psychiatrist in the morning.

Chapter Two

The Queerest Art

In the United States, the "gay nineties" bore witness to an unprecedented efflorescence of cultural productions by or about lesbians and
gay men. Dozens of independent films were released—from *Go Fish* to
Chasing Amy, from *The Incredibly True Adventure of Two Girls in Love* to
Watermelon Woman—that feature lesbian protagonists. The major studios, meanwhile, discovered the commercial potential of women coded
as lesbian or bisexual in lurid melodramas like *Basic Instinct* and *Single
White Female.* Hollywood's fascination with lesbians (especially if they
happen to be psychopaths) was paralleled by a flirtation with gay men
and/or male homoeroticism in a number of high-profile, critically well-
received films—from *Philadelphia* to *The Talented Mr. Ripley,* from *As
Good as It Gets* to *American Beauty*—that aspire to the category of art.
In 1997, *Ellen* became the first sitcom to feature a lesbian hero, while
Ellen DeGeneres's simultaneous coming out provided fodder for countless editorials, sermons, and talk shows. Although *Ellen* was unable to
make a go of it, a year later *Will and Grace* turned camp into highly successful, Emmy-winning, primetime entertainment. k.d. lang, Melissa
Etheridge, and the Indigo Girls amassed devoted fans. The Pet Shop
Boys and George Michael managed to retain their niche market. Even
disco made a comeback.

In what remains of elite culture, books by lesbian and gay writers, including Dorothy Allison, Michael Cunningham, Gore Vidal, Jeanette
Winterson, and Edmund White, garnered glowing reviews in the mainstream press. And in the theater, which occupies a somewhat less ele-

vated position in the cultural hierarchy, gay men and lesbians were productive, visible, and honored as never before. *Angels in America,* having amassed the Pulitzer Prize, two best-play Tonys, and other prestigious awards, chalked up a groundbreaking Broadway run, a national tour, and countless productions in regional theaters. But Tony Kushner was by no means the only widely produced out gay or lesbian playwright in America. Terrence McNally, Paula Vogel, Margaret Edson, Nicky Silver, Jon Robin Baitz, Paul Rudnick, Lanford Wilson, and Craig Lucas have all enjoyed successful, high-profile productions in New York and remain among the most widely produced contemporary American playwrights. Downtown (or on the West coast), meanwhile, Split Britches, Maria Irene Fornes, Lisa Kron, the Five Lesbian Brothers, Holly Hughes, Pomo Afro Homos, Carmelita Tropicana, Kiki and Herb, Lypsinka, Tim Miller, and David Greenspan (to name only the most well established) continued to break new ground by producing work that was often far more experimental than that of their uptown kin. Although long a sanctuary for closeted lesbians and gay men, the U.S. theater truly came out in the 1990s. Even Stephen Sondheim tiptoed out of the closet. And many of the most prominent playwrights, directors, actors, and other theater artists proclaimed themselves proudly, joyously—and matter-of-factly—queer.

A reclamation of a formerly stigmatized term, *queer* (as adjective or noun) functioned during the 1990s as a deeply utopian designation: a locus of refusal; an unbinding of psychic, sexual, and social energy; a destabilizing third term; a principle of radical democratization; a postmodernist renovation of camp; an affront to the bipolar system of gender and sexuality; a way of transcending both assimilationist and anti-assimilationist politics; a privileged mode of subversion. In Eve Kosofsky Sedgwick's now-classic theorization, it signifies less a fixed identity than a principle of polysemy: "'Queer' can refer to: the open mesh of possibilities, gaps, overlaps, dissonances and resonances, lapses and excesses of meaning when the constituent elements of anyone's gender, of anyone's sexuality aren't made (or *can't be* made) to signify monolithically." And while sexual and gendered differences have historically been the privileged markers of that which passes for queer, Sedgwick emphasizes that "a lot of the most exciting recent work around 'queer' spins the term outward along dimensions that can't be subsumed under gender and

sexuality at all," including "race, ethnicity," and "postcolonial national-
ity."[1] And because *queer* enjoys the distinction—in theory, at least—of
being gender neutral, it can be used to describe male, female, and transgendered identities. In its 1990s formulation, *queer* represented an attempt to open up a vista of multiple, shifting, and gloriously polymorphous bodies, pleasures, and sites of resistances and to problematize
1970s-style identity politics and the minoritizing discourses associated
with lesbian-feminism and gay liberation. In this way it became part of
a new and seductively universalizing discourse that could include under
its rainbow banners anyone willing to renounce the claims and prerogatives of heteronormativity.

And although the category "queer" clearly functioned (and continues
to function) as a utopian fantasy, queer organizations and initiatives
during the 1990s were often dominated (much like the activist group
Queer Nation, which did so much to disseminate the new queer politics
and culture) by the persons, agendas, and styles of white, middle-class,
gay men.[2] Moreover, as Jill Dolan notes, "the insistent anti-hegemonic
pose of 'queer' can also be a ruse for not taking responsibility for the va-
garies of a movement, a style, a life."[3] Too often, a self-congratulatory
queer identification—the politics of lifestyle—has functioned as a substitute for a commitment to radical social change. And like the identity
politics that it at once embraces and problematizes, a queer politic too
often, as Wendy Brown notes, "may specifically abjure a critique of class
power and class norms precisely insofar as these identities are established *vis-à-vis* a bourgeois norm of social acceptance, legal protection
and relative material comfort."[4]

Although cognizant of its problems, I believe that "queer" remains a
provocative way for thinking about the intersection between certain theatrical forms and certain sexual subjects. It functions as a useful hermeneutic for analyzing an American theater in which the boundaries between the traditional and the experimental have become increasingly
porous and in which ostensibly stable meanings and identities (sexual or
otherwise) are routinely displaced by notions of mutability, instability,
and polyvalence. In its contemporary use, it suggests a mode of excessive
and self-conscious theatricality that has long been linked to sexual deviance. At the same time, the flowering of an explicitly queer dramaturgy is a reminder that "queer" is a performative designation, one that

privileges doing over being, action over intention. Queerness, in other words, is constituted in and through its practice. It is less a fixed attribute of a given text or performance than a transient disturbance produced between and among text, actor, director, and spectator. It might be said to be an effect of knowledge, or lack of it, in relation to dissident sexual desires and identities. And it remains, some thirty years after Stonewall, an effect generated by the closet, by a tacit recognition—"I know you know"—or a tacit misrecognition—"I know something you don't know." For as Sedgwick emphasizes, the closet is not a site that a self-identified lesbian or gay man can conclusively and definitively leave. One is always in the process of coming out.

The association of queerness with theater is by no means novel. As a number of historians have pointed out, theaters have long and notoriously been associated with queer bodies and pleasures. Both the early Kabuki and Elizabethan stages were routinely attacked for aiding and abetting same-sex sexual practices. By the end of the nineteenth century, as Alan Sinfield observes, "theatre bars and adjacent public houses" in London's West End were widely "known as places for same-sex encounters."[5] Surveying the New York scene, George Chauncey notes that a "gay enclave had quietly developed in Times Square before the 1920s because the theater and the district's other amusement industries attracted large numbers of gay men who worked as chorus boys, actors, stagehands, costume designers, and publicity people; waiters and club performers; busboys and bellhops." Less discreetly during the same period, Times Square had become "one of the city's most significant centers of male prostitution." And "homosexuality, along with other unconventional sexual behavior," was tolerated by theater professionals in part because they "themselves [were] often stigmatized because of the unconventional lives they led as theater workers."[6] By midcentury, one scandal sheet, *Tip-Off* magazine, featured an article titled, "Why They Call Broadway the 'GAY' White Way," in which it lamented that "homosexuals have gained . . . a stranglehold on the theater."[7]

At many times and in many places in North America and Europe, theater has been considered a coterie art that holds a special attraction for lesbian and gay spectators. The musical theater, in particular, has in popular mythology been adjudged a sacred preserve of gay men, who have been among its most important producers and who remain, as Stacy

Wolf notes, its "most visible devotees."[8] Much recent critical writing on musical theater is rife with references to its queer subcultural appeal. In what is far and away the most sophisticated analysis of its appeal, *Place for Us,* D. A. Miller analyzes the numerous intersections between the conventions of the midcentury musical and the tastes and experiences—the secret codes and fantasies—of a generation of gay men. He also compellingly details the contradictory seductions by which the musical works its magic, its way of both provoking and foreclosing an identification with the figure of the Star Mother.[9] Wolf, meanwhile, attempts to reclaim the musical for lesbian (and feminist) spectators by pointing out that female characters in midcentury musicals are offered up less as "objects of desire" than as "strong, dominating women," as characters, in other words, whose presence undermines the distinction between identification and desire.[10]

Yet the queer character of theater depends on more than its historical associations with lesbians and gay men as producers and consumers. It can also be seen, I will argue, as an effect of theater's ontology. In comparison with other arts (especially film), theater is queer in part because of its particular mode of address and its uncanny ability to arouse a spectator's mutable and mutating investments. More provocatively than film, theater challenges the heterosexualizing, Oedipal imperative that (according to the Freudian family romance) would definitively separate identification (with the parent of the same sex) from desire (for the parent of the other sex and, later, a surrogate for that parent). Delighting instead in confounding identification and desire, theater unleashes an Oedipal scandal.

To describe theater as the queerest art is akin to describing music as the most emotional art or literature as the most intellectual. It is, in other words, a universalizing judgment of value and taste that is predicated less on an analysis of the functioning of each medium than on an evaluation of certain discrete bodies of canonical texts. Indeed, the very notion that any of these arts has a distinctive and unchanging essence is undermined both by the extensive, heterogeneous, worldwide histories of each, as well as by the many aesthetic revolutions waged during the last century in the name of modernism (and whatever has allegedly succeeded modernism). It is at best hazardous to make such sweeping claims, for they inevitably erase or marginalize certain varieties of cultural productions that don't fit the model. The diligent historian will always be able to reel off a string of counterexamples. I am reluctant therefore to make any more than the most provisional claim to theater's status as the queerest art. Rather than argue for theater's irreducible queerness, I want to try on the notion by studying the recent history and sociology of theater as a distinctive form of cultural production in the United States and examining recent theorizations of theater's ontology, particularly in relation to that of film. I want, in other words, to analyze what it might mean to consider theater the queerest art. Which avenues of inquiry does this designation open up, and which does it close down? Who is served by this universalizing claim? If it turns out that theater can indeed stake a claim to a plenipotent queerness, so much the better for the Tony Kushners of this world. And so much the worse for the Pat Robertsons.

The Particular and the Universal

Since the decline of vaudeville, the rise of the talkie, and the subsequent emergence of television, theater has been—and remains—a middlebrow and marginalized form of cultural production in the United States. In regional theaters, subscription bases continue to decline and, with them, the adventurousness of most artistic directors.[11] And while Broadway is thriving, it does so either by reviving what are now regarded as classic plays and musicals (usually from the 1940s and 1950s) or by mimicking mass culture and transforming cinematic high jinks into stage spectacle, turning *Footloose* and *Saturday Night Fever* into lucrative Broadway properties. Most new Broadway (and even off-Broadway) plays either come ready-made for cable television, like Wendy Wasserstein's *An American Daughter* or Donald Margulies's *Dinner with Friends,* or are British imports. Like the American musical comedy, which was bludgeoned into submission by the British megamusical in the 1980s, new American drama has been virtually vanquished on the Great White Way. And while serious drama does retain a foothold off-Broadway and in the nonprofit theaters, it does not have the same cultural capital as other forms of literature. The only American playwright to win a Nobel Prize, Eugene O'Neill, secured his reputation during a period when theater was far more central culturally than it became after World War II. Playwrights now rarely become the figureheads of the literary world or the emblems of literature as an elite cultural practice, in the way that novelists like William Faulkner, Toni Morrison, or Philip Roth do. Moreover, unlike poetry, with its dependence on small presses and a highly specialized and professionalized readership, theater is a manifestly commercial and public art. Dependent upon the many laborers who must perform the playwright's text, it has long been regarded as a minor art form.

The small audience that attends professional theater today, whether commercial or more experimental venues, is overwhelmingly middle- or upper-middle-class and decidedly liberal in its social attitudes. It also must be relatively affluent, insofar as live theater is far more expensive than movies or cable TV. As a form of cultural production, theater (especially since the controversy over NEA funding for the arts began in 1988) has been distinguished from mass culture in part by its many and often highly sexualized representations of gay men. By way of contrast, gay men in film and TV (in *In and Out,* for example) are usually so defined by their gender deviance, not by homoerotic desire, which has barely registered on Hollywood's radar. Unlike their gay brethren, lesbians (and lesbian eroticism) provide a kind of spicy divertissement that is arguably less threatening than male homoeroticism to the many straight men who produce and consume these works. In Hollywood during the 1990s, lesbians became the height of chic—stylish, sexy, and consumable commodities guaranteed to titillate (this development neatly complements and extends the long history of lesbian pornography marketed to straight men). Even a film like *Bound,* with its duo of triumphantly lethal lesbians, manages to control and contain these resistant subjects to some extent at least through the scopophilia of the cinematic apparatus and their positioning by the end of the film as narcissistic doubles. Unlike Hollywood product, however, theater, with its more ambitious cultural designs, often strives to produce gay men and lesbians as agents, highly empathic figures, and desiring subjects.

At this point, I want to turn my attention to two plays, Tony Kushner's *Angels in America* and Terrence McNally's *Love! Valour! Compassion!,* that, despite their many differences, set the standard during the early 1990s for a putatively queer Broadway theater that allows spectators to participate in what has all the trappings, but little of the sub-stance, of a transgressive project. The fact that both widely produced plays feature gay men—rather than lesbians—is symptomatic of the fact that the very category "queer" in the commercial theater designates as a rule plays by and/or about gay men. The more adventurous, provocative, and highbrow of the two, *Angels* works actively to interrogate and un-dermine the binary opposition between public and private and, indeed, to expose the presence of (usually closeted) gay men in American polit-ical culture. But the play's millennialism (not unlike that, ironically, of the Christian right) functions to reassure audiences that History has a meaning and that they can awaken from the nightmare of the past. Al-though *Love! Valour! Compassion!,* in its reinvention and opening up of gay domestic drama, does not question the opposition between public and private, it is, like *Angels,* committed to a utopian vision of commu-nity and a teleology of redemption. Yet unlike *Angels,* it does not attempt to reimagine gay male subjectivity or problematize racial, gendered, or class-based norms, preferring instead to exploit, proudly and voyeuristi-cally, the buff bodies and physical endowments of (the actors playing the roles of) upwardly mobile gay men. Like the identity politics to which they remain indentured, both plays restrict transgression to the cultural and sexual realms and respectfully forswear any critique of an expansive liberal pluralism that is all too eager to accept these men as producers and, more especially, consumers of cultural diversity.[12] In short, this pu-tatively queer theater often functions, whether on Broadway or in re-gional theaters, to titillate well-heeled audiences, queer and straight alike, and reassure them of their hip, liberal values.

Lesbian playwrights and characters, in contrast, remain almost invis-ible on Broadway and in regional theaters. Only Paula Vogel and Mar-garet Edson (whose works have been showcased off-Broadway and awarded Pulitzer Prizes) have managed to have their plays widely per-formed. Yet Vogel's most successful plays and Edson's *Wit* are heterosex-ualized dramas—or at least seem so to the untutored eye. Most lesbian writers and performers flourish downtown in more modest arenas, where their presence (like that of their gay brethren on Broadway) has become virtually synonymous with a variety of edgy performance that challenges the canons of realism as well as bourgeois social, political, and sexual mores. And while lesbian performance may be marginalized, the downtown performance circuit is able to offer artists like Holly Hughes or Split Britches a measure of control over the means of production that Broadway (and even off-Broadway) writers sacrifice to the more corporatized interests of the large producing organizations.

The success of gay men on Broadway and in regional theaters is in part the result of the work of their many distinguished—and closeted—forebears. Although the Western theater, at least since its professionalization during the early modern period, has been relatively hospitable to a wide variety of social and sexual dissidents, gay men in particular have played leading roles in U.S. theater since World War II. Although critics dared not reveal the sexual orientation of several rather eminent theater artists during the height of McCarthyism in the late 1940s and 1950s, some relished casting not-so-subtle aspersions against especially Tennessee Williams, whose writings, in the words of an anonymous reviewer for *Time* magazine, read "too frequently as if the chapters of *Psychopathia Sexualis* had been raided for TV skits."[13] By 1961, however, prominent critics like Howard Taubman (in the *New York Times*) began to acknowledge "the increasing incidence and influence of homosexuality on New York's stage" and decry the "indirection" practiced by playwrights, which, he alleged, "distorts human values." Taking up the mantle of the tolerant liberal that *Times* critics have historically worn, he opined that homosexuality is "a fact of life" and that "nothing human should be alien to an enlightened theatre." The problem with homosexuality, therefore, is less its avowal than its disguise. In Taubman's opinion, crypto-homosexuals produce those malodorous closet dramas that invariably turn a woman into an "unpleasant," "exaggerated" grotesque and a man "into a ragingly lustful beast or . . . a limp, handsome neutral creature of otherworldy purity."[14] Five years later, Stanley Kauffmann (also in the *Times*) virtually named names by observing that "three of the most successful American playwrights of the last twenty years are (reputed) homosexuals." (It hardly required a private detective to fill in the names Tennessee Williams, William Inge, and Edward Albee.) And like Taubman, he argued for a tolerant, liberal theater in which the "homosexual dramatist must be free to write truthfully of what he [*sic*] knows, rather than try to transform it to a life he does not know."[15]

Taubman's and Kauffmann's positions are demonstrably homophobic insofar as they demand that these—implicitly male—homosexual writers, unlike their heterosexual brethren, are fit to write only of what they "know," that is, homosexuality. (According to this essentialist prescription, a male writer should write only about men, an African American writer only about African Americans, etc. And isn't there something more than a little absurd in assuming that even the queerest writer could survive and prosper in the United States during the heyday of McCarthyism, the domestic revival, and *The Donna Reed Show* without acquiring some passing familiarity with heterosexuality?) Most important, their arguments are based on an association of homosexuality with the "distorted," "neurotic," and minoritized and of heterosexuality with the universal.[16] While the homosexual artist should be restricted to writing about perverts, the heterosexual can be trusted with the depiction of all kinds of persons. The former gives a skewed version of society while the latter offers an ostensibly more balanced and healthy assessment. Yet a mere glance at social histories of the Cold War era suggests that the portraits of U.S. culture limned by Williams, Inge, and Albee are far less distorted than Taubman and Kauffmann suggest.[17] Indeed, the representations of discontented marriages, of characters who "represent something different from what they purport to be," and of "the lurid violence that seems a sublimation of social hatreds" describe all too well the very real disturbances that sustained and threatened the Cold War consensus but that the arbiters of culture (and producers of *The Donna Reed Show*) routinely preferred to ignore.[18] Indeed, the gay male playwrights of the 1950s and 1960s achieved their renown (and notoriety) in large part because of their ability to construct plays that, for most theatergoers at least, were read as all too true fictions.

Yet the continued association of the heterosexual with the universal and the homosexual with the particular has been an obstinate mythology that was bolstered by the emerging gay commercial theater of the late 1960s and 1970s. The very plea for tolerance advanced by Mart Crowley's *The Boys in the Band* depends on the construction of the gay male as a deviant subject who should be embraced by an expansive liberal pluralism on condition that he lock his perversions away and minimally disrupt the sequestration of private from public. In relation to this tradition, the greatest and most radical contribution of the queer theater of the 1990s (and in particular of *Angels in America* and *Love! Valour! Compassion!*) has been its reconstruction of the gay man as a universal subject. In these texts, homosexual subjectivities are produced as representative not of the perverse but the normative, not of the subversive but the national. This project is particularly unmistakable in Kushner's "Gay Fantasia on National Themes," with its queering of U.S. political culture. But it is also dramatized in a running gag in *Love! Valour! Compassion!* in which the British-born James discovers a book that "gives the names of all the gay men and lesbians in this country in alphabetical order, from the pre-Revolutionary period (Pocahontas, I think her name was) right up to now, someone called Dan Rather."[19] These two plays thereby work rather slyly to fulfill what Monique Wittig describes as the Proustian project of making "'homosexual' the axis of categorization from which to universalize."[20] At the same time, however, even these universalizing projects must be recognized as producing a counterfeit universal insofar as the "homosexual" in these texts remains a white, male, middle-class subject whose racialized identity is clearly foregrounded by the presence of Belize and Ramon, each of whom represents an idealized fantasy: perfectly radical politics and perfectly fuckable body, respectively. Yet intriguingly, this counterfeit universalism also guarantees that this queered national identity will have a certain global purchase. For *Angels in America* and *Love! Valour! Compassion!* became during the 1996–97 season the two most widely produced U.S. plays in Western European theaters.[21] In a world increasingly held hostage to an American-style globalized economy, and in a Europe increasingly seduced by *la mode américaine,* these texts would seem to epitomize a new queer culture whose very American-ness is the proof of its transnational character.

While Kushner and McNally win Tony awards, a more avant-gardist mode of performance has been institutionalized in alternative venues. Dominated by lesbians rather than white gay men, this queer theater is explicitly deconstructionist in its strategies. Rather than attempt to universalize the queer subject, it delights in deconstructing subjectivity, or rather, in revealing the disruptions and divisions that structure all subjectivities. For Holly Hughes, for example, performance is a privileged medium for examining the processes by which identities are socially produced. All of her work stages the Other within the self (or the Other that structures the self) and remembers a lost, forgotten tongue, like her "mother's invented French," that can be used to articulate (lesbian) desire.[22] Calling attention to the indispensability of narrative for the construction of subjectivity, Hughes uses the stage—standing, as she puts it, in the beams of "light shining out of [the audience's] eyes"—to dramatize both the contingent nature of performance and the performative nature of identity.[23] Like the work of so many other downtown performers, Hughes's is highly self-reflexive and designed to cast the audience as a collective before whom the performer testifies and, thus, as an active, if silent, accessory to the production of her identity. It is queer, however, less because of its subject matter than because of its method. It testifies to the fact that by the late 1980s, self-identified queer performers had appropriated and expanded the techniques of deconstructionist performance developed during the previous decade (by the Wooster Group, Richard Foreman, and Mabou Mines, among many others) in order to take possession of a mode of self-presentation that at once asserts and problematizes identities and desires. For Hughes is as much concerned with absence, with that which defies representation, as she is with trying to carve out a space for an autonomous, dissident subject (and this technique clearly distances her work from the affirmative lesbian-feminist project of the 1970s). At the same time, her deconstructionist politics lead her not to look for an escape from an oppressive (in this case, heteronormative) culture but to use the contradictions always already at play within heteronormativity to undermine its epistemological priority and privilege. Much like the subversive readings of Freud that proliferate throughout queer and feminist theory, the new queer performance attempts less to prove that perverts are normal than to demonstrate that all desire is perverted. Simultaneously, it dramatizes the recognition that performance (as a staging of the Other within the self) is, by definition, a rather queer preoccupation.

If one can consider the new queer theater (stretching from the WOW Cafe to Broadway) to be in any way a unified category, it would seem to be because of its attempt to problematize the putative oppositions between dissident and normative sexualities, on the one hand, and between a realist and an avant-gardist dramaturgy, on the other. For the more closely one analyzes these binarisms, the less securely they seem to hold. Thus, for example, despite their commercial successes, both *Angels in America* and *Love! Valour! Compassion!* rehearse strategies that question minoritized sexual identities and undermine the conventions of domestic realism. Both exploit direct address; both shuffle temporal sequence; both dramatize a mixture of memory, fantasy, and desire; both intercut scenes in an almost cinematic way; both feature drag; both spectacularize the male body; both demonstrate the volatile relationship between the private and the public. At the same time, both plays—like the works of their more avant-gardist kin—work to foreground and problematize performance itself. Both attempt to reimagine community (or family, to take up the discourse of domestic realism) and to universalize a (white) queer subjectivity. So too, the deconstructionist strategies of the avant-garde function both to particularize the performing subject and to produce her or him as the paradigm of subjectivity tout court. By rehearsing a problematic associated with a particular, abjected identity, Holly Hughes coincidentally dramatizes the impossibility of stabilizing any and all identities. By performing a fragmented social and personal history of African American gay men and the particular issues facing them, Pomo Afro Homos illuminate the difficulty of producing any affirmative (racial or sexual) minoritized identity.

Whether in its uptown or downtown guises, then, the new queer theater has become a metonym for postnaturalistic performance in the United States. It thereby represents in a particularly clear and incisive form both the situation of theater as a bastard art (which is to say, as a product of the unnatural intercourse of high and low) and the necessary slippage (both on- and offstage) between self and Other. Placing formal innovation at the service of a deconstructed performing subject, this theater refuses the certainties of the neorealisms and cultural nationalisms of the 1970s in favor of pluralism, undecidability, and anti-essentialism. And although it has unashamedly moved far beyond the closet dramas of the 1950s, its fascination with innuendo, instability, and absence allows it, in ingenious ways, to reimagine and reinvent the conventions so subtly deployed by Tennessee Williams (and others) to undermine and decenter a heteronormative dramaturgy. In this sense, the godparents of the new queer theater are not Mart Crowley and Jane Chambers but the great closet dramatists from Oscar Wilde to Tennessee Williams, Gertrude Stein to Jane Bowles, who, recognizing that absence is the purest way of safeguarding pathologized and criminalized subjects, chose to stage the very unrepresentability of an affirmative homosexuality.

Writing and Reading Out

The ascendency of a deconstructionist queer theater in the United States and of a universalized queer subject marks a rupture with the gay and lesbian drama that emerged around Stonewall and is best exemplified by plays like Crowley's *The Boys in the Band* and Chambers's *Last Summer at Bluefish Cove*. For although many queer playwrights acknowledge their debt to this work, they are also insistent on interrogating the relationship between the sexual identity of the cultural producer and his or her work. This tendency became particularly clear at the "Reading and Writing Out" panel that I moderated at a 1995 Center for Lesbian and Gay Studies (CLAGS) Queer Theatre conference. The writers on the panel, Janis Astor del Valle, Maria Irene Fornes, Joan Shenkar, Nicky Silver, and Chay Yew, represented an extremely heterogeneous grouping. And while Silver's project is arguably the most universalizing (and commercial) and Fornes's the most deconstructionist, all these playwrights have produced work that disrupts a facile opposition between these terms. Despite their diverse backgrounds, ages, races, and points of view, all agree that identity—sexual or otherwise—is always a problem. Fornes understands it to be so vexed because it is in large part unconscious; it is "so delicate and so elusive" as to be virtually inaccessible to the writing subject.[24] Astor del Valle argues that identity is "ever-evolving," while Yew notes that he "never intended to be categorized" and "hate[s] being categorized." Shenkar, meanwhile, observes that "when you sit down to face that blank sheet of paper, you are reduced. The best thing you can do is to erase yourself." Rather than affirming a preexistent, full subject, queer playwriting always seems (as it did in the closet dramas of fifty years ago) to erase the self, producing the writer as a supplement to a polyvalent and incomplete text.

In elaborating on the idea of self-erasure, Fornes uses a provocative metaphor, noting that writing "is like your fingerprints." For her, writing remains a unique and enigmatic enterprise—unique because all fingerprints are different and enigmatic because "you have no idea what they look like." And fingerprints, although quite literally at one's fingertips, are taken for granted, a mass of indeterminate swirls to the untrained eye. Yet they are also understood to be the distinctive signature of the individual. "Wherever you go, you are leaving your mark," leaving a trace behind that can be used to finger you. Both alien and incriminating, fingerprints are a privileged marker of identity, which for Fornes is an "elusive," "mysterious," and irrecoverable property, "so hidden from yourself." And although writing clearly bears a privileged relation to the production of identity, it does not function to stabilize it or lend it coherence. Writing, she adds, is a "search inside, . . . but you search inside you for an imaginary other." Writing, like performance, is a quest less for the self than for an Other who stands in for the self, a fantasy double (a theatrical character, persona, or phantasm) that always manages to exceed the subject. Writing, in short, represents not a stabilization but a disarticulation of identity.

If theater is the queerest art, perhaps it so because writing and performance always function to disarticulate and disrupt identity—whether the identity in question is that of the playwright, the performer, or the spectator. The performer is the most obviously destabilized of this group insofar as he or she is always playing a role, always literally giving breath to an Other within the self. And the slippage between playwright and text is, as Fornes alleges, a function of the fact that on some level the writer never knows what he or she is doing. But the disarticulation of the spectator is effected rather differently from both, by the specificity of the theatrical apparatus. In what remains one of the most provocative comparisons between theater and cinema, Christian Metz argues that although theater has a materiality and a facticity that film (being "closer to phantasy") lacks, the most crucial difference between the two lies in their construction of the spectator.[25] Since the "spectator is absent" from that peculiar mirror that constitutes the film screen, "it is always the other who is on the screen; as for me, I am there to look at him [*sic*]." Unlike the theatrical spectator, the cinematic spectator is "*all-perceiving*" and yet takes "no part in the perceived," remaining "absent from the screen." He becomes a depository, a "second screen" for this "perceived-imaginary material" (48). He is so completely occupied with looking that "the spectator *identifies with himself*, with himself as a pure act of perception," which is to say, as the one who discovers "himself" watching the Other silently in the dark (49). (Countless critics of Metz, beginning with Laura Mulvey, emphasize that because the spectator is masculinized by the apparatus, Metz's use of masculine pronouns represents far more than a conventionalized figure of speech.)[26] Because the spectator identifies most of all with the camera (not a character), the cinematic apparatus succeeds in reconstructing him as a "a kind of transcendental subject" whose "presence often remains diffuse, geographically undifferentiated, unevenly distributed over the whole surface of the screen; or more precisely *hovering*" (49, 54). The very "foundation" of the cinema is thus "identification with one's own look." (This would explain why so many of the most celebrated and idiomatic films, like Hitchcock's *Vertigo* and *Rear Window,* are explicitly about looking.) Metz emphasizes that the identifications with characters made by the cinematic spectator are only "secondary" or "tertiary," in contrast with those of the theatrical spectator, which are first and foremost with the impersonated characters who populate the stage (56). (This would explain why so many of the most celebrated and idiomatic plays, from *Hamlet* to *Six Characters in Search of an Author,* are explicitly about impersonation and role playing.)

While Metz's analysis of theatrical spectatorship is clearly based upon his acquaintance with European realistic and naturalistic theater, he is correct, I believe, to discern that empathic identification—or disidentification, for that matter—with characters tends to be foundational in theater in a way that it is not in cinema.[27] André Bazin makes a similar point when he insists that "the human being is all-important in the theater," which, as a medium, "acts on us by virtue of our participation in a theatrical action." To his way of thinking, "theater calls for an active individual consciousness while the film requires only a passive adhesion."[28] The theatrical character, in other words, demands a level of spectatorial investment that is qualitatively different from that demanded by his or her cinematic (or televisual) counterpart. Even in plays that clearly attempt some kind of Brechtian distanciation (like *Angels in America*), the spectator must, if the play is going to work, actively identify with at least one of the characters (as opposed to the act of looking). At the same time, I would like to suggest that the act of identification in the theater is by no means consistent and immutable. Rather, it is as unstable, improvisatory, and unpredictable as the theatrical event itself. For theater is distinguished from film not only on account of the changes that take place between one performance and the next but also because of the relatively nonhierarchical nature of the stage picture. Even the most carefully composed tableau does not focus the spectatorial gaze quite as authoritatively as the cinematic shot (at least in Hollywood narrative cinema), in part because each spectator is given a different perspective on the action. Moreover, the theatrical image is far more dependent on a dialogical relationship between setting and human subject, between container and the thing contained. And stage directors, designers, and actors constantly exploit the knowledge that the spectator's gaze will always wander among characters and setting. In fact, is not spectatorial pleasure in the theater partly the result of a necessarily errant eye?

The concept of errancy is important, I believe, because it accounts both for the quality—and instability—of the spectator's primary identifications with characters and for the tacit contract between actor and spectator. For when Metz describes actor and spectator in the theater as "the two protagonists of an authentic perverse couple," he means that the actor knowingly (and exhibitionistically) consents to a specularized relationship, deliberately presenting him- or herself to the spectator (63). The actor, moreover, always vies with the other actors for the spectator's attention (and usually empathy as well). At the same time, unlike most novels and many films, plays (except in rare instances) do not use a narrator to provide a seamless narration or to adopt an unwavering attitude toward the dramatic action. Even when they do (as, for example, in Brecht's *Caucasian Chalk Circle* or Paula Vogel's *How I Learned to Drive*), the narrator more often than not is untrustworthy, opening up rather than foreclosing multiple points of view. As a result, the spectator's identification with characters remains far more unstable and unpredictable than in narrative forms (among which I would include cinema).

The analyses by both Metz and Bazin of the differences between theater and cinema emphasize the materiality of the theatrical performance and of the actor in relation to his or her cinematic image. For there is no question that the presence of the living actor is responsible for producing the almost magical effects that Bazin endeavors to describe by using metaphors drawn from the lexicon of fire and passion. The cinematic image may be manufactured simply by the projection of light on a reflective screen, but theater is both literally and figuratively inflammatory. In Bazin's (imaginary) theater, performance takes place on the far side "of a wall of fire—that fiery frontier between fantasy and reality which gives rein to Dionysiac monsters while protecting us [spectators] from them." The actor, meanwhile, "burns" with a "fire" that is "at once that of his inner passion and of that focal point [as described by the glare of the footlights] at which he stands. He lights up in each member of his audience an accomplice flame."[29] For Bazin (almost in echo of Artaud), theater is a medium for the production of monsters and their doubles; it is a place in which passion spreads from actor to spectator. It is a site in which the spectator passionately identifies with a character (who can never be conclusively separated from the actor impersonating the character) in all of his or her living, breathing materiality and presence. And it is doubtless for this reason that while "cinema calms the spectator, the theater excites him" and so arouses his desires.[30] Unlike cinema, theater—in all its phonocentric glory—is unable to extinguish the fire it lights, unable to quell the fantasmatic investment that the spectator makes in a character, and unable conclusively to separate that investment from the spectator's own burning (if partly unconscious) desires. Theater, in other words, mobilizes an erotic cathexis with both character and actor that is qualitatively different from that of film.

In relation to cinema, theater spectatorship provides an almost irresistible challenge to that law of Oedipus that would definitively segregate identification (wanting to be someone) from desire (wanting to have someone). (And it bears recalling here that Freud's theorization of the Oedipus complex is named after a play.) For how, in watching *Cat on a Hot Tin Roof*, for example, can one separate one's identification with Maggie and Brick (this gloriously charismatic couple who, at least initially, take a stand against the tyranny of the commodity and the nuclear family) from one's desire for these gloriously spectacularized and fetishized creatures who, to borrow a page from Bazin, burn with passion before us? One might well believe that this inevitable confusion of identification with desire renders theater a rather peculiar, if not to say queer, art. Not only does this confusion describe an Oedipal scandal, but it also suggests the difficulty for the spectator in maintaining a stable and unambiguous sexual identity. How is even the most compulsively heterosexualized of male spectators to ensure that he will not desire that washed-up, alcoholic quarterback lounging about the stage in a white silk bathrobe? For sexual identities remain arguably the most unstable of all identities—in part because of the polymorphous, unpredictable, and uncontrollable nature of desire itself; in part because they are (usually) among the most privatized and invisible of identities. And sitting in a theater in the darkness allows one to fantasize and make certain erotic investments that one would be loath to make in the light of day.

As Judith Butler points out in her celebrated deconstruction of the sex/gender system, all gender identities represent a kind of drag performance insofar as all are produced through acts of impersonation. There is "no original or primary gender that drag imitates, but *gender is a kind of imitation for which there is no original;* in fact, it is a kind of imitation that produces the very notion of the original as an *effect* and consequence of the imitation itself." And heterosexuality (like the bipolar system of gender it requires) is itself a performance that imitates "a phantasmatic ideal of heterosexual identity." In one of Butler's most clever moves, she depathologizes homosexuality by theorizing heterosexuality as a kind of obsessive-compulsive disorder. It is "a compulsive and compulsory repetition that can only produce the *effect* of its own originality."[31] At the same time, drawing on Freud's theories of mourning and melancholia, she emphasizes that any and all ostensibly fixed sexual identities are haunted by those they are compelled to repudiate. Thus heterosexuality is always predicated on lost—and unmourned— homosexual cathexes. For, as she notes, "the giving up of the object is not a negation of the cathexis, but its internalization and, hence, preservation."[32] Expressing distinct discomfort with any fixed sexual identity (because it is always based on disavowal), she tries to advance the possibility of multiple and mutating identifications. Preferring not to disavow "something like heterosexuality or bisexuality," she proposes instead a kind of queerness that would be founded upon "a set of identificatory and practical crossings between these [and all other] categories that renders the discreteness of each equally suspect."[33] Since both heterosexuality and homosexuality are predicated on a repudiation of their opposites, Butler attempts to valorize those queer identities that are the product of these "crossings" not only because they alone can acknowledge the necessarily plural and contradictory constitution of all subjects (who always take up multiple positionalities) but also because they enable the formation of political communities and coalitions. "It may be," she suggests, "only by risking the *incoherence* of identity that connection is possible."[34]

In theater, the possibility—nay, the necessity—of multiple identifications and desires in real time and in real space—across genders, sexualities, races, and classes—renders it a particularly utopian medium. And I must take issue here with David Harvey, who argues that, of all forms of cultural production, "the novel, as an exploration of possible worlds . . . has now become the primary site for the exploration of utopian sentiments and sensibilities."[35] For while it is true that narrative fiction has historically occupied itself more explicitly with utopian (and dystopian) fantasies, the theatrical apparatus also and always produces possible—and alternative—worlds. And while *Angels in America* may be the clearest recent example of a utopian theatrical fiction, it is by no means unique. Moreover, it seems to me that the quality of theater's utopian explorations distinguishes them from the novel's. For unlike narrative fiction, theater happens in real (as well as narratological) spaces and is populated by real (as well as narratological) bodies. Theater, moreover, at least in its realist modes, is predicated on an opposition between two different spaces—onstage and off—and two different modes of materialization—visible and invisible, present and absent. And it is absence, quite precisely, that becomes a placeholder for an unimaginable otherness. So when Prior Walter's ceiling opens up and an Angel descends, that utopian visitation has a spatiotemporal facticity that cannot be achieved in the novel (or on film). Moreover, the theatrical spectator always has the opportunity to take up multiple positions and desire multiple partners; to identify or conjugate—secretly, in the dark—with many characters; to enjoy what Butler calls "the *pleasure* produced by the instability" of erotic categories.[36] And this instability is redoubled by the fact that the spectator is never able definitively to separate a character from the actor playing the role. So one always identifies with and desires both a clearly designated absence (a character) and a material presence (an actor). Moreover, as Metz and Bazin imply, since the theatergoer is always more or less conscious of playing the role of spectator together with the rest of the audience, he or she always retains more of his or her social being sitting in the darkened theater than the filmgoer does. As a result, the theater is the site, as Metz notes, in which "a true 'audience'" is constituted, "a temporary collectivity" made all the more efficacious both by the physical presence of actors' bodies as well as by the actors' awareness that they are being overseen, that they are participating willingly in the formation of "an authentic perverse couple."[37]

Spaces of Hope

Whether on Broadway or off, a new theater emerged during the late 1980s and the 1990s that both deconstructs and universalizes the queer subject and represents a utopian project dedicated to spectatorial pleasure, to the crossings of identifications and desires, to a queer colonization of the public sphere, and to community formation. The ascendency of this new theater is historically linked, I believe, to social developments of the period: to the power of identity politics among those who consider themselves to be on the left, to the rise of queer nationalism in the streets and queer theory in the academy, and to the escalating struggle for lesbian and gay civil rights. It is also linked to contemporaneous developments in American theater: to a rapprochement between the avant-gardist modes of the 1960s and a more realistic drama that never went completely out of fashion; and to the ascendancy of a decentralized, non-profit, bourgeois theater that demands this kind of play. This new theater is demonstrably salutary for those making it. Lesbians and gay men in the theater simply have more opportunities to work uncloseted than they did twenty years ago. And the relatively affluent consumers of theater with a taste for the sexually adventurous have more offerings from which to choose.

But one must be wary of falling into a triumphalist swoon. The new American queer theater is also a sign that lesbian and gay politics have become increasingly assimilationist and increasingly oriented toward the conspicuous consumption of images. For much of what passes for queer theater (like *Love! Valour! Compassion!*) remains a relatively cliquish dramaturgy that usually addresses a coterie audience or those already sympathetic to its cause. As a result, much queer theater may be considered analogous to what Dennis Lim calls "gaysploitation," that "breed of gay [independent] film (predominantly American) that favors postures over ideas, titillation over eroticism, anodyne affirmation over thoughtful provocation."[38] As I have argued, much of this theater, like gaysploitational films, tends to privilege and appeal to white, middle-class subjects, producing them as the axis from which to universalize. And these subjects sometimes function (as they do on *Will and Grace*) as a pretext for a particular kind of campy wit that clearly appeals to many straight-identified spectators. As a result, the new queer theater too often prefers to naturalize and glamorize the consumption of commodities and almost invariably ignores the increasingly inequitable distribution of wealth in the United States and the many perverts who cannot afford a house in the Hamptons or even a night out at the theater. For the new queer theater has also and arguably become increasingly reformist. As a result, it is clearly an expression of those identity politics that, having displaced the New Left during the early 1970s, remain dependent, as Brown notes, "upon the demise of a *critique* of capitalism and of bourgeois cultural and economic values."[39] And one might recall here that heady moment in the early 1990s when—in the wake of Queer Nation, *Gender Trouble, Paris Is Burning,* and Madonna's *Sex* book—everything and everyone suddenly seemed queer. But this queer moment was the result of more than a renewal of AIDS activism or a salutary backlash against the Christian right. For this moment (memorialized in texts like *Angels in America, Love! Valour! Compassion!,* and Sedgwick's *Tendencies*) coincides with what I would call a national identity crisis that is itself linked to the collapse of historical Communism and the attenuation of the opposition between East and West. For it was in that moment that "queer" emerged as a utopian trope (in contradistinction to the often anticapitalist program of the earlier gay liberation and lesbian-feminist movements) that appropriates corporate strategies to reimagine a nation of sexual outlaws who are defined at least as much by what they consume as by the people they fuck.

The delineation of a queer theater that challenges cultural and sexual norms is further complicated by the emergence since the early 1990s of a vital, popular subculture that I would label "queer wannabe," if I did not believe that "queer" by definition deconstructs (or hopes to deconstruct) the opposition between the authentic and the copy. A number of filmmakers, actors, playwrights, and, most prominently, rock musicians have flirted with queer or bisexual identities and/or desires in their works (and less frequently, or at least less openly, in their private lives). Going all the way back to the glam rock of the 1970s, singers like David Bowie, Mick Jagger, Elton John, Alice Cooper, Lou Reed, and Prince have played with bisexuality, drag, and flamboyant theatricality as ways of making their work seem edgy, shocking, seductive, and relatively highbrow. Twenty-five years later the highbrow aspirations may have become attenuated, but Ricky Martin never completely lays to rest the rumors that he is gay, while Sinéad O'Connor bolsters her sales and polishes her bad-girl image by coming out as lesbian. Hollywood players, meanwhile, remain a notoriously closeted lot, while Hollywood product benevolently pushes its message of tolerance, antihomophobia, and multiculturalism. And straight-identified actors like Tom Hanks, Robin Williams, Patrick Swayze, Tom Selleck, and Wesley Snipes prove both their liberalism and their daring by playing the part of gay men in popular feature films. In mass culture, queerness most often functions as a way of elevating what used to be called lowbrow entertainment. By providing a frisson of danger and excitement and a whiff of high style, it remains one of the most efficient ways of accruing symbolic capital in Hollywood. At the same time, the changes taking place in mass culture are an indication of the growing normalization of sexual dissidence in the United States. These changes are certainly linked both to the increasing visibility of lesbians and gay men in the media and the public sphere and to the embrace by lesbians, gay men, and their many allies of more assimilationist political goals (for example, gay marriage) and strategies (for example, increased participation in electoral politics).

Despite the success of Broadway plays like *Angels in America, Love! Valour! Compassion!,* and *Rent,* the prosperity of a queer theater is by no means uncontroversial. In fact, its rise has coincided with what can only be described as a backlash against plays that flaunt dissident sexualities. This is particularly true on Broadway. Terrence McNally relates a telling anecdote: "Someone told me about the night *Kiss of the Spiderwoman* and *Angels* both won Tony Awards—the parents of a playwright that didn't win said, 'What have they got against normal people?'"[40] Producers have attempted to answer this question by increasing the quota of British and Anglo-Irish plays on Broadway. This drama doubtlessly appeals to theatergoers and critics alike because it brings to the American theater a different and more archaic kind of symbolic capital—a whiff of elite, Europeanized culture. It is also resolutely heterosexualized, at least all that makes it to Broadway. During the 1999–2000 season, the conflict between middlebrow American spectacle and more highbrow British drama was played out in the contest for the Tony Award for Best Play. Among the four nominees, the two serious contenders were Claudia Shear's *Dirty Blonde* and Michael Frayn's *Copenhagen.*[41] While Frayn's is, I believe, much the better play, its triumph at the Tonys is also sympto-

matic of a preference for relatively elitist—and safely heterosexualized—
entertainment in a certain sector of the American theater. Shear's play,
about the idolization of Mae West by two devoted fans, is a study of the
power of identification, of the desire to become a highly sexualized Hollywood icon. And although the play finally devolves into a neatly heterosexualized romance between two Mae West wannabes (it's not very
dirty, or very blonde), it is an intensely corporeal piece of theater in
which transgressive, transvestite, and exorbitant bodies parade across a
pastel pink stage. Like so much of what passes for queer theater, it exu-
berantly stages the impossibility of separating desire from identification.

Frayn's play, by way of contrast, is a highly intellectualized, three-
dimensional enactment of undecidability (that bears a more than passing likeness to the kind of play that Harold Pinter was writing in the
1960s). Providing multiple and contradictory versions of a real meeting
that took place between Niels Bohr and his former pupil, Werner Heisenberg, in occupied Copenhagen in 1941, it stages the Heisenberg uncertainty principle, the impossibility of ever knowing what really happens
between two figures, despite—or, more accurately, because of—their own
subsequent rationalizations. Considering that the play is quite precisely
about materialization (the Heisenberg principle is a theory of particles,
positing an inverse relationship between the knowledge of the position of
a particle and its velocity), *Copenhagen* is an almost astonishingly dematerialized piece of theater. (Frayn has explained that he initially conceived
it as a radio play.) The relatively neutral setting and rather dowdy, func-
tional costumes help to focus attention not on corporeality (it is hard to
believe that the characters, all of them parents, have a clue about sex) but
on the ideas that circulate among them. Even Bohr's wife, Margrethe,
who is predictably excluded from philosophical debate and functions as
the play's version of a moral conscience, remains little more than a walking, talking idea. Yet it is precisely by virtue of its dematerialization, its
abstraction, and its engagement with quantum physics that *Copenhagen*
neatly performs a fashionable, deconstructionist undecidability and once
again allows Broadway audiences to exercise their minds and participate
vicariously in the dramas of "normal people."

Despite the fact that *Copenhagen* is light-years away from what I have
been describing as queer theater, Margrethe's predictable marginalization all too neatly dovetails with the fact that the new queer theater has

done little to redress the long history of the exclusion of women as playwrights, protagonists, directors, and designers in prestigious, commercial venues. Almost invariably, gay men have achieved levels of visibility and power in the theater that are routinely denied to women, whether straight or lesbian. At the "Reading and Writing Out" panel I moderated, this gender inequality was vividly and cruelly reenacted. Silver and Yew sat on one side of me, while Astor del Valle, Fornes, and Shenkar sat on the other (I did not plan this partitioning). As Jill Dolan describes the scene, two "sides" quickly emerged, and as they became "more ideological," it looked "as though a schoolyard brawl was about to be staged":

> Silver and Yew laughed and whispered when the women talked, and Silver began each of his comments with a parody of something one of the women before him had volunteered. Shenkar's and Fornes's faces expressed their displeasure with Silver's camping, and in their remarks took care to distinguish themselves from this category "queer," especially if Silver was the defense's exhibit A.[42]

Not only were Silver and Yew far less amusing than they imagined, but they were also far less articulate than the women they mocked. Unfortunately, however, this ugly performance was hardly a unique event. Rather, an offstage and more subtle and insidious version of it holds sway in countless theaters across the United States. And this denigration of women tends to be echoed by the relative exclusion of both lesbians and gay men of color from major administrative and artistic positions in prestigious theaters (the New York Shakespeare Festival is the most obvious exception to this rule). Until women and persons of color are able to procure the same highly visible forums as white gay men in which to present their work, a truly universalized and democratized queer theater will remain a utopian fantasy.

Or to shift the terms of the argument, perhaps the problem is a matter less of the identity of the cultural producer than of the political character of the project he or she undertakes. In that case, a new—and truly universalized—queer theater might be predicated less on avowedly queer identities than on desires marked as being fantastic, luxurious, and perverse: desires for radical change, for a new space in which to live and love, for a more equitable global settlement, for a redistribution of wealth, for a new mode of theatrical (and economic) production. The vast majority of the makers of queer theater about whom I have been writing are so categorized on the basis of their acknowledged sexual identities. But if queer theater is, as I suggest, largely a formal designation, why not include José Rivera, Mac Wellman, and Suzan-Lori Parks among its luminaries? For like Tony Kushner or Paula Vogel, these playwrights insistently disrupt the conventions of mimetic realism while imagining the erotic as a locus of transformative power. Why must a queer theater remain fixated on the imaginary stability of that most unstable of identities? And why not acknowledge the fact that a writer's work will always exceed, and often belie, his or her avowed identity? White men—whether gay or straight, Terrence McNally or Jonathan Larson—are quite capable of producing a theater that is not only queer but also feminist, antiracist, antihomophobic, and anticapitalist. Maybe some day they will.

Chapter Three

The Haunted Stages
of Modernity

To hail the beginning of a new era is to inaugurate a rupture in time. Thus, George H. W. Bush in 1992 wrapped himself in the mantle of a sage and declared that with the fall of the Soviet empire, "the world has known changes of almost biblical proportions."[1] And indeed, all of Bush's State of the Union addresses of the early 1990s overflowed with a visionary rhetoric of progress and revolution, repeatedly referencing "democracy's advance," "a new world order," and "a dramatic and deeply promising time in our history."[2] Pundits, meanwhile, cheered what they took to be the millennial new age, one *Wall Street Journal* columnist exulting: "'thanks to the democracy of the market' and the widespread ownership of stock, 'the U.S. is now closer to [the] Marxian ideal[!] than any society in history.'"[3] Some ten years later, George W. Bush, now occupying the White House, recycled his father's discourse of transfiguration with a vengeance. Responding to a devastating attack on the World Trade Center and the Pentagon, he declared a new war on terrorism and ended the defensive military posture that had been the official—if not always actual—United States foreign policy since World War II in favor of willful preemption and unapologetic empire building.

Although these discourses of Bush *père* and *fils* seem intent on defining America as "the beacon of freedom in a searching world" and disavowing all imperial ambitions, they are incapable, I believe, of laying the ghosts of colonialism to rest.[4] It may be true that the end of the bipolar global settlement left the United States, as Samir Amin observes, "with a 'world-view' monopoly and the (military) means to try to administer it."[5] And there is no question that the ever-growing economic polarization produced by capitalist globalization, the proliferation of weapons of mass destruction, and the emergence of new media and social technologies have produced increasingly effective ways of controlling, terrifying, and immiserating innocent populations. Although these achievements may seem unprecedented, they are far less novel, I want to argue, than they at first appear. Similarly, U.S. foreign policy since September 11, 2001, represents less a new initiative than a reconfirmation of what had long been in effect a distinctively American brand of unilateralism. These strategies and technologies thereby represent less a radical break with former policies than the fulfillment of a particular historical logic, a kind of monstrous repetition of the past. And despite a widespread—and arguably premature—disillusionment with Marxism, Marx's celebrated (if somewhat gothic) account of the burden of history seems to have acquired a new veracity: "The tradition of all the dead generations weighs like a nightmare on the brain of the living."[6]

The 150 years since Marx penned these words have witnessed a proliferation of nightmares that I can hardly begin to enumerate. And despite the many recent attempts to consign the Cold War, communism, liberalism, the welfare state, and colonialism to the dustbin of history, the past is not so easily killed off. Like a zombie, history is coming back to stalk us, and perhaps nowhere as insistently as on the stage. For the plays that fill U.S. theaters are full of ghosts—revivals of *Hamlet,* Ibsen, and *A Christmas Carol* notwithstanding. From the surprisingly placable apparition of Ethel Rosenberg in *Angels in America* to the unquiet spirit of Uncle Peck in *How I Learned to Drive,* from the anxious specter of Jelly Roll Morton in *Jelly's Last Jam* to the luminous vision of Sarah Brown Eyes in *Ragtime,* the American theater is truly a haunted stage.

Why, I wonder, is it so haunted? What exactly has disturbed it so? Why do these emanations from different times and places frequent our stages? And finally, what is the relationship between these ghosts and history itself, which, like the repressed, seems to have unaccountably returned and taken up residence in America's theaters?

Theater and Mass Culture

The haunting of the stage is undoubtedly a complicated phenomenon with as many causes as there are ghosts. And there is no question that today's theater is by no means unique in its fascination with things mysterious and unexplained. Mass culture also bore witness to a revival of the occult during the nervous 1990s, although its ghosts tend to be much more flamboyant and frankly horrifying than those that haunt the stage. Stephen King remained a synonym for "best-seller," *The X-Files* racked up Emmy awards, and the latest incarnations of *Alien* or *Scream* filled the local multiplexes. *The Blair Witch Project* pulled off the marketing coup of the decade, while *The Sixth Sense* became a surprise box-office smash that was nominated for six Academy Awards. As the *New York Times* notes, the psychological horror film is once again in vogue.[7] And occult genres are popular in part because they do more than arouse awe and terror. They also becalm anxieties. For virtually all horror films end with the defeat or destruction of the monstrous Other. No less an authority than Stephen King maintains that

> horror fiction is really as Republican as a banker in a three-piece suit. The story is always the same in terms of development. There's an incursion into taboo lands, there's a place where you shouldn't go, but you do. . . . And the same thing [always] happens inside: you look at the guy with three eyes, . . . or whoever it happens to be. And when you come out, well, you say, "Hey, I'm not so bad. I'm all right. A lot better than I thought." It has the effect of reconfirming values, or reconfirming self-image.[8]

Although King may oversimplify, he is correct to note that horror usually functions as an ironically conservative and comforting experience insofar it is always about mastering the unknown, controlling the uncontrollable, attaching a shape and a name to formless and nameless fears. And it is little wonder that the first hour of a horror movie is always far more frightening than the second and that the vague intimations of an alien presence are far more unsettling than the slime-dripping monster that belatedly rears its ugly head. For horror cannot be vanquished until it is descried. Once seen and comprehended, it is a thing whose inevitable defeat will prove the hero's—and our own—provisional mastery and power.

At the same time, however, horror does more than help us tame our private demons. It is also a means for a society to assuage cultural fears by exercising a fantasmatic control over those things that are apparently out of control. As Robert Sklar points out, the success of "the horror genre, one of the oldest in the movies, has always been cyclical." It has enjoyed its greatest popularity during "moments of extreme social and cultural dislocation"—in Germany after World War I, in the United States during the depths of the Great Depression and the height of 1950s nuclear panic.[9] The resurgence of the occult during the last decade of the twentieth century and the first decade of the twenty-first may well be linked to new anxieties circulating in the West. In the wake of the Cold War, as the geopolitical equilibrium of forty-five years gave way to a more unpredictable world order, limited and local wars have proliferated while fears of terrorism and chemical, biological, and nuclear weapons have been used to justify the remilitarization of U.S. society and an almost unprecedented attack on civil liberties. Confronting these developments, and seeing the alien queen or Godzilla killed off, Americans can imagine their triumph, however provisionally, over their own monstrous enemies—be they Saddam Hussein, Slobodan Milosevic, Osama bin Laden, or the next despot du jour.

The recent occult revival may also represent the flip side of a new wave of spirituality linked to the New Age movement. The 1990s bore witness to the burgeoning of a multibillion-dollar industry that betrays what trend spotters call a spiritual renaissance, as manifested by a rekindled interest in Asian philosophies and religions, meditation, alternative medicine, twelve-step programs, and various religious fundamentalisms. During a period of doubt and insecurity, when there seems to be such a hunger on the part of so many to believe, both the new spirituality and the occult fixate on questions of superhuman agency. As Noël Carroll points out, "The experience of supernatural horror in the arts is frequently analogized to religious experience."[10] The appearance of ghosts, angels, and monsters in a wide range of cultural productions thus functions ironically to confirm that there is an order to the universe and a meaning to life and death. It suggests there are patterns and even moments of clarity in human history. It proves there's someone out there who cares.

While this renewed popularity of both the occult and the spiritual may be of some use in explaining a surge in theatrical ghosts, spirits function rather differently, I believe, in theater and in mass culture. For one thing, theater cannot compete with cinema in terms of the sheer spectacle of horror. Its ghosts and supernatural apparitions tend therefore to be less gruesome and frightening—and more psychological— than those that populate film. Second, although there are undeniable similarities between theater and cinema, the two occupy very different cultural niches. Tony Kushner and David Cronenberg may use similar devices, but the differences between the media they use and the audiences they attract guarantee that these devices will produce dissimilar meanings and effects. It is important therefore to consider the relative positions of theater, on the one hand, and film and television, on the other, in the hierarchically organized fields of cultural production.

Perhaps the most obvious distinction between theater and mass culture is the former's considerably higher admission price. A ticket to Broadway or a regional theater can cost up to twenty times the price of a movie ticket or four times that of a month of cable TV. Surveys, not surprisingly, have shown that most regular theatergoers have far more disposable income than the average moviegoer. Theater's costliness means that it remains a more specialized art form and that its audiences (like those for many independent films) are often well-educated and highly professionalized spectators. They pride themselves on their taste for work that is by and large more aesthetically adventurous, confrontational, and politically liberal than Hollywood product. They go to the theater, in other words, because it has far greater cultural and symbolic capital and is more likely to tackle serious social issues in serious ways. (The exceptions to this pattern are the megamusicals and dance spectaculars, which, delivering a sumptuously wrapped package, appeal to a wider audience than most so-called straight theater and provide essentially a more expensive—and live—version of mass culture.)

Popular movies like *Titanic* or *Star Wars* (as well as a growing number of domestic dramas like *Forrest Gump* or *Pleasantville*), although relying on tried and true formulas and old-fashioned plots, have come in recent years increasingly to depend on special effects. Computer-generated images and sounds allow filmmakers to guarantee that their product will be bigger, shinier—and, most important, newer—than anything that has come before. Theater, in contrast, remains curiously wedded to the past. Not only is it one of the oldest performing arts, but its legacy seems far grander than its somewhat precarious present state. Most regional theater companies anchor their seasons on the classics—from Shakespeare to Tennessee Williams, Ibsen to Rodgers and Hammerstein—while Broadway has been deluged over the past decade by so many revivals that the Tony Awards have had to invent new categories for them. At the same time, the American theater has not become, as much opera has, a museum in which the classics are annually trotted out in fancy dress.

The lifeblood of theater remains new plays, plays that give relatively elite, knowledgeable audiences an opportunity to see debated, and to debate themselves, pressing social issues. The vitality of social drama does not mean that Brecht's activist (and revolutionary) theater is alive and well and living in America. But it does mean that some theater remains a forum for the examination of difficult and contentious issues, that, for example, racist institutions, sexual violence, homophobia, and even the workings of capitalism are interrogated more openly and vigorously in theater (as well as, it must be admitted, in some independent film) than in mass culture. At least since the 1920s, with the success of Eugene O'Neill and, later, the Federal Theatre Project and the Group Theatre, and continuing with the flowering of off-off-Broadway in the 1960s, the stage has been positioned as a critical, if not exactly oppositional, force in American culture. And the most honored and well-known playwrights—from Williams, Miller, and Albee to Kushner and Vogel—have invariably acquired their renown in part by challenging received opinions. The status of theater as both critique and public forum has encouraged a number of playwrights, like Kushner and Vogel, to become forceful public advocates and intellectuals, penning opinion columns and op-ed pieces and speaking out against various attempts to curtail civil liberties and freedom of speech. Given this history, it is little wonder that conservatives in the U.S. Congress have targeted the National Endowment for the Arts for extinction and that theater artists in particular, especially the so-called NEA Four, have been caricatured as wanton and indecent destroyers of what passes, in some quarters at least, for traditional American values. And while Congress has yet to extinguish adventurous and daring art in this country, the decline in public funding (combined with the clamor of the Christian Coalition and other right-wing activists) has succeeded in intimidating some theater companies into designing more conservative seasons.

Memory and History

Given theater's historically critical footing, it is unlikely, it seems to me, that ghosts on the stage simply becalm King's "Republican . . . in a three-piece suit" and reinforce the status quo. (Even in mass culture, this process of reassurance is complex and uneven insofar as no horror film is ever able completely to put to rest all the demons it has raised.) But before analyzing exactly what ghosts enable a playwright to do, I want to consider theater's uniqueness as a medium that is quite literally haunted in a way that film and television can never be.

For theater is distinguished from mass-cultural forms by more than its penchant for social critique. It is also the most literary of the performing arts, and plays have long (and misleadingly) been considered a branch of literature. Despite the high profiles of certain directors and designers, playwrights and their plays are usually taken to be the generative forces behind almost all productions on what Derrida calls the theological stage, that physical—and metaphysical—space in which "a primary logos" is not literally present on "the theatrical site" but "governs it from a distance." Performances on the theological stage—which is to say, our own stage—will always be evanescent, but the written word of the "author-creator" is imagined both as a divine injunction and as a kind of time capsule, a tomb in which are interred both his or her own ideas, predilections, and emotions and the remains of a vanished time and culture.[11] (It is little wonder that the citizens of Grover's Corners include a copy of *Our Town*, that most celebrated of ghost plays and the very text in which they appear, in the cornerstone of their new bank.) If the play-text is indeed a kind of memorial, then theatrical performance must be akin to awakening the dead. For both performing and reading are ways of remembering; they jog the memory and help restore what has been lost. But if performance is an act of remembering, it must also remember what was never really there. For in bringing a written text to life, performance always reveals that the text is incomplete, that it is composed of what are, in effect, dead words. Yet as a form of resuscitation, it must revivify this incompletely realized artifact in relation to the desires, fantasies, and beliefs of the absent playwright—which can be endlessly hypothesized but never really known—and to those of the living actors, designers, and director. Performance based on a written text thus always (and uneasily) occupies two historical moments, the moment in which it was written and that in which it is performed. Negotiating between past and present, the theological stage always dramatizes not the coincidence but the gap between written text and performance, writer and director, character and actor. Theater, in short, is always about the impossibility of representing what was never fully there in the first place. Performance is always in thrall to a written text that is not quite alive yet not quite dead. Film may be haunted by the absent actor whose luminous reincarnation fills the screen, but theater is haunted by the absent author-creator whose text functions as a kind of ghost, mediating between death and life.

Given the status of the dramatic text as a memorial, an incomplete project, a specter, it is little wonder that the theater, from Greek and Renaissance tragedy to Japanese Nō, has long been linked to the occult and populated by ghosts. As Marvin Carlson notes, "one of the universals of performance, both East and West, is its ghostliness, its sense of return, the uncanny but inescapable impression imposed upon its spectators that *we are seeing what we saw before.*"[12] Actors may be passing before our eyes, but they are of necessity only standing in for those imaginary beings who, like the ghost of King Hamlet, vanish before we can touch them. As Mac Wellman's *Crowbar* so vividly suggests, every performance, like every theater building, is haunted by what has come before, by the ghosts of characters and actors who have trod the boards. Entering a suburban multiplex, whose walls are inevitably plastered with posters announcing ever more glorious coming attractions, we are swept into the future, dazzled by technology, computer animation, digital sound, or at the least, the play of light on a brilliantly blank screen. But entering a theater, either a Broadway house or a repertory theater, whose walls are invariably dotted with posters and photographs of previous productions, we walk into a past that is haunted by the spirits of dedicated artists. Theater, despite recent advances in sound and lighting technologies, remains curiously antitechnological, a place for those who do and those who act—in the broadest sense, a site for reimagining and remaking the self. For if film is preoccupied with technology, fantasy, and plotting, then theater is preoccupied with character, with the richness of a human subject about whom one fact is indisputable: he or she is going to die. Yet, as Joseph Roach notes, it is the very mortality of the actor that allows him or her to stake a claim for a kind of immortality:

> Even in death actors' roles tend to stay with them. They gather in the memory of audiences, like ghosts, as each new interpretation of a role sustains or upsets expectations derived from the previous ones. This is the sense in which audiences may come to regard the performer as an eccentric but meticulous curator of cultural memory, a medium for speaking with the dead.[13]

In the act of curating cultural memory, the performer not only conserves the theatrical past but also and ironically commemorates both his or her own mortality and the mortality of the performance itself. For all performance, as Peggy Phelan reminds us, "becomes itself through disappearance."[14] It silently acknowledges its evanescence, the fact that it is a unique and fleeting occasion that can never be preserved or reiterated. Like Prince Hamlet, it always dies at the end of the last act.

At the close of what Henry Luce in 1941 announced somewhat belatedly to be the American Century and the beginning of a new century, as the theater continues to be positioned as a relatively elitist alternative to film and television, it has become a place to meet both our own past and that of our culture. For it is my contention that ghosts are so important on our stages in part because they serve as a sign of theater's self-consciousness as a medium and its highbrow aspirations. Unlike cinema, in which ghosts are almost invariably the sign of a cheesy horror film, theater routinely uses ghosts as a deconstructive trope in which memory and history intersect, two processes, Pierre Nora argues, that now "appear"—in this age of identity politics—"to be in fundamental opposition" to each other.[15] Memory, as Nora explains, is now understood to be spontaneous, a part of lived experience. Connecting us with the past, it fills us out. It gives us an identity. It is alive, immediate, and concrete. It is communicated through the body, through gesture, words, and rituals. Memory is in our blood, in our genes; it is "a bond tying us to the eternal present" as well as the past. History, on the other hand, is assumed to come to us from without. It is reconstructed through cultural narratives we read or watch or listen to. It "belongs to everyone and to no one, whence its claim to universal authority."[16] Even our own memories become history only when, in effect, they are no longer ours, when we meet them again in someone else's representations. For no matter how vibrant or how densely populated by the sweating, teeming masses, history always has something vaguely abstract about it.

The theatrical ghost is a figure uniquely positioned in relation to both memory and history. As a token of memory, the ghost is usually intensely personalized, emanating from and materializing characters' fears and desires (and playing off of our own as well). For like Uncle Peck, or Jelly Roll Morton, or Sarah Brown Eyes, the ghost returns almost ritualistically to tell characters (and audiences) what they know but would rather forget. It is thus a concrete manifestation of fears and desires that, because they have never been resolved, literally haunt a character. Dating back at least to classical Greece, the ghost has usually been imagined as a tortured soul who has not yet found peace but who walks the earth seeking satisfaction.[17] The ghost, in short, is unfulfilled and only appears to those figures who are themselves unfulfilled. For the ghost is a token of an intensely personal loss, a loss so great or so painful that one is loath to acknowledge it. And coming to peace with the ghost means coming to terms with this disavowed loss in such a way that it is both internalized and transformed, as if by magic, into a kind of profit. Thus, *How I Learned to Drive* is about learning that what has been lost can never be struck from one's memory, that L'il Bit must live always with the unexpectedly comforting reflection of Uncle Peck in her rearview mirror. It demonstrates that Peck is also her own reflection, a double, a shadow self, a figure who has taken root inside her and yet stands apart, watching her from a distance.

Like Peck, virtually every ghost in the contemporary theater signals a crisis in the constitution of the subject, for whom the ghost represents an Other who has been lost and yet is imagined to inhere both inside and outside the self. For these bereaved subjects (and, as I have learned, for many playwrights as well), the ghost functions as a symptom of a melancholic process whereby the subject attempts to incorporate that which he or she has lost.[18] In Freud's essay "Mourning and Melancholia," he describes both these conditions as "the reaction to the loss of a loved person, or to the loss of some abstraction."[19] The difference between the two consists in the fact that "melancholia is in some way related to an unconscious loss," unlike "mourning, in which there is nothing unconscious about" it.[20] In both cases, however, the experience of loss compels the subject, as Judith Butler explains, "to incorporate that other into the very structure of the ego, taking on attributes of the other and 'sustaining' the other through magical acts of imitation." But because the melancholic (unlike the mourner) refuses to relinquish the love-object, "internalization becomes a strategy of magically resuscitating the lost object, not only because the loss is painful, but because the ambivalence felt toward the object requires that the object be retained until the differences are settled."[21] It is precisely this act of melancholic sustenance that is dramatized in *How I Learned to Drive* and *Ragtime*. Yet these plays also suggest that the very act of calling up theatrical ghosts represents a form of derepression. It thereby allows for the transformation of melancholia into mourning, unconscious into conscious. It is little wonder then that both *How I Learned to Drive* and *Ragtime* should end with gestures of putting the past to rest in what counts as something of a triumph for the survivors.

But the theatrical ghost is more than just an illustration of Freud's theories of loss and subject formation. It is also symptomatic of the persistence of history during a period when it is fashionable to deride it, whether history be understood in Marxian terms as a chronicle of struggle among classes, peoples, and nations or more broadly, as Nora explains, as that which "binds itself strictly to temporal continuities, to progressions and to relations between things."[22] For the ghost is not only a product of highly subjective, personal memories but also an embodiment of social, political, and economic forces. The ghost need not be that of a public figure like Ethel Rosenberg, but it nonetheless serves as a representative and reminder of the skirmishes that constitute history—skirmishes, for example, between Reagan's cocky henchmen and guilty liberals or between African Americans and a racist fire chief in New Rochelle. Insofar as each skirmish has a winner and a loser, the ghost usually represents a casualty of history. For it is almost always numbered among the losers. It may not imagine itself a victim, but its refusal to die, to disappear, leads one to suspect that it has in some way been wronged or oppressed. Thus, for example, the spectral figures of Ethel Rosenberg and Sarah Brown Eyes are the spirits whom the victors would rather forget. *Angels in America* resurrects Ethel Rosenberg to incite both Roy Cohn and the audience to remember the injustices perpetrated by McCarthyism in the name of national security. And *Ragtime* calls up Sarah as a reminder of the racialized violence that remains a legacy of slavery and continues to ravage American society. One of these figures is historical, while the other may be a product of fantasy, but both roam the earth because they cannot be consigned neatly to another time and another place. Rather, they function as the sign of the haunting of the present by the past, the living by the dead.

Insofar as the theatrical ghost functions as a historical referent, as a representative of what Marx calls the "tradition of all the dead generations," this ghost is less an incorporeal essence than that which Derrida (following Marx) designates a specter, an impossible conjunction of spirit and flesh whose persistence on the stage (and off) testifies to the fact that we still live with the ghosts of those persons and social institutions we thought we had put behind us. Located on the threshold between two worlds, two orders of being, and two temporalities, the specter is proof that the past lives in all of us and that we are both its products and its makers. It is the sign, as Derrida notes, glancing at Marx and at *Hamlet,* that "*to be* . . . means . . . to inherit."[23] For the specter is "a paradoxical incorporation, the becoming-body, a certain phenomenal and carnal form of the spirit. It becomes . . . some 'thing' that remains difficult to name: neither soul nor body, and both one and the other."[24] As a figure endlessly undoing the opposition between flesh and spirit, the carnal and the abstract, this almost nameless "thing" ends up deconstructing the opposition between memory and history. Or more precisely, it represents the site and the occasion for the transformation of memory into history, the individual into the collective, the particular into the universal. It represents the persistence of the past, the intractability of the Other, "the furtive and ungraspable visibility of the invisible."[25] It demonstrates that what is memory one moment can be history the next. For as we watch the spectacle, in a darkened auditorium, of other people remembering, we see memory changed into history as the struggles in which they participate and the society in which they play their parts are illuminated. We see memory and experience suddenly problematized, dematerialized, rendered untrustworthy, a kind of phantom limb produced by an individual consciousness unaware that it is a historical construction.

Living as we do in a culture obsessively foreseeing the end, a uniquely forgetful culture that regards last month's headlines as a dusty chronicle—Monica who?—the theater has become for some writers a site for *re-membering,* literally piecing together what has been lost. As a marginalized and endangered form of cultural production, the American theater is haunted in so many ways: by its own more glorious past, by the culture that it both critiques and helps prop up, by the written texts of vanished author-creators, and by characters who are in turn stricken with memory. It is haunted by the fact that it is no longer a central feature of U.S. culture. It is haunted by the 1960s, the last truly progressive era—one in which so many prominent theater artists came of age and to whose utopian promises they continue to hearken. Yet a mere glance at recent U.S. history reveals that these promises have consistently and brutally been betrayed. For America itself is haunted by the disillusionment and the losses of the past thirty years: by the ever-widening disparity between rich and poor, black and white; by the backlash against feminism and affirmative action; by the increasing power of social and fiscal conservatives; by the studied blindness of most Americans to their nation's many imperialist enterprises; and by the gradual whittling away of possibilities for and incitements to change.

But the ghosts in recent plays are even more than the woeful traces of what was once an activist culture. They also function as the signs of a crisis of political representation. For so many of these specters are criminalized or pathologized subjects. Ethel Rosenberg, Sarah Brown Eyes, and Uncle Peck are all accused of having violated those laws intended to produce normative social, political, and sexual subjects. They are all, in short, constructed as slightly queer, whatever their sexual orientation may be. They remain the abjected ones—sometimes damned, sometimes redeemed, but always irreclaimable. It is little wonder then that most of the ghosts who populate American stages are feminized. If not female characters, they are men who more often than not are marked as sexual or gender deviants. Defying that representational regime that imagines women as pure materiality, these ghosts are decorporealized, on the side of spirit rather than flesh. Exposing the limits of both political and theatrical representation, they are literally without bodies, disallowed full participation—full presence—as subjects. Rather, they haunt the texts, the stages, and the social body, a queer minority relentlessly exposed to the violence of the law.

Modernism and Imperialism

In the hands of at least some practitioners, theater (in part because of its history as a critical practice) has attempted more conscientiously than most other forms of cultural production to keep utopian impulses alive. And this has become a particularly difficult—and important—project during a period when alternatives to capitalism and commodity culture seem increasingly foreclosed. For it is the specter, as *Angels in America* so clearly suggests, that in keeping the past alive also announces the promise of a radically different future. As Derrida emphasizes, the spectral—and utopian—character of the promise "will always keep within it . . . this absolutely undetermined messianic hope at its heart," this hope for "an alterity that cannot be anticipated." "The very place of spectrality," therefore, must always be left empty "in memory of the hope," in memory of an unimaginable future. Following in the footsteps of those peerless tragedians, Hamlet, Marx, and Walter Benjamin, Derrida envisions history itself as a kind of theater in which one forever awaits the appearance of a ghost and in which memory functions to keep both past and future alive. History is always incomplete, a site of absence, loss, horror, betrayal. Taking up these betrayals, the real theater, as *Angels in America* so compellingly demonstrates, can become a site of "infinite promise," a place for "awaiting what one does not expect . . . any longer," for re-membering what has never happened.[26]

Despite their undeniable spectral and spectacular power, Ethel Rosenberg, Sarah Brown Eyes, Uncle Peck, and Jelly Roll Morton are in the end only ghosts, that is, a sign of the increasing inaccessibility of a living past in an era that is profoundly antihistoricist. As analysis of the past has in recent years given way more and more to a fetishization of

experience, as history has been displaced more and more by nostalgia—
a whiff of the past from which social struggles have been conveniently
excised—we can now imagine history only as an intervention from
without, an *Invasion of the Body Snatchers,* or as a specter that suddenly
materializes to confront a frightened and amnesiac population. As if to
acknowledge and treat this amnesia, the theater has, in the hands of at
least a few practitioners, become a space in which to remember what we
have forgotten. Yet even in commemorating the utopianism of the
1960s, in valorizing the revolutionary praxis that has historically been
inscribed in the very idea of America, the American theater—like the
culture of which it is a part—has been ill disposed to confront the increasingly arrogant imperial posturing of the United States as the last remaining superpower. With the exception of a handful of playwrights,
American writers have been curiously insular, even isolationist in their
concerns. This isolationism has many correlations and causes. It seems
linked in part to a refusal on the part of the major media outlets to critique the U.S. role on the world stage. Few American writers are committed to investigating the increasingly globalized post–Cold War economy and the exploitative relations between the First and Third Worlds.
For the displacement of the proletariat of the First World to the sweat-
shops of the Third may have set the class struggle out of our line of vision, but it has by no means erased it. And it may well be that the specter
haunting the American theater, the ghost that most writers cannot see,
is this new proletariat that cannot even be represented directly but that
instead makes itself known through surrogates—those abjected ones on
the fringes of plays that happen to have the word "America" in their titles,
persons of color with the names of developing countries like Belize (in
Angels in America) or Brazil (in *The America Play*)—that provocatively
reference this unseen presence.

   This displacement of imperial relations in recent American plays
marks the sign, I believe, not of a break but of a continuity with the
canons of modern drama. For contemporary plays are hardly the only
texts in which one discovers ghosts. As Derrida suggests, modernity itself,
as inaugurated and instantiated by *Hamlet,* represents a kind of spectral
drama. And there is no question that the stage, from the early modern
through the romantic periods, often called up spirits. But beginning in

the late nineteenth century, with the development of a modernist drama with highbrow ambitions that explicitly interrogates and sets itself apart from both tradition and popular culture, the theater became a far more ambiguously and disturbingly spectral site. In the experimental dramas of Maeterlinck, Wedekind, Strindberg, Cocteau, O'Neill, and many others, the early modernist stage defined itself as a space in which to problematize presence, which is to say, to interrogate and deconstruct the oppositions between past and present, here and there, self and Other, spirit and flesh, text and performance, the real and the hallucinatory, the living and the dead. If, throughout the twentieth century, this tradition—and I think that is the correct word to describe it—remained the dominant strain of what has been canonized as modern drama, its hegemony testifies to what surely must be seen as an aestheticizing and etherealizing tendency within modernism and within theater. (Brecht's historicist and materialist theater, in contrast, could be described as, if not exactly a theater without ghosts, then at least a theater that goes to great lengths both to illuminate and to debunk the claims of both theology and the undead.) This etherealizing tendency, moreover, has by no means been merely an undesirable side effect of modernism. On the contrary, it has been crucial for the production of those utopian figurations and intimations of the sublime that have been indispensable to modernist drama and for the elevation of theater in the cultural hierarchy just as it was being challenged (and nearly overwhelmed) by an explosion of mass-cultural forms. Ghosts, in other words, have functioned since the birth of modernism as a sign of theater's seriousness, self-reflexivity, and highbrow aspirations.

Yet early modernist plays are not the only spectral dramas that fill play anthologies and modern drama classes. For within the dominant, aestheticizing strain of Western theatrical modernism, there is a second prominent collection of canonical ghost plays that is the product of what has misleadingly been labeled the theater of the absurd. The characters who people the plays of Beckett, Genet, and Ionesco are invariably haunted by the desires of and for others who remain either unseen or inaccessible, others who are neither altogether present nor altogether absent but who represent the promise of an impossible return, like the Orator in *The Chairs;* the growing corpse in *Amédée;* or, most famously,

Godot. Beckett, in particular, is so central to the modernist canon in part because he problematizes theatrical presence in a way that both recapitulates and defamiliarizes the achievements of early modernism.

If I am correct, the canon of modern drama is in fact marked by a triple efflorescence of ghost plays. The first dates from the years 1885 until, say, 1925; the second from the 1950s and early 1960s; and the third from the 1990s. And I want to argue, moreover, that this latest flowering represents not only a formal reiteration but, more important, the fulfillment of a certain globalizing logic. For the three periods of ghost plays—all of these plays, it must be noted, the products of metropolitan cultures—also correspond to three distinct phases of Western imperialism. The first phase marks European imperialism's triumph after the Berlin Conference of 1884, when, as Fredric Jameson notes, "a significant structural segment of the economic system as a whole is now located elsewhere," in colonies in Africa or Asia. As a result, "daily life in the metropolis . . . can no longer be grasped immanently; it no longer has its meaning, its deeper reason for being, within itself." And "artistic content," in its turn, "will now henceforth always have something missing about it." Metropolitan modernism, with its formal disjunctions and constitutive absences, must then quite precisely "live. . . this formal dilemma," a dilemma it can neither compass nor solve, through a ritual displacement.[27] How else, for example, is one to understand Cocteau's *The Wedding on the Eiffel Tower,* in which the General is inexplicably devoured on the eponymous Tower by a lion that "is actually in Africa" and, hence, "a simple mirage"?[28] What is this if not the impossible revenge of a colonized subject who is imaginable only as a decorporealized, trompe l'oeil image?

The second phase, the so-called theater of the absurd, should be described more accurately as the theater of decolonization, or the theater that emerged when the violence of anticolonial struggle was sublimated as metaphysics. This is the drama of disorientation that resulted when Europe's relations with its former colonies were radically altered and the metropolitan capitals suffered an unprecedented identity crisis, which is to say, a crisis of economic and military power, of memory, and of place. How else, for example, is one to make sense of the obsessive attempts of Ionesco's blundering bourgeois to determine whether a rioting rhinoceros is, in their words, "African" or "Asiatic"? Why else would their frustration then lead them to an increasingly heated dispute over whether "Asiatics" are "bright yellow" or "white . . . like us"?[29] Like the rhinoceroses, the formerly colonized masses are imagined as representing both an unprecedented threat to "us" and an incomprehensible otherness—dangerous, foreign, and out of control.

The third phase of ghost plays, and arguably the most monstrous repetition of all, is the drama of neocolonialism, which signals the replacement of occupying armies by the pinstriped brigades of the World Bank, the International Monetary Fund, and the World Trade Organization. While the first two phases focus on relations between Europe and its colonies, the last marks a geographical shift. For with the fall of the Soviet Union, the triumph of neoliberalism, and the increasing mobility and internationalization of capital, there is no question that the United States has become the new imperial hub whose bankers, CEOs, and politicians structure relations of global domination on the American plan, despite, as David Harvey notes, unprecedented "geographical dispersal and fragmentation of production systems, divisions of labor, and specializations of tasks." Yet this neocolonialism no more represents a radical break with the past, and with imperialism, than postmodernism does with the discourses of modernism, or the new ghost play does with the old. For as Harvey emphasizes, despite the proliferation of discourses trumpeting a new globalized economy, "there has not been any fundamental revolution in the mode of production and its associated social relations." Even the development of new information technologies cannot disguise a "reassertion of early nineteenth-century capitalist values coupled with a twenty-first century penchant for pulling everyone (and everything that can be exchanged) into the orbit of capital while rendering large segments of the world's population permanently redundant in relation to the basic dynamics of capital accumulation."[30] I would argue in fact that postmodernism—and the huge mass-mediated apparatus that trumpets its achievements—represents less a momentous epistemological shift than it does an attempt to divert attention away from increasingly uneven patterns of capital accumulation and economic development toward the cultural and the social. Within this global context, the ghost plays of both the 1990s and the 1890s emblematize what might be called, with a nod to George Lucas, the dark side of imperial triumphalism, the repressed anxieties that return unwelcomed to haunt the metropolitan conscience.

If I am correct that the very category "modern drama" is in fact a product of imperialism, then its existence is predicated upon a certain disavowal, a refusal to credit the corporeal existence and the labor power of those nearly invisible Others who haunt its margins. Is it any wonder then that in all these modern dramas, the ghost remains an enigma? For like the category "native," which, Fanon reminds us, is also a product of imperialism, the ghost is both utterly material and utterly dematerialized, a nearly invisible producer at the beck and call of the prosperous few and yet one whose realm, language, and social relations remain mysterious and mystified.

The Visor Effect

Although my analysis of American drama's isolationism may suggest that I am reproaching already marginalized cultural producers for their refusal to acknowledge those more marginalized than they, I am more concerned with drawing attention to the spectral consequences of a particular economic and cultural logic. Convincing playwrights to critique the international division of labor is not likely to alter the latter's structure. And I believe it is a mistake to look to even a would-be dissident theater as a way of producing social and economic change. Indeed, when I hear critics and artists calling—always with the best intentions—for an aggressively feminist or antiracist or antihomophobic theater, I wonder why we want the theater to redeem us. I don't particularly enjoy watching right-wing art. And I do believe that theater, like all art, can be crucial in keeping utopian promises alive. But it is a mistake to look to theater to solve problems that can be solved only in the political arena. Is not the desire on the part of so many playwrights and theorists to agitate for a politically redemptive theater a symptom of a profound disillusionment with real-world politics? Those cultural producers whom Bourdieu rightly dubs a "dominated fraction of the dominant class" feel so completely disempowered because they are.[31] But storming the barricades at Berkeley Rep can lead to real political and economic change only through the most impossibly tortuous of routes.

Although I think it is a mistake to look to the theater to redeem us, I want finally to consider one more ghostly consequence of the theater and its implications for theorizing spectatorship. This is what Derrida (referencing the ghost of King Hamlet hidden in armor) calls "the *visor effect*." According to Derrida, the visor effect is produced by the opposing positions on stage of specter and living character. This effect, which is a kind of theatrical version of a one-way mirror, is generated by the theatrical specter who can look at a living character yet never itself be seen. Having the ability to watch even as it remains not quite flesh, the specter retains a certain resistance to a scopic regime. And even when materialized, like the ghost of King Hamlet, it wears a kind of veil. "A spectral asymmetry," Derrida notes, "interrupts all specularity," disjoining the one who watches from the one who is watched. The visor effect thereby both protects the insubstantial substance of the specter and ensures the visibility of his or her all-too-human antagonist. Unlike King Hamlet, Uncle Peck and Ethel Rosenberg may be quite visible to those whom they visit, but like the murdered king, they always hold something back in order to retain a certain mystery and authority that Derrida connects specifically to paternal law: "To feel ourselves seen by a look which it will always be impossible to cross, that is the *visor effect* on the basis of which we inherit from the law" (Derrida, *Specters of Marx*, 6–7). So it is the spectral presence of this paternal signifier, this deity whom one cannot quite make out, that compels obedience and guarantees the transmission of authority. Aligning vision and domination, the visor effect guarantees the persistence and reproduction of patriarchal spectacles, among which one must include the theological stage. The spectral Uncle Peck, after all, is the architect of the photo shoot that functions as a kind of mirror stage for L'il Bit, splitting her into two, turning her into both subject and object. And Peck will always remain an unseen presence in L'il Bit's rearview mirror, like an imperious passenger invisibly giving directions to his chauffeur.

In being revealed as the not-quite-hidden face of the Father, the specter also becomes an image of the absent author-creator. Both specter and author, after all, are imagined as those who control the action silently, impermeably, autocratically. The one hovers above the stage while the other watches from the wings. Yet both are in the know. At the same time, this distinction between seeing and being seen, knowing and being known, also describes the ontology of the realist stage (as inaugurated by *Hamlet*), which is always predicated on a "spectral asymmetry," a differentiation between those who look and those who are being looked at. For Li'l Bit finds herself being gazed upon by many sets of eyes. As a character, she is overseen by the specter of her late uncle and the ghost of her absent author-creator. And as an actor, she is looked at by spectators, those spectral Others who see and yet remain silent and unseen. In other words, the very ontology of the realist theater guarantees that the spectators will see themselves reflected in the eyes of the specter.[32] Both *spectator* and *specter*, after all, are derived from the Latin verb *spectare*, meaning "to look, to behold," and both denote subjects whose primary function is to see yet who remain, in a sense, invisible. Specters and spectators alike—(mis)recognizing themselves in the vigilant eyes of the Other.

So this stage—overrun by ghosts, overseen by an absent author-creator, gazed upon by a spectral audience—designates not only the realist theater at the end of one millennium and the beginning of another. It also describes the stage of history at a moment when the messianic promise has become increasingly spectral, which is to say, elusive. For there is no question that history—in the age of infomercials, reality TV, and Jerry Springer—has become utterly theatricalized. People more and more believe themselves to be passive spectators of the historical pageant. Yet to draw out this analogy a bit further, I would like to suggest that both the contemporary stage and the producers of the spectacle we call history have perhaps underestimated the agency of the spectator. For it is easy to overlook the fact that both theater and history are finally the productions of collectives and communities. As the ghost of Jelly Roll Morton belatedly learns, both transform an "I" into a "we." Theater, on the one hand, turns individual spectators into a group that assembles to work out their desires and fears. Unlike the cinema, which for most people represents an intensely privatized experience, the theater creates as if by magic a temporary community out of the multitude assembled to watch the ghosts tread the boards. History, on the other hand, as Marx has taught us, also interpellates individualized subjects as collectives, classes, social formations.

Even *Wall Street Journal* columnists may have to admit that the United States has yet a way to go before it realizes the "Marxian ideal" thanks to a mass political movement that started in Seattle at the end of 1999. Since the protests over the neocolonialist policies of the World Trade Organization, a left-wing activism has been reborn whose flamboyant tactics look back to the 1960s but whose message recalls the workers' struggles of the 1930s. In Seattle, Washington, and Genoa, protesters are decrying the new international division of labor and producing a theater in the streets that promises both to move the workers of the world to center stage again and to endow the seemingly immobilized watchers of history with a kind of agency. This activist theater aims thereby not to banish but to honor the specters of all the dead generations. This new theater of the streets promises once again to turn the abject and silent ones into actors on the stage of history. All they—or perhaps I should say, we—need is the will and the opportunity. No audition necessary. No talent required.

Part II: Closet Dramas

Chapter Four

Ambivalence, Utopia, and a Queer Sort of Materialism

how *angels in america* reconstructs the nation

Critics, pundits, and producers have placed Tony Kushner's *Angels in America: A Gay Fantasia on National Themes* in the unenviable position of having to rescue the American theater. The latter, by all accounts, is in a sorry state. It has attempted to maintain its elite cultural status despite the fact that the differences between "high" and "low" have become precarious. On Broadway, increasingly expensive productions survive more and more by mimicking mass culture, either in the form of mind-numbing spectacles featuring singing cats, falling chandeliers, and dancing dinnerware or plays, like *The Heidi Chronicles* or *Prelude to a Kiss,* whose style and themes aspire to "quality" television. In regional theaters, meanwhile, subscriptions continue to decline, and with them the adventurousness of artistic directors. Given this dismal situation, *Angels in America* has almost singlehandedly resuscitated a category of play that has become almost extinct: the serious Broadway drama that is neither a British import nor a revival.

Not within memory has a new American play been canonized by the press as rapidly as *Angels in America.*[1] Indeed, critics have been stumbling over each other in an adulatory stupor. John Lahr hails *Perestroika* as a "masterpiece" and notes that "not since Williams has a playwright announced his poetic vision with such authority on the Broadway stage."[2] Jack Kroll judges both parts "the broadest, deepest, most searching American play of our time," while Robert Brustein deems *Millennium Approaches* "the authoritative achievement of a radical dramatic artist with a fresh, clear voice."[3] In the gay press, meanwhile, the play is viewed as testifying to the fact that "Broadway now leads the way in the industry with its unapologetic portrayals of gay characters."[4] For both Frank Rich and John Clum, *Angels* is far more than just a successful play; it is the marker of a decisive historical shift in American theater. According to Rich, the play's success is in part the result of its ability to conduct "a searching and radical rethinking of the whole esthetic of American political drama."[5] For Clum, the play's appearance on Broadway "marks a turning point in the history of gay drama, the history of American drama, and of American literary culture."[6] In its reception, *Angels*—so deeply preoccupied with teleological process—is itself positioned as both the culmination of history and as that which rewrites the past.

Despite the enormity of the claims cited earlier, I am less interested in disputing them than in trying to understand why they are being made—and why *now*. Why is a play featuring five gay male characters being universalized as a "turning point" in the American theater and minoritized as the preeminent gay male artifact of the 1990s? Why is it both popular and "radical"? What is the linkage between the two primary sources for the play's theory of history and utopia—Walter Benjamin and Mormonism? And what does this linkage suggest about the constitution of the nation? Finally, why has queer drama become *the* theatrical sensation of the 1990s? I hope it's not too perverse of me to attempt to answer these questions by focusing less on the construction of queer subjectivities per se than on the field of cultural production in which *Angels in America* is situated. After all, how else would one practice a queer materialism?

The Angel of History

The opposite of nearly everything you say about *Angels in America* will also hold true: *Angels* valorizes identity politics; it offers an antifoundationalist critique of identity politics. *Angels* mounts an attack against ideologies of individualism; it problematizes the idea of community. *Angels* submits liberalism to a trenchant examination; it finally opts for yet another version of American liberal pluralism. *Angels* launches a critique of the very mechanisms that produce pathologized and acquiescent female bodies; it represents yet another pathologization and silencing of women. A conscientious reader or spectator might well rebuke the play, as Belize does Louis: "You're ambivalent about everything."[7] And so it is. The play's ambivalence, however, is not simply the result of Kushner hedging his bets on the most controversial issues. Rather, it functions, I believe—quite independently of the intent of its author—as the play's political unconscious, playing itself out on many different levels: formal, ideological, characterological, and rhetorical. (Frank Rich refers to this as Kushner's "refusal to adhere to any theatrical or political theory.")[8] Yet the fact that ambivalence—or undecidability—is the watchword of this text (which is, after all, *two* plays) does not mean that all the questions it raises remain unresolved. On the contrary, I will argue that the play's undecidability is, in fact, always already resolved because the questions that appear to be ambivalent in fact already have been decided consciously or unconsciously by the text itself. Moreover, the relentless operation of normalizing reading practices works to reinforce these decisions. If I am correct, the play turns out (*pace* Frank Rich) to adhere all too well to a particular political theory.

Formally, *Angels* is a promiscuously complicated play that is very difficult to categorize generically. Clum's characterization of it as being "like a Shakespearean romance" is doubtlessly motivated by the play's rambling and episodic form, its interweaving of multiple plotlines, its mixture of realism and fantasy, its invocation of various theological and mythological narratives, as well as by its success in evoking those characteristics that are usually associated with both comedy and tragedy.[9] Moreover, *Perestroika*'s luminous finale is remarkably suggestive of the beatific scenes that end Shakespeare's romances. There is no question, moreover, that the play deliberately evokes the long history of Western dramatic literature and positions itself as heir to the traditions of Sophocles, Shakespeare, Brecht, and others. Consider, for example, its use of the blindness/insight opposition and the way that Prior Walter is carefully constructed (like the blind Prelapsarianov) as a kind of Teiresias, "going blind, as prophets do."[10] This binarism, the paradigmatic emblem of the tragic subject (and mark of Teiresias, Oedipus, and Gloucester), deftly links cause and effect—because one is blind to truth, one loses one's sight—and is used to claim Prior's priority, his epistemologically privileged position in the text. Or consider the parallels often drawn in the press between Kushner's Roy Cohn and Shakespeare's Richard III.[11] Or Kushner's use of a fate motif, reminiscent of *Macbeth*, whereby Prior insists that Louis not return until the seemingly impossible comes to pass, until he sees Louis "black and blue" (2:89). Or Kushner's rewriting of those momentous moral and political debates that riddle not just classical tragedy (*Antigone, Richard II*) but also the work of Brecht and his (mainly British) successors (Howard Brenton, David Hare, Caryl Churchill). Or the focus on the presence/absence of God that one finds not just in early modern tragedy but also in so-called absurdism (Beckett, Ionesco, Stoppard). Moreover, these characteristics tend to be balanced, on the one hand, by the play's insistent tendency to ironize and, on the other, by the familiar ingredients of romantic comedies (ill-matched paramours, repentant lovers, characters suddenly finding themselves in unfamiliar places, plus a lot of good jokes). Despite the ironic/comic tone, however, none of the interlaced couples survives the onslaught of chaos, disease, and revelation. Prior and Louis, Louis and Joe, Joe and Harper have all parted by the end of the play, and the romantic dyad (as primary social unit) is replaced in the final scene of *Perestroika* by a utopian concept of (erotic) affiliation and a new definition of family.

Angels in America's title, its idea of utopia, and its model for a particular kind of ambivalence are derived in part from Benjamin's extraordinary meditation, "Theses on the Philosophy of History," written shortly before his death in 1940. Composed during the first months of World War II, with fascism on its march across Europe, the darkness (and simultaneous luminosity) of Benjamin's "Theses" attest not only to the seeming invincibility of Hitler but also to the impossible position of the European left, "stranded," as Terry Eagleton notes, "between social democracy and Stalinism."[12] In this essay, Benjamin sketches a discontinuous theory of history in which "the services of theology" are enlisted in the aid of reconceiving "historical materialism."[13] Opposing the universalizing strategies of bourgeois historicism with historical materialism's project of brushing "history against the grain" (257), he attempts a radical revision of Marxist historiography. Suturing the Jewish notion of Messianic time (in which all history is given meaning retrospectively by the sudden and unexpected coming of the Messiah) to the Marxist concept of revolution, Benjamin reimagines proletariat revolution not as the culmination of a conflict between classes, or between traditional institutions and new forms of production, but as a "blast[ing] open" of "the continuum of history" (262). Unlike traditional Marxist (or idealist) historiographers, he rejects the idea of the present as a moment of "transition" and instead conceives it as *Jetztzeit:* "time filled by the presence of the now" (261), a moment in which "time stands still and has come to a stop" (262). Facing *Jetztseit,* and opposing all forms of gradualism, Benjamin's historical materialist is given the task not of imagining and inciting progressive change (or a movement toward socialism) but of "blast[ing] a specific era out of the homogeneous course of history" (263).

The centerpiece of Benjamin's essay is his explication of a painting by Paul Klee, which becomes a parable of history, of the time of the Now, in the face of catastrophe (which for him means all of human history):

> A Klee painting named "Angelus Novus" shows an angel looking as though he is about to move away from something he is fixedly contemplating. His eyes are staring, his mouth is open, his wings are spread. This is how one pictures the angel of history. His face is turned toward the past. Where we perceive a chain of events, he sees one single catastrophe which keeps piling wreckage upon wreckage and hurls it in front of his feet. The angel would like to stay, awaken the dead, and make whole what has been smashed. But a storm is blowing from Paradise; it has got caught in his wings with such violence that the angel can no longer close them. This storm irresistibly propels him into the future to which his back is turned, while the pile of debris before him grows skyward. This storm is what we call progress. (257–58)

In Benjamin's allegory, with its irresolvable play of contradictions, the doggedly well-intentioned angel of history embodies both the inconceivability of progress and the excruciating condition of the Now. Poised (not unlike Benjamin himself in Europe in 1940) between the past, which is to say "catastrophe," and an unknown and terrifying future, he is less a heavenly actor than a passive observer, "fixedly contemplating" that disaster which is the history of the world. His "Paradise," meanwhile, is not the site of a benign utopianism but a "storm" whose "violence" gets caught under his wings and propels him helplessly into an inconceivable future that stymies his gaze.

Benjamin's allegory of history is, in many respects, the primary generative fiction for *Angels in America.* Not only is its Angel clearly derived from Benjamin's text (although with gender-reassignment surgery along the way—Kushner's Angel is "Hermaphroditically Equipped"), but so is its vision of Heaven, which has *"a deserted, derelict feel to it,"* with *"rubble . . . strewn everywhere"* (2:48; 121). And the play's conceptualizations of the past, of catastrophe, and of utopia are clearly inflected by Benjamin's "Theses," as is its linkage between historical materialism and theology. Moreover, rather than attempt to suppress the contradictions that inform Benjamin's materialist theology, Kushner expands them. As a result, the ideas of history, progress, and paradise that *Angels in America* invokes are irreducibly contradictory (often without appearing to be so). Just as Benjamin's notion of revolution is related dialectically to catastrophe, so are *Angels*'s concepts of deliverance and abjection, ecstasy and pain, utopia and dystopia, necessarily linked. Kushner's Angel (and her/his heaven) serve as a constant reminder both of catastrophe (AIDS, racism, homophobia, and the pathologization of queer and female bodies, to name only the play's most obvious examples) and of the perpetual possibility of the millennium's approach, or the possibility in the words of Ethel Rosenberg (unmistakably echoing Benjamin), that "history is about to crack wide open" (1:112). And the concept of utopia/dystopia to which s/he is linked guarantees that the vehicle of hope and redemption in *Angels*—the prophet who foresees a new age—will be the character who must endure the most agony: Prior Walter, suffering from AIDS and Louis's desertion.

Within the economy of utopia/dystopia that *Angels* installs, the greatest promise of the millennium is the possibility of life freed from the shackles of hatred, oppression, and disease. It is hardly surprising, therefore, that Roy Cohn is constructed as the embodiment and guarantor of dystopia. Not only is he the paradigm of bourgeois individualism—and Reaganism—at its most murderous, hypocritical, and malignant, but he is the one with the most terrifying vision of the "universe," which he apprehends "as a kind of sandstorm in outer space with winds of mega-hurricane velocity, but instead of grains of sand it's shards and splinters of glass" (1:13). It is, however, a sign of the play's obsessively dialectical structure that Roy's vision of what sounds like hell should provide an uncanny echo of Benjamin's "storm blowing from Paradise." Yet even this dialectic, much like the play's ambivalences, is deceptive insofar as its habit of turning one pole of a binarism relentlessly into its opposite (rather than into a synthesis) describes a false dialectic. Prior, on the other hand, refusing the role of victim, becomes the sign of the unimaginable, of "the Great Work" (2:148). Yet, as with Roy, so Prior's privileged position is a figure of contradiction, coupling not just blindness with prophecy, but also history with an impossible future, an ancient lineage (embodied by Prior 1 and Prior 2) with the millennium yet to come, and AIDS with a "most inner part, entirely free of disease" (1:34). Moreover, Prior's very name designates his temporal dislocation, the fact that he is at once too soon and belated, both that which anticipates and that which provides an epilogue (to the Walter family, if nothing else, since he seems to mark the end of the line). Prior Walter also serves as the queer commemoration of the Walter that came before—Walter Benjamin—whose revolutionary principles he both embodies and displaces insofar as he marks both the presence and absence of Walter Benjamin in this text.[14]

Throughout *Angels in America,* the utopia/dystopia coupling (wherein disaster becomes simultaneously the marker for and incitement to think Paradise) plays itself out through a host of binary oppositions: heaven/hell, forgiveness/retribution, communitarianism/individualism, spirit/flesh, pleasure/pain, beauty/decay, future/past, homosexuality/heterosexuality, rationalism/indeterminacy, migration/staying put, progress/stasis, life/death. Each of these functions not just as a set of conceptual poles in relation to which characters and themes are worked out and interpreted but also as an *oxymoron,* a figure of undecidability whose contradictory being becomes an incitement to think the impossible—revolution. For it is precisely the conjunction of opposites that allows what Benjamin calls "the flow of thoughts" to be given a "shock" and so turned into "the sign of a Messianic cessation of happening" (262–63). The oxymoron, in other words, becomes the privileged figure by which the unimaginable allows itself to be imagined.

In Kushner's reading of Benjamin, the hermaphroditic Angel becomes the most crucial site for the elaboration of contradiction. Because her/his body is the one on which an impossible—and utopian—sexual conjunction is played out, s/he decisively undermines the distinction between the heterosexual and the homosexual. With her/his "eight vaginas" and "Bouquet of Phalli" (2:48), s/he represents an absolute otherness, the impossible Other that fulfills the longing for both the maternal and paternal (or in Lacanian terms, both demand and the Law). On the one hand, as the maternal "Other," s/he is constituted by "demand . . . as already possessing the 'privilege' of satisfying needs, that is to say, the power of depriving them of that alone by which they are satisfied."[15] On the other hand, "as the law of symbolic functioning," s/he simultaneously represents the "Other embodied in the figure of the symbolic father," "not a person but a place, the locus of law, language and the symbolic."[16] The impossible conjunction of the maternal and paternal, s/he provides Prior with sexual pleasure of celestial quality—and gives a new meaning to safe sex. At the same time, s/he also fills and completes subjectivity, being the embodiment of and receptacle for Prior's "Released Female Essence" (2:48).

Although all of these characteristics suggest that the Angel is constructed as an extratemporal being, untouched by the ravages of passing time, s/he comes (quite literally for Prior) already culturally mediated. When s/he first appears at the end of *Millennium*, Prior exclaims, "*Very Steven Spielberg*" (1:118). Although his campy ejaculation is clearly calculated as a laugh line, defusing and undercutting (with typical postmodern cynicism) the deadly earnestness of the scene, it also betrays the fact that this miraculous apparition is in part a product of the culture industry and that any reading of her/him will be mediated by the success of Steven Spielberg and his ilk (in films like *Close Encounters of the Third Kind* and *E.T.*) in producing a particular vision of the miraculous—with lots of bright white light and music by John Williams. To that extent, the appearance of the Angel signals the degree to which utopia—and revolution!—have now become the product of commodity culture. Unlike earlier periods, when utopia tended to be imagined in terms of production (rather than consumption) and was sited in a preceding phase of capitalism (for example, in a preindustrial or agrarian society), late capitalism envisions utopia through the lens of the commodity and—not unlike Walter Benjamin at his most populist—projects it into a future and an elsewhere lit by that *"unearthly white light"* (1:118) that represents, among other things, the illimitable allure of the commodity form.[17]

Although the construction of the Angel represses her/his historicity, the heaven s/he calls home is explicitly the product (and victim) of temporality. Heaven is a simulacrum of San Francisco on April 18, 1906, the day of the Great Earthquake. For it is on this day that God "abandoned" his angels and their heaven *"and did not return"* (2:51). Heaven thus appears frozen in time, *"deserted and derelict,"* with *"rubble strewn everywhere"* (2:121). The Council Room in Heaven, meanwhile, *dimly lit by candles and a single great bulb"* (which periodically fails), is a monument to the past, specifically to the New Science of the seventeenth century and the Enlightenment project to which it is inextricably linked. The table in the Council Room is *"covered with antique and broken astronomical, astrological, mathematical and nautical objects of measurement and calculation."* At its center sits a *"bulky radio, a 1940s model in very poor repair"* (2:128) on which the Angels are listening to the first reports of the Chernobyl disaster. Conflating different moments of the past and distinct (Western) histories, Heaven is a kind of museum, not the insignia of the Now, but of *before,* of an antique past, of the obsolete. Its decrepitude is also symptomatic of the Angels' fear that God will never return. More nightmare than utopia, marooned in history, Heaven commemorates disaster, despair, and stasis.

Because of its embeddedness in the past, the geography of Heaven is a key to the complex notion of temporality that governs *Angels in America.* Although the scheme does not become clear until *Perestroika,* there are two opposing concepts of time and history running through the play. First, there is the time of the Angels (and of Heaven), the time of dystopian "STASIS" (2:54) as decreed by the absence of a God who, Prior insists, "isn't coming back" (2:133). According to the Angel, this temporal paralysis is the direct result of the hyperactivity of human beings: "YOU HAVE DRIVEN HIM AWAY! YOU MUST STOP MOVING!" (2:52), the Angel enjoins Prior, in the hope that immobility will once again prompt the return of God and the forward movement of time. Yet this concept of time as stasis is also linked to decay. In the Angel's threnody that ends the Council scene, s/he envisions the dissolution of "the Great Design, / The spiraling apart of the Work of Eternity" (2:134). Directly opposed to this concept is human temporality, of which Prior, in contradistinction to the Angel, becomes the spokesperson. This time—which is also apparently the time of God—is the temporality connected with Enlightenment epistemologies; it is the time of "Progress," "Science," and "Forward Motion" (2:132; 2:50). It is the time of "Change" (2:13) so fervently desired by Comrade Prelapsarianov and the "neo-Hegelian positivist sense of constant historical progress towards happiness or perfection" so precious to Louis (1:25). It is the promise fulfilled at the end of *Perestroika* when Louis, apprehending "the end of the Cold War," announces, "The whole world is changing!" (2:145). Most important, the time of "progress, migration, motion," and "modernity" is also, in Prior's formulation, the time of "desire," because it is this last all-too-human characteristic that produces modernity (2:132). Without desire (for change, utopia, the Other), there could be no history.

Despite the fact that this binary opposition generates so much of the play's ideological framework, and that its two poles are at times indistinguishable, it seems to me that this is one question on which *Angels in America* is not ambivalent at all. Unlike the Benjamin of the "Theses on the Philosophy of History," for whom any concept of progress seems quite inconceivable, Kushner is devoted to rescuing Enlightenment epistemologies at a time when they are, to say the least, extremely unfashionable. On the one hand, *Angels in America* counters attacks from the pundits of the right, wallowing in their post–Cold War triumphalism, for whom socialism, or "the coordination of men's activities through central direction," is the road to "serfdom."[18] For these neoconservatives, "we already live in the millennial new age," we already stand at "the end of history," and, as a result, in Francis Fukuyama's words, "we cannot picture to ourselves a world that is *essentially* different from the present one, and at the same time better."[19] Obsessed with "free markets and private property," and trying desperately to maintain the imperialist status quo, they can only imagine progress as regression.[20] On the other hand, *Angels* also challenges the orthodoxies of those poststructuralists on the left by whom the Marxian concept of history is often dismissed as hopelessly idealist, as "a contemptible attempt" to construct "grand narratives" and "totalizing (totalitarian?) knowledges."[21] In the face of these profound cynicisms, *Angels* unabashedly champions rationalism and progress. In the last words of *Perestroika*'s last act, Harper suggests that "in this world, there is a kind of painful progress. Longing for what we've left behind, and dreaming ahead" (2:144). The last words of the epilogue, meanwhile, are given to Prior, who envisions a future in which "we" (presumably gay men, lesbians, and persons with AIDS) "will be citizens." *"More Life"* (2:148), he demands.

Kushner's differences with Benjamin—and the poststructuralists—over the possibility of progress and his championing of modernity (and the desire that produces it) suggest that the string of binary oppositions that are foundational to the play are perhaps less undecidable than I originally suggested. Meaning is produced, in part, because these oppositions are constructed as interlocking homologies, each an analogy for all the others. And despite the fact that each term of each opposition is strictly dependent on the other and, indeed, is produced by its other, these relations are by no means symmetrical. Binary oppositions are always hierarchical—especially when the fact of hierarchy is repressed. *Angels* is carefully constructed so that communitarianism, rationalism, progress, and so forth, will be read as being preferable to their alternatives: individualism, indeterminacy, stasis, and so forth ("the playwright has been able to find hope in his chronicle of the poisonous 1980s").[22] So at least as far as this string of interlocked binary oppositions is concerned, ambivalence turns out to be not especially ambivalent after all.

At the same time, what is one to make of other binarisms—most notably, the opposition between masculine and feminine—toward which the play seems to cultivate a certain studied ambivalence? On the one hand, it is clear that Kushner is making some effort to counter the long history of the marginalization and silencing of women in American culture generally and in American theater, in particular. Harper's hallucinations are crucial to the play's articulation of its central themes, including questions of exile and of the utopia/dystopia binarism. They also give her a privileged relationship to Prior, in whose fantasies she sometimes partakes and with whom she visits Heaven. Her unequivocal rejection of Joe and expropriation of his credit card at the end of the play, moreover, signal her repossession of her life and her progress from imaginary to real travel. Hannah, meanwhile, is constructed as an extremely independent and strong-willed woman who becomes part of the new extended family that is consolidated at the end of the play. Most intriguingly, the play's deliberate foregrounding of the silencing of the Mormon Mother and Daughter in the diorama is symptomatic of Kushner's desire to let women speak. On the other hand, *Angels* seems to replicate many of the structures that historically have produced female subjectivity as Other. Harper may be crucial to the play's structure, but she is still pathologized, like so many of her antecedents on the American stage (from Mary Tyrone to Blanche DuBois to Honey in *Who's Afraid of Virginia Woolf?*). With her hallucinations and "emotional problems" (1:27), she functions as a scapegoat for Joe, the displacement of his sexual problems. Moreover, her false confession that she's "going to have a baby" (1:41) not only reinforces the link in the play between femininity and maternity but also literally hystericizes her. And Hannah, despite her strength, is defined almost entirely by her relationship to her real son and to Prior, her surrogate son. Like Belize, she is given the role of caretaker.

Most important, the celestial "sexual politics" (2:49) of the play guarantees that the feminine remains Other. After his visitation by the Angel, Prior explains that "God . . . is a man. Well, not a man, he's a flaming Hebrew letter, but a male flaming Hebrew letter" (2:49). In comparison with this masculinized, Old Testament–style, "flaming"(!) patriarch, the Angels are decidedly hermaphroditic. Nonetheless, the play's stage directions use the feminine pronoun when designating the Angel, and s/he has been played by a woman in all of the play's various American premieres. As a result of this clearly delineated gendered difference, femininity is associated (in Heaven at least) with "STASIS" and collapse, while a divine masculinity is coded as being simultaneously deterministic and absent. In the play's pseudo-Platonic—and heterosexualized—metaphysics, the "orgasm" of the Angels produces (a feminized) "protomatter, which fuels the [masculinized] Engine of Creation" (2:49).

Moreover, the play's use of doubling reinforces this sense of the centrality of masculinity. Unlike Caryl Churchill's *Cloud 9* (surely the locus classicus of genderfuck), *Angels* uses cross-gender casting only for minor characters. And the crossing of gender works in one direction only. The actresses playing Hannah, Harper, and the Angel take on a number of male heterosexual characters while the male actors double only in masculine roles. As a result, it seems to me that *Angels,* unlike the work of Churchill, does not denaturalize gender. Rather, masculinity—which, intriguingly, is always already queered in this text—is produced as a remarkably stable, if contradictory, essence that others can mime but that only a real (i.e., biological) male can embody. Thus, yet another ambivalence turns out to be always already decided.

The American Religion

The nation that *Angels in America* fantasizes has its roots in the early nineteenth century, the period during which the United States became constituted, to borrow Benedict Anderson's celebrated formulation, as "an imagined political community, . . . imagined as both inherently limited and sovereign."[23] For not until the 1830s and 1840s, with the success of Jacksonian democracy and the development of the ideology of Manifest Destiny, did a sense of an imagined community of Americans begin to solidify, due to a number of factors: the consolidation of industrialization in the Northeast; the proliferation of large newspapers and state banks; and a transportation revolution that linked the urban centers with both agricultural producers and markets abroad.[24]

It is far more than coincidence that the birth of the modern idea of America coincided with what is often called the Second Great Awakening (the First had culminated in the Revolutionary War). During these years, as Klaus Hansen relates, "the old paternalistic reform impulse directed toward social control yielded to a romantic reform movement impelled by millennialism, immediatism, and individualism." This movement, in turn, "made possible the creation of the modern American capitalist empire with its fundamental belief in religious, political, and economic pluralism."[25] For those made uneasy (for a variety of reasons) by the new Jacksonian individualism, this pluralism authorized the emergence of alternative social and religious sects, both millennialist evangelical revivals and new communities like the Shakers, the Oneida Perfectionists, and, most prominently and successfully, the Mormons.[26] As Hansen emphasizes, "Mormonism was not merely one more variant of American Protestant pluralism but an articulate and sophisticated counterideology that attempted to establish a 'new heaven and a new earth.'" Moreover, "both in its origins and doctrines," Mormonism "insisted on the peculiarly American nature of its fundamental values" and on the identity of America as the promised land.[27]

Given the number and prominence of Mormon characters in the play, it should come as little surprise that Mormonism, at least as it was originally articulated in the 1820s and 1830s, maintains a very close relationship to the epistemology of *Angels in America*. Many of the explicitly hieratic qualities of the play—the notion of prophecy, the sacred book, as well as the Angel her/himself—owe as much to Mormonism as to Walter Benjamin. Even more important, the play's conceptualization of history, its millennialism, and its idea of America bring it startlingly close to the tenets of early Mormonism. Indeed, it is impossible to understand the concept of the nation with which *Angels* is obsessed (and even the idea of queering the nation!) without understanding the constitution of early Mormonism. Providing Calvinism with its most radical challenge during the National Period, it was deeply utopian in its thrust (and it remains so today). Indeed, its concept of time is identical to the temporality for which *Angels in America* polemicizes. Like *Angels,* Mormonism understands time as evolution and progress (in that sense, it is more closely linked to Enlightenment epistemologies than romantic ones) and holds out the possibility of unlimited human growth: "As man is God once was: as God is man may become."[28] Part of a tremendous resurgence of interest in the millennium between 1828 and 1832, Mormonism went far beyond the ideology of progress implicit in Jacksonian democracy (just as *Angels*'s millennialism goes far beyond most contemporary ideologies of progress).[29] Understood historically, this utopianism was in part the result of the relatively marginal economic status of Joseph Smith and his followers, subsistence farmers and struggling petits bourgeois. Tending "to be 'agin the government," these early Mormons were a persecuted minority and, in their westward journey to Zion, became the subjects of widespread violence, beginning in 1832 when Smith was tarred and feathered in Ohio.[30] Much like present-day lesbians and gay men—although most contemporary Mormons would be appalled by the comparison—Mormons were, throughout the 1830s and 1840s, attacked by mobs, arrested on false charges, imprisoned, and murdered. In 1838, the governor of Missouri decreed that they must be "exterminated" or expelled from the state. In 1844, Smith and his brother were assassinated by an angry mob.[31]

The violent antipathy toward early Mormonism was in part the result of the fact that it presented a significant challenge to the principles of individualist social and economic organization. From the beginning, Mormonism was communitarian in nature and proposed a kind of ecclesiastical socialism in which "those entering the order were asked to 'consecrate' their property and belongings to the church." To each male would then be returned enough to sustain him and his family, while the remainder would be apportioned to "'every man who has need.'" As Hansen emphasizes, this organization represents a repudiation of the principles of laissez-faire and an attempt "to restore a more traditional society in which the economy was regulated in behalf of the larger interests of the group."[32] This nostalgia for an earlier period of capitalism (the agrarianism of the early colonies) is echoed by Mormonism's conceptualization of the continent as the promised land. Believing the Garden of Eden to have been sited in America and assigning all antediluvian history to the western hemisphere, early Mormonism believed that the term "'New World' was in fact a misnomer because America was really the cradle of man and civilization."[33] So the privileged character of the nation is linked to its sacred past, and—as with Benjamin—history is tied to theology. At the same time, this essentially theological conceptualization of the nation bears witness to the "strong affinity," noted by Anderson, between "the nationalist imagining" and "religious imaginings."[34] As Timothy Brennan explains it, "nationalism largely extend[s] and modernize[s] (although [does] not replace) 'religious imaginings,' taking on religion's concern with death, continuity, and the desire for origins."[35] Like religion, the nation authorizes a reconfiguration of time and mortality, a "secular transformation of fatality into continuity, contingency into meaning."[36] Mormonism's spiritual geography was perfectly suited to this process, constructing America as both origin and meaning of history. Moreover, as Hans Kohn has pointed out, modern nationalism has expropriated three crucial concepts from those same Old Testament mythologies that provide the basis for Mormonism: "the idea of a chosen people, the emphasis on a common stock of memory of the past and of hopes for the future, and finally national messianism."[37]

This conceptualization of America as the site of a blessed past and a millennial future represents—simultaneously—the fulfillment of early nineteenth-century ideas of the nation and a repudiation of the ideologies of individualism and acquisitiveness that underwrite the Jacksonian marketplace. Yet, as Sacvan Bercovitch points out, this contradiction was at the heart of the nationalist project. As the economy was being transformed "from agrarian to industrial capitalism," the primary "source of dissent was an indigenous residual culture," which, like Mormonism, was "variously identified with agrarianism, libertarian thought, and the tradition of civic humanism." These ideologies, "by conserving the myths of a bygone age" and dreaming "of human wholeness and social regeneration," then produced "the notion of an ideal America with a politically transformative potential." Like the writers of the American Renaissance, Mormonism "adopted the culture's *controlling* metaphor— 'America' as synonym for human possibility"—and then turned it against the dominant class. Both producing and fulfilling the nationalist dream, it "portray[ed] the American ideology, as all ideology yearns to be portrayed, in the transcendent colors of utopia."[38] A form of dissent that ultimately (and contradictorily) reinforced hegemonic values, Mormonism reconceived America as the promised land, the land of an already achieved utopia, and simultaneously as the land of promise, the site of the millennium yet to come.

I recapitulate the early history of Mormonism because I believe it is crucial for understanding how *Angels in America* has been culturally positioned. It seems to me that the play replicates both the situation and project of early Mormonism with an uncanny accuracy and thereby documents the continued validity of both a particular regressive fantasy of America and a particular understanding of oppositional cultural practices. Like the projects of Joseph Smith and his followers, *Angels* has, from the beginning, on the levels of authorial intention and reception, been constructed as an oppositional and even "radical" work. Structurally and ideologically, the play challenges the conventions of American realism and the tenets of Reaganism. Indeed, it offers by far the most explicit and trenchant critique of neoconservativism to have been produced on Broadway. It also provides the most thoroughgoing—and unambivalent—deconstruction in memory of a binarism absolutely crucial to liberalism, the opposition between public and private. *Angels* demonstrates conclusively not only the constructedness of the difference between the political and the sexual but also the murderous power of this distinction. Yet, at the same time, *not despite but because of these endeavors,* the play has been accommodated with stunning ease to the hegemonic ideology not just of the theatergoing public but of the democratic majority—an ideology that has become the *new* American religion, liberal pluralism.[39]

The old-style American liberalisms, variously associated (reading from left to right) with trade unionism, reformism, and competitive individualism, tend to value freedom above all other qualities (the root word for *liberalism* is, after all, the Latin *liber,* meaning "free"). Taking the "free" individual subject as the fundamental social unit, liberalism has long been associated with the principle of laissez-faire and the "free" market and is reformist rather than revolutionary in its politics. At the same time, however, because liberalism, particularly in its American versions, has always paid at least lip service to equality, certain irreducible contradictions have been bred in what did, after all, emerge during the seventeenth century as the ideological complement to (and justification for) mercantile capitalism. Historically, American liberalism has permitted dissent and fostered tolerance—within certain limits—and guaranteed that all men in principle are created equal (women were long excluded from the compact, as well as African American slaves). In fact, given the structure of American capitalism, the incommensurability of its commitment both to freedom and equality has proven a disabling contradiction, one that liberalism has tried continually, and with little success, to negotiate. Like the bourgeois subject that is its production and raison d'être, liberalism is hopelessly schizoid.

The new liberalism that has been consolidated in the United States since the decline of the New Left in the mid-1970s (but whose antecedents date back to the first stirrings of the nation) marks the adaptation of traditional liberalism to a post–welfare state economy. Pursuing a policy of regressive taxation, its major constituent is the corporate sector—all others it labels "special-interest groups" (despite certain superficial changes, there is little fundamental difference between the economic and foreign policies of Reagan/Bush, Clinton, and George W. Bush). In spite of its corporatism, however, and its efficiency in redistributing the wealth upward, liberalism speaks the language of tolerance. Unable to support substantive changes in economic policy that might in fact produce a more equitable and less segregated society, it instead promotes a *rhetoric* of pluralism and moderation. Reformist in method, it endeavors to fine-tune the status quo while at the same time acknowledging (and even celebrating) the diversity of American culture. For the liberal pluralist, America is less a melting pot than a smorgasbord. He or she takes pride in the ability to *consume* cultural difference—now understood as a commodity, a source of boundless pleasure, an expression of an exoticized Other. And yet, for him or her, access to and participation in so-called minority cultures is entirely consumerist. Like the new, passive racist characterized by Hazel Carby, the liberal pluralist uses "texts"—whether literary, musical, theatrical, or cinematic—as "a way of gaining knowledge of the 'other,' a knowledge that appears to replace the desire to challenge existing frameworks of segregation."[40]

Liberal pluralism thus does far more than tolerate dissent. It actively enlists its aid in reaffirming a fundamentally conservative hegemony. In doing so, it reconsolidates a fantasy of America that dates back to the early nineteenth century. Liberal pluralism demonstrates the dogged persistence of a *consensus politic that masquerades as dissensus.* It proves once again, in Bercovitch's words, that

> the American way is to turn potential conflict into a quarrel about fusion or fragmentation. It is a fixed match, a debate with a foregone conclusion: you must have your fusion and feed on fragmentation too. And the formula for doing so has become virtually a cultural reflex: you just alternate between harmony-in-diversity and diversity-in-harmony. It amounts to a hermeneutics of laissez-faire: all problems are obviated by the continual flow of the one into the many, and the many into the one.[41]

According to Bercovitch, a kind of dissensus (of which liberal pluralism is the contemporary avatar) has been the hallmark of the very idea of America—and American literature—from the beginning. In this most American of ideologies, an almost incomparably wide range of opinions, beliefs, and cultural positions are finally absorbed into a fantasy of a utopian nation in which anything and everything is possible, in which the millennium is simultaneously at hand and indefinitely deferred. Moreover, the nation is imagined as the geographical representation of that utopia which is both everywhere and nowhere. For as Lauren Berlant explains, "the contradiction between the 'nowhere' of utopia and the 'everywhere' of the nation [is] dissolved by the American recasting of the 'political' into the terms of providential ideality, 'one nation under

God.'"[42] Under the sign of the "one," all contradictions are subsumed, all races and religions united, all politics theologized.

Dissensus and the Field of Cultural Production

It is my contention that *Angels*'s mobilization of a consensual politic (masquerading as *dis*sensual) is precisely the source not only of the play's ambivalence but also of its ability to be instantly recognized as part of the canon of American literature. Regardless of Kushner's intentions, *Angels* sets forth a project wherein the theological is constructed as a transcendent category into which politics and history finally disappear. For all its commitment to a historical-materialist method, for all its attention to political struggle and the dynamics of oppression, *Angels* finally sets forth a liberal pluralist vision of America in which all, not in spite but because of their diversity, will be welcomed into the new Jerusalem (to this extent, it differs sharply from the more exclusionist character of early Mormonism and other, more recent millennialisms). Like other apocalyptic discourses, from Joseph Smith to Jerry Falwell, the millennialism of *Angels* reassures an "audience that knows it has lost control over events" not by enabling it to "regain . . . control" but by letting it know "that history *is* nevertheless controlled by an underlying order and that it has a purpose that is nearing fulfillment." It thereby demonstrates that "*personal* pain," whether Prior's or that of the reader or spectator, "is subsumed within the pattern of history."[43] Like Joseph Smith, Tony Kushner has resuscitated a vision of America as both promised land and land of infinite promise. Simultaneously, he has inspired virtually every theater critic in the United States to a host of salvational fantasies about theater, art, and politics. And he has done all this at a crucial juncture in history, at the end of the Cold War, as the geopolitical order of forty-five years collapsed.

Although the events of September 11, 2001, precipitated a seemingly endless war against terrorism, this crusade in fact dates back at least to the 1991 Gulf War and represents the successor to the Cold War. As the makers of U.S. foreign policy well understand, the struggle against terrorism—rather than a specific foe—provides a justification for an almost endless expansion of the already immense military machine as well as the national security state apparatus. Because terrorism (like globalization) has been constructed as a transnational phenomenon, it challenges the integrity and sovereignty of the nation-state far more effectively than the Soviet empire ever could and produces a kind of free-floating fear that has enormous political usefulness. If nothing else, *Angels in America* attests both to the continuing anxiety over national definition and mission and to the importance of an ideological means of assuaging that anxiety. In *Angels,* a series of political dialectics (which are, yet again, false dialectics) remains the primary means for producing this ideological fix, for producing dissensus, a sense of alternation between "harmony-in-diversity and diversity-in-harmony." The play is filled with political disputation—all of it between men since women, unless in drag, are excluded from the political realm. Most is centered around Louis, the unmistakably ambivalent, ironic Jew, who invariably sets the level of discussion and determines the tenor of the argument. If with Belize he takes a comparatively rightist (and racist) stance, with Joe he takes an explicitly leftist (and antihomophobic) one. And while the play unquestionably problematizes his several positions, he ends up, with all his contradictions, becoming by default the spokesperson for liberal pluralism, with all *its* contradictions. Belize, intriguingly, functions unlike the white gay men as an ideological point of reference, a kind of "moral bellwether," in the words of one critic.[44] Because his is the one point of view that is never submitted to a critique, he becomes, as David Román points out, "the political and ethical center of the plays." The purveyor of truth, "he carries the burden of race" and so seems to issue from what is unmistakably a "white imaginary" ("This fetishization," Román notes, "of lesbian and gay people of color as a type of political catalyst is ubiquitous among the left").[45] He is also cast in the role of caretaker, a position long reserved for African Americans in "the white imaginary." Even Belize's name commemorates not the Name of the Father, but his status as a *"former drag queen"* (1:3), giving him an identity that is both performative and exoticized. He is the play's guarantee of diversity.

The pivotal scene for the enunciation of Louis's politics, meanwhile, is his long discussion with Belize in *Millennium* that begins with his question, "Why has democracy succeeded in America?" (1:89), a question whose assumption is belied by the unparalleled political and economic power of American corporatism to buy elections and from which Louis, as is his wont, almost immediately backs down. (His rhetorical strategy throughout this scene is to stake out a position from which he immediately draws a guilty retreat, thereby making Belize look like the aggressor.) Invoking "radical democracy" and "freedom" in one breath, and crying "fuck assimilation" (1:89–90) in the next, he careens wildly between a liberal discourse of rights and a rhetoric of identity politics. Alternating between universalizing and minoritizing concepts of the subject, he manages at once to dismiss a politics of race (and insult Belize) and to assert its irreducibility. Yet the gist of Louis's argument (if constant vacillation could be said to have a gist) is his disquisition about the nation:

This reaching out for a spiritual past in a country where no indigenous spirits exist—only the Indians, I mean Native American spirits and we killed them off so now, there are no gods here, no ghosts and spirits in America, there are no angels in America, no spiritual past, no racial past, there's only the political. (1:92)

For Louis, America hardly exists as a community (whether real or imagined). Rather, for this confused liberal, America is defined entirely by its relationship to the "political." With characteristic irony, Kushner chooses to present this crucial idea (which does, after all, echo the play's title) in the negative, in the form of a statement that the rest of the play aggressively refutes. For if nothing else, *Angels in America*—like *The Book of Mormon*—demonstrates that there are angels in America, that America is in essence a utopian and theological construction, a nation with a divine mission. Politics is by no means banished insofar as it provides a crucial way in which the nation is imagined. But it is subordinated to utopian fantasies of harmony in diversity, of one nation under a derelict God.

Moreover, this scene between Louis and Belize reproduces millennialism in miniature, in its very structure, in the pattern whereby the political is finally subsumed by utopian fantasies. After the spirited argument between Louis and Belize (if one can call a discussion in which one person refuses to stake out a coherent position an argument), their conflict is suddenly overrun by an outbreak of lyricism, by the intrusion, after so much talk about culture, of what passes for the natural world:

> BELIZE: All day today it's felt like Thanksgiving. Soon, this . . . ruina-
> tion will be blanketed white. You can smell it—can you smell it?
> LOUIS: Smell what?
> BELIZE: Softness, compliance, forgiveness, grace. (1:100)

Argumentation gives way not to a resolution (nothing has been settled) but to the ostensible forces of nature: snow and smell. According to Belize, snow (an insignia of coldness and purity in the play) is linked to "softness, compliance, forgiveness, grace," in short, to the theological virtues. Like the ending of *Perestroika,* in which another dispute between Louis and Belize fades out behind Prior's benediction, this scene enacts a movement of transcendence whereby the political is not so much resolved as covered by the snow. In the American way, contradiction is less disentangled than immobilized. History gives way to a concept of cosmic evolution that is far closer to Joseph Smith than to Walter Benjamin.

In the person of Louis (who is, after all, constructed as the most empathic character in the play), with his unshakable faith in liberalism and the possibility of "radical democracy," *Angels in America* assures that the (liberal) theatergoing public that a kind of liberal pluralism remains the best hope for change.[46] Revolution, in the Marxist sense, is rendered virtually unthinkable, oxymoronic. Amid all the political disputation, there is no talk of social class. Oppression is understood in relation not to economics but to differences of race, gender, and sexual orientation. In short: *an identity politic comes to substitute for Marxist analysis.* There is no clear sense that the political and social problems with which the characters wrestle might be connected to a particular economic system (Comrade Prelapsarianov is, after all, a comic figure). And despite Kushner's avowed commitment to socialism, an alternative to capitalism, except in the form of an indefinitely deferred utopia, remains absent from the play's dialectic.[47] Revolution, even in Benjamin's sense of the term, is evacuated of its political content, functioning less as a Marxist hermeneutic tool than as a *trope,* a figure of speech (the oxymoron) that marks the place later to be occupied by a (liberal pluralist?) utopia. *Angels* thus falls into line behind the utopianisms of Joseph Smith and the American Renaissance and becomes less a subversion of hegemonic culture than its reaffirmation. As Berlant observes, "the temporal and spatial ambiguity of 'utopia' has the effect of obscuring the implications of political activity and power relations in American civil life."[48] Like "our classic texts" (as characterized by Bercovitch), *Angels* has a way of conceptualizing utopia so that it may be adopted by "the dominant culture . . . for its purposes." "So molded, ritualized, and controlled," Bercovitch notes (and, I would like to add, stripped of its impulse for radical economic change), "utopianism has served . . . to diffuse or deflect dissent, or actually to transmute it into a vehicle of socialization."[49]

The ambivalences that are so deeply inscribed in *Angels in America,* its conflicted relationship to various utopianisms, to the concept of America, to Marxism, Mormonism, and liberalism, function, I believe, to accommodate the play to what I see as a fundamentally conservative and paradigmatically American politic—dissensus, the "hermeneutics of laissez-faire." Yet it seems to me that the play's ambivalence (its way of being, in Eve Kosofsky Sedgwick's memorable phrase, "kinda subversive, kinda hegemonic") is finally less a question of authorial intention than of the peculiar cultural and economic position of this play (and its writer) in relation to the theater, theater artists, and the theatergoing public in the United States.[50] On the one hand, the Broadway and regional theaters remain in a uniquely marginal position in comparison with Hollywood. The subscribers to regional theaters continue to dwindle while more than half of Theatre Communications Group's sample theaters in their annual survey "played to smaller audiences in 1993 than they did five years ago." Moreover, in a move that bodes particularly ill for the future of new plays, "workshops, staged readings and other developmental activities decreased drastically over the five years studied."[51] On the other hand, serious Broadway drama does not have the same cultural capital as other forms of literature. Meanwhile, the relatively small public that today attends professional theater in America is overwhelmingly middle-class and overwhelmingly liberal in its attitudes. Indeed, theater audiences are in large part distinguished from the audiences for film and television on account of their tolerance for works that are more challenging both formally and thematically than the vast majority of major-studio releases or prime-time miniseries.

Because of its marginal position, both economically and culturally, theater is a privileged portion of what Pierre Bourdieu designates as the literary and artistic field. As he explains, this field is contained within a larger field of economic and political power, while, at the same time, "possessing a relative autonomy with respect to it." It is this *relative autonomy* that gives the literary and artistic field—and theater in particular—both its high level of symbolic forms of capital and its low level of economic capital. In other words, despite its artistic cachet, it "occupies a *dominated position*" with respect to the field of economic and political power as a whole.[52] And the individual cultural producer (or theater artist), insofar as he or she is a part of the bourgeoisie, represents a "dominated fraction of the dominant class."[53] The cultural producer is thus placed in an irreducibly contradictory position—and this has become particularly clear since the decline of patronage in the eighteenth century and the increasing dependence of the artist on the vicissitudes of the marketplace. On the one hand, he or she is licensed to challenge hegemonic values insofar as it is a particularly effective way of accruing cultural capital. On the other hand, the more effective his or her challenge, the less economic capital he or she is likely to amass. Because of theater's marginality in American culture, it seems to be held hostage to this double bind in a particularly unnerving way: the very disposition of the field guarantees that Broadway and regional theaters (unlike mass culture) are constantly in the process of having to negotiate this impossible position.

What is perhaps most remarkable about *Angels in America* is that it has managed, against all odds, to amass significant levels of both cultural and economic capital. And while it by no means resolves the contradictions that are constitutive of theater's cultural positioning, its production history has become a measure of the seemingly impossible juncture of these two forms of success. Just as the play's structure copes with argumentation by transcending it, so does the play as cultural phenomenon seemingly transcend the opposition between economic and cultural capital, between the hegemonic and the counterhegemonic. Moreover, it does so, I am arguing, by its skill in both reactivating a sense (derived from the early nineteenth century) of America as the utopian nation and mobilizing the principle of ambivalence—or more exactly, dissensus—to produce a vision of a once and future pluralist culture. And although the text's contradictory positioning is to a large extent defined by the marginal cultural position of Broadway, it is also related specifically to Tony Kushner's own class position. Like Joseph Smith, Kushner represents a dominated—and dissident—fraction of the dominant class. As a white gay man, he is able to amass considerable economic and cultural capital despite the fact that the class of which he is a part remains relatively disempowered politically (according to a 1993 survey, the average household income for gay men is 40 percent higher than that of the average American household).[54] As an avowed leftist and intellectual, he is committed (as *Angels* demonstrates) to mounting a critique of hegemonic ideology. Yet as a member of the bourgeoisie and as the recipient of two Tony Awards, he is also committed—if only unconsciously—to the continuation of the system that has granted him no small measure of success.

A Queer Sort of Nation

Although I am tempted to see the celebrity of *Angels in America* as yet another measure of the power of liberal pluralism to neutralize oppositional practices, the play's success also suggests a willingness to recognize the contributions of gay men to American culture and to American literature, in particular. For as Eve Sedgwick and others have argued, both the American canon and the very principle of canonicity are centrally concerned with questions of male (homo)sexual definition and desire.[55] Thus, the issues of homoeroticism, of the anxiety generated by the instability of the homosocial/homosexual boundary, of coding, of secrecy and disclosure, and of the problems around securing a sexual identity remain pivotal for so many of the writers who hold pride of place in the American canon, from Thoreau, Melville, Whitman, and James to Hart Crane, Tennessee Williams, and James Baldwin—in that sense, the American canon is always already queered. At the same time, however, unlike so much of the canon, and in particular the canon of American drama, *Angels in America* foregrounds explicitly gay men. No more need the reader eager to queer the text read subversively between the lines, or transpose genders, as is so often done to the work of Williams, Inge, Albee, and others. Since the 1988 controversies over NEA funding for exhibitions of Mapplethorpe and Serrano, and the subsequent attempt by the Endowment to

revoke grants to the so-called NEA Four (three of whom are queer), theater, as a liberal form, has been distinguished from mass culture in large
part by virtue of its queer content. In the twenty-first century, a play without a same-sex kiss may be entertainment, but it can hardly be considered
a work of art. It appears that the representation of (usually male) homosexual desire has become the privileged emblem of that endangered
species, the serious Broadway drama. But I wonder finally how subversive
this queering of Broadway is when women, in this play at least, remain
firmly in the background. What is one to make of the remarkable ease
with which *Angels in America* has been accommodated to that lineage of
American drama (and literature) that focuses on masculine experience
and agency and produces women as the premise for history, as the ground
on which it is constructed? Are not women sacrificed—yet again—to the
male citizenry of a (queer) nation?

If Kushner, following Benjamin's prompting (and echoing his masculinism), attempts to "brush history against the grain" (257), he does
so by demonstrating the crucial importance of (closeted) gay men in
twentieth-century American politics—including, most prominently, Roy
Cohn and two of his surrogate fathers, J. Edgar Hoover and Joseph
McCarthy. By so highlighting the (homo)eroticization of patriarchy, the
play demonstrates the always already queer status of American politics
and, most provocatively, of those generals of the Cold War (and American imperialism) who were most assiduous in their denunciation of political and sexual dissidence. Moreover, unlike the work of most of Kushner's predecessors on the American stage, *Angels* does not pathologize gay
men. Or more exactly, gay men as a class are not pathologized. Rather,
they are revealed to be pathologized circumstantially: first, by their construction (through a singularly horrific stroke of ill luck) as one of the
"risk groups" for HIV; and second, by the fact that some remain closeted
and repressed (Joe's ulcer is unmistakably the price of disavowal). So, it
turns out, it is not homosexuality that is pathological, but its *denial.* Flagrantly uncloseted, the play provides a devastating critique of the closeted
gay man in two medicalized bodies: Roy Cohn and Joe Pitt.

If *Angels in America* queers historical materialism (at least as Benjamin
understands it), it does so by exposing the process by which the political
(which ostensibly drives history) intersects with the personal and sexual
(which ostensibly are no more than footnotes to history). Reagan's pres-

idency and the neoconservative hegemony of the 1980s provide not just the background to the play's exploration of ostensibly personal (i.e., sexual, marital, medical) problems but the very ground on which desire is produced. For despite the trenchancy of its critique of neoconservativism, *Angels* also demonstrates the peculiar sexiness of Reagan's vision of America. Through Louis, it demonstrates the allure of a particular brand of machismo embodied by Joe Pitt: "The more appalling I find your politics the more I want to hump you" (2:36). And if the Angel is indeed "a cosmic reactionary" (2:55), it is in part because her/his position represents an analogue to the same utopian promises and hopes that Reagan so brilliantly and deceptively exploited. Moreover, in this history play, questions of male homosexual identity and desire are carefully juxtaposed against questions of equal protection for lesbians and gay men and debates about their military service. Louis attacks Joe for his participation in "an important bit of legal fag-bashing," a case that upholds the U.S. government's policy that it's not "unconstitutional to discriminate against homosexuals" (2:110). And while the case that Louis cites may be fictional, the continuing refusal of the courts in the wake of *Bowers v. Hardwick* to consider lesbians and gay men a suspect class, and thus eligible for protection under the provisions of the Fourteenth Amendment, is anything but.[56] Unilaterally constructing gay men as a suspect class (with sexual identity substituting for economic positionality), *Angels* realizes Benjamin's suggestion that it is not "man or men but the struggling, oppressed class itself [that] is the depository of historical knowledge" (260). More decisively than any other recent cultural text, *Angels* queers the America of Joseph Smith—and Ronald Reagan—by placing this oppressed class at the very center of American history; by showing it to be not just the depository of a special kind of knowledge; but by recognizing the central role that it has had in the construction of a national subject, polity, literature, and theater. On this issue, the play is not ambivalent at all.

Chapter Five

The Sadomasochist in the Closet

sam shepard, robert bly, and the new white masculinity

Twenty years ago, fresh from his brooding performance as Chuck Yeager in *The Right Stuff*, Sam Shepard spoke balefully about masculinity and violence to the *New York Times:*

> There's something about American violence that to me is very touching. In full force it's very ugly, but there's also something very moving about it, because it has to do with humiliation. There's some hidden, deeply rooted thing in the Anglo male American that has to do with inferiority, that has to do with not being a man, and always, continually having to act out some idea of manhood that invariably is violent. This sense of failure runs very deep.[1]

For the Shepard of this melancholy confession, masculinity is neither an instinct nor a quality that the male subject possesses by birthright. Rather, it is performative, a masquerade that must ceaselessly be reiterated, "act[ed] out." Founded not on presence but on lack, masculinity compensates for "inferiority," "humiliation," and "failure," qualities to which it is ineluctably linked in Shepard's economy of desire. Like the elusive phallus, masculinity is never possessed by the male subject but is perpetually misplaced, the emblem of an anxiety that is in turn linked to a violence toward which Shepard maintains an astonishing ambivalence, finding it as "touching" as it is "ugly."

134

At the same time that Shepard was setting forth his ideas about masculine inadequacy, other men across the United States were beginning to feel the pinch. A former B-movie star was breathing new life into heroic Cold War mythologies as president, while Rambo stalked the jungles of Vietnam in search of POWs allegedly forsaken by the American government. Coincidentally, a men's movement was beginning to cohere that later attracted a large and devout following. Under the aegis of Robert Bly, a poet and former peace advocate whose best-selling manifesto, *Iron John,* fortuitously revived his flagging literary career, the movement was (and is) committed to the recovery of a wild and primordial masculinity that the reputedly feminized culture of late capitalism has repressed. During the 1980s, Bly refined his philosophy (drawn variously from Jung, Joseph Campbell, various pop psychologists, and, to a lesser extent, Freud) and his workshop techniques (inspired by consciousness-raising groups of the 1960s, twelve-step programs, various religious and tribal rituals, and the so-called masculinity therapy of the 1970s).[2] In 1990 he appeared in a PBS documentary with Bill Moyers, "A Gathering of Men," which catapulted him—and the men's movement of which he was dubbed the "patron saint"—into the mainstream.[3]

What is the connection, I wonder, between Shepard's musings on humiliation and violence and the pseudoliterary event known as *Iron John*? What is the link between the masculine identities that Shepard and the men's movement so obsessively fantasize? Why did these cultural productions emerge at the same time? And, finally, why do the fragmented and disorderly male subjects produced by Shepard and Bly characteristically turn their violent and murderous instincts against themselves— masochistically, suicidally? What is concealed in the fractured, would-be hero of their work, the one who, like Kosmo in Shepard's *Mad Dog Blues,* "has a sadomasochist hid in his closet"?[4]

Let me begin by examining the men's movement, whose bible, *Iron John,* is an extraordinarily disordered and eclectic text, part sociology, part anthropology, part pop psychology, part holy writ, part self-help manual. Indiscriminately combining fairy tales with New Age spiritualism, Native American myths with an inaccurate cultural critique, it has such an improvisatory quality and is so deeply conflicted and overgeneralized that it is often difficult to pin down ideologically. It is also filled with gross historical, sociological, and anthropological errors, often

citing theories that were discredited a generation ago.[5] The gist is as fol-
lows. According to Bly—a biological essentialist if there ever was one—
the women's movement of the late 1960s and 1970s reversed traditional
gender roles by producing what he labels "the 'soft male'": "a nice boy
who pleases not only his mother but also the young woman he is living
with."[6] In rhetoric remarkably evocative of that decrying the smothering
"Momism" of the 1950s, Bly deplores the state of those feckless men
whose power has been sapped by "strong women who positively radiate
energy" (3).[7] Since the onset of the Industrial Revolution, Bly argues, the
"love unit most damaged . . . has been the father-son bond," whose health
he believes decisive for the production of a strong, healthy male. Unless a
son makes "a clean break from the mother," he will always end up as a
heterosexualized wimp, "afraid" of his own masculinity (19, 25). As a cure
for this gender inversion (which retains more than a whiff of the opprobrium traditionally attached to "sexual inversion"), Bly urges a recupera-
tion of "the deep masculine," the primitive and "true radiant energy" that
all men "*instinctive*[ly]" know and possess, the "Wild Man" whom the
purportedly effeminizing culture of late capitalism has locked away in a
cage (8). For several hundred dollars, a man can join Bly on a weekend
retreat to unlock the "Wild Man," don a mask, crawl around like an ani-
mal, recite myths, volunteer personal confessions, endure the heat of a
Native American sweatbox, and beat drums until he is exhausted.[8]

Bly's followers passionately defend his program and maintain that the
men's movement has made them more open emotionally and taught them
more gentle ways in which to be assertive. "We tried to be kind to women,
and they don't love us for it," one man notes. "We got weak, and we need
to be strong again." Bly's detractors, meanwhile, insist that the men's
movement is primarily a reaction against the women's movement and represents an attempt to recoup and reconsolidate the masculine prerogatives
that have been threatened by feminist critiques and the limited economic
achievements of women in certain spheres. Susan Faludi argues that "the
true subject of Bly's weekends, after all, is not love and sex, but power—
how to wrest it from women and how to mobilize it for men."[9] Taking a
longer historical view, Suzanne Gordon observes, "You cannot equate the
systematic domination of women for centuries, . . . the violence against
women, the restrictions of women's talents and options . . . with any
amount of pain and suffering and confusion that modern men may feel."[10]

Susan Faludi's reading of the men's movement as part of the antifeminist backlash is difficult to refute. Although the movement tends
to see itself as a "parallel development" rather than a "reactionary response," and although Bly himself attempts to distinguish between his
wing and the "antifeminist" one, *Iron John* suggests that feminism is primarily responsible for producing the problems that the men's movement seeks to alleviate and repeatedly positions men as the victims of
feminism.[11] Yet the more closely one examines the text, the more one
notices that the apparently stabilized and hierarchical gender roles it attempts to institute are, in fact, profoundly contradictory. Masculinity in
Iron John is by no means singular and integral. It is not simply the "Wild
Man energy" that Bly insists "leads to forceful action undertaken ... with
resolve" (8). Rather, it is endlessly conflicted; wounded; riven by pain,
doubt, and darkness; always set in a deeply ambivalent relationship to
the categories of nature and culture, inside and outside, masculine and
feminine.

What I find most intriguing about *Iron John* is that its rhetoric de-
ranges the opposition between masculinity and femininity, the very one
that monopolized American culture during the domestic revival that followed World War II, during which femininity was squarely positioned on
the side of "nature," sexuality, and irrationality, whereas masculinity was
equated with "culture," intellect, and reason. According to the logic of
Cold War America, it was the task of men to control, domesticate, and ra-
tionalize women and their dark sexuality, to ensure that "feminine"
would forever remain a synonym for "submissive."[12] But by the early
1970s the balance began to shift, as the women's movement began to
challenge men's domination of the workplace and the appalling disparity
in wages between men and women. As men began to feel increasingly
threatened economically, masculinist discourse began to reposition them
so that they too could lay claim to the state of "nature," to a raw physical
and sexual power that purportedly antedates cultural apparati. Thus, Bly
consistently imagines women as the driving force of an enculturation
that robs the male subject of his "Wild Man" energy. As a corollary to this,
Iron John repeatedly associates with masculinity those very characteristics
that were linked in Cold War culture to the feminine, in effect reconstructing masculinity—and what irony there is in this move!—on the
very terrain of femininity. According to Bly, the "Wild Man" is "wet,

moist, foresty, ignorant, [and] leafy" (232), while "the deep masculine" is a place of shadows and silence, a dark continent of sexuality and power into which a man must descend, "protected by the *instinctive* one who's underwater" and sustained by "the *nourishing* dark" (8, 6).

Yet *Iron John* is not content simply to invert the binary opposition between "nature" and "culture." On the contrary, the text consistently contradicts its avowed plans and inadvertently betrays an old-fashioned misogyny that sees women as deceitful, dangerous, and in need of domestication. *Iron John* ceaselessly attempts to negotiate these contradictions by forcing male subjectivity to inhere both inside and outside civilization, by making men the guardians of "nature" and "culture," sexuality and rationality, simultaneously. It accomplishes this sleight of hand by making conflict the very ground of subjectivity and culture: "We know each man has a woman inside him, and each woman has a man inside him" (98). In Bly's fantasy, the male subject is necessarily split into male and female, light and dark, strong and weak, good and evil. The resolution that Bly proposes for this schizophrenia represents a stunning obfuscation: "To live between we stretch out our arms and push the opposites as far apart as we can, and then live in the resonating space between them" (175). Even Bly's pseudopoetry is incapable of disguising the fact that male subjectivity in *Iron John* is invariably turned against itself and exists in a constant state of war with itself—it is little wonder that the "inner warrior" is in many ways *the* crucial trope for Bly. More than any other, the "inner warrior" seems to stand in for male subjectivity, for the notion that a man will always be at battle with himself—or at least with the feminine part of the self. And it is precisely in this sense that male subjectivity in Bly is always turned against itself in a deeply masochistic way, dedicated to the violent subjugation of the Other within the self, that feminine part always lurking within the male subject and threatening to disrupt his best-laid plans.

Killer's Head

Suicide in B-Flat, first performed at the Yale Repertory Theatre in 1976, is often read as one of Sam Shepard's most "tantalizing," "inventive," and "enigmatic" plays.[13] It is also invariably interpreted as being both a doc-

umentation of the process of artistic production and an interrogation—
and indictment—of the commodity status of the work of art. While I do
not dispute this interpretation, I prefer to see it as an analysis, or psychoanalysis, if you prefer, of what for Shepard, for Bly, and for the culture of which they are a part is the primal scene of masculinity.

Structurally, *Suicide* looks like an absurdist episode of *Dragnet*. It
brings two detectives, Pablo and Louis, to the scene of a murder, complete with the outline of a man's sprawled body drawn on the floor, and
then documents their interrogation of witnesses and reconstructions of
the killer's motives. The play ends with the ostensible reenactment of the
crime and the apprehension of the murderer. Yet this summary omits
the most original aspect of Shepard's play. Unlike most whodunits, *Suicide* pivots around the simultaneous presence and absence of the man
who (if we are to believe the play's title) is simultaneously murderer and
victim. About halfway through the play, Niles, the jazz musician, enters,
both visible and invisible to the others in the room, both dead and not
dead, both suicide and killer who blew off someone else's/his own face.
At the appearance of this doubled subject, the dramatic action is itself
doubled and turned back upon itself as Niles (together with his accomplice, Paullette, playing Virgil to his Dante) reenacts the suicide/murder.
Past is superimposed onto present, mortem onto postmortem. Unlike
the traditional crime drama (or the well-made play, for that matter),
which moves backward toward the disclosure of a past that conclusively
settles the present, this work leaves Niles's crime to the last insoluble. Is
he a suicide, murderer, or victim of a frame-up? Is he dead or on the
lam? Is the body present or absent, self or Other?

Shepard's deconstruction of the formal tenets and parameters of the
whodunit is redoubled by a deep perturbation in the play's production of
subjectivity. All of the characters are unremittingly destabilized. The two
detectives are clearly farcical doubles (dubbed "bogus Bogarts" and "daffy
dicks" by critics), not only of each other but also of Niles, whose death
they unwittingly reenact.[14] Petrone and Laureen, Niles's musician friends,
are also produced as extensions of Niles, characters uniquely capable of
telling his story, inhabiting his space, playing his music, reading his mind.
Niles, meanwhile, the dead/not dead hero, is quite unlike the unitary subject that dominates most detective fiction. Rather, he is a collection of dis-
parate selves (musician, murderer, suicide, cowboy, tuxedoed swell,

among others), each of which he wants to kill off. "They're crowding me up," Niles exclaims. "They've gotten out of control. They've taken me over and there's no room left for me."[15] At the same time, Niles's status as a jazz musician gives him a privileged relationship to African American culture. And although Niles's race is never specified in the text—which means he is assumed to be white—his presence/absence in the stage space is signified by a white outline painted on the dark stage floor. He is constructed, like so many of Shepard's musician-hipster heroes (and like so many white males who pose as victims), as an imitation black man, a 1970s counterpart to the White Negro of the 1950s.

The production of these doubles in the play is insistently linked to a level of psychic violence that cannot easily be accommodated by the conventions of parodic comedy. The titular suicide, for example, seems clearly the symptom of an intense, virtually ubiquitous emotional violence whose foundation is never fully illuminated. One way of interpreting the suicide is as a realization of that most controversial of all the Freudian drives, the death instinct, which "rushes" the organism "forward so as to reach the final aim of life as swiftly as possible."[16] As initially formulated in 1920 in *Beyond the Pleasure Principle*, the death instinct in many ways functions as a linchpin to the Freudian system. Set in opposition to the life instinct (or eros), it "is held to represent the fundamental tendency of every living being to return to the inorganic state" and is characterized by Freud as the cardinal instinct, indeed, as the "factor which determines the actual *principle* of all instinct."[17] By means of this formulation, Freud for the first time was able not only to explicate the logic of masochism (a "perversion" for which he formerly could find "no satisfactory explanation") but also to theorize an original erotogenic masochism that is not dependent on an inversion of the aggressive instinct.[18] In "The Economic Problem in Masochism" (1924) Freud consequently redefined masochism as a conjuncture of the death instinct with the libido, which is to say, as that part of the death instinct that "remains within the organism and is 'bound' there libidinally."[19]

In this context, *Suicide in B-Flat*, with its rush toward self-destruction and its doubled characters, seems a remarkably clear and conclusive playing out of masochistic fantasy. As Freud and his followers have pointed out, masochism is defined by a particular narrativization of the self. According to Laura Mulvey's celebrated formulation, "sadism demands a story, depends on making something happen, forcing a change in another person, a battle of will and strength, victory/defeat, all occurring in a linear time with a beginning and end."[20] So too with masochism. Indeed, masochism, of all the so-called perversions, is the one most dependent on fantasy and on a fully enunciated (if partly unconscious) scenario through which humiliation and pain are transformed into pleasure. Theodore Reik, meanwhile, in the most encyclopedic of the psychoanalytical works on masochism, details scores of fantasies and scenarios. For Reik, the masochistic subject works like a playwright, producing a highly ritualized and symbolic "scene" that "corresponds . . . to the staging of a drama."[21] This scene (or ritual) depends for its effectiveness on endless reiteration: "A change or disturbance of this masochistic ritual diminishes its lust-value."[22] Reik emphasizes that this scene, furthermore, is always on display, always being performed for a real or imagined audience, always accompanied (not unlike the Brechtian scene) by a gesture of showing, of demonstrating. And although "the demonstrative feature is essential to . . . masochism," the audience may be a willing participant in the drama or even the masochistic subject him- or herself.[23] Reik observes that "frequently young men—rarely women—practice self-flagellation before a mirror."[24] Moreover, this scene (like the setting for *Suicide in B-Flat*) retains "a certain theatrical flavor" and the self-conscious "character of a performance."[25] Furthermore, the fantasies documented by Reik suggest that the emblematic masochistic drama, like a whodunit, always aims to prolong suspense and that "masochistic tension vacillates more strongly than any other sexual tension between the pleasurable and the anxious."[26]

The formulation of the masochistic subject is always marked by a split within subjectivity itself. As Freud explains: "The most remarkable feature of this perversion is that its active and passive forms are habitually found to occur together in the same individual. . . . A sadist is always at the same time a masochist."[27] So in any masochistic subject, there is always a sadistic part that fantasizes the infliction of pain and identifies with the real or imagined tormentor and a properly masochistic part that delights in its own humiliation. Yet even this binary structure is, to my mind, insufficient to explain the complexity of masochistic subjectivity. As Reik points out, the bipolarity is always supplemented by a third term, a spectator, whether real or imagined, whose voyeuristic delight in the masochist's pleasurable pain redoubles it. Moreover, as Reik emphasizes, because the spectatorial position is always to some extent introjected, the masochist is always, as it were, performing in front of a mirror for his or her own exquisitely cruel pleasure.[28] If Reik is correct, then, there are three parts to the masochistic subject: sadist, masochist, spectator; one desiring to hurt, the second to be hurt, the third to watch the spectacle; each delighting to be simultaneously self, Other, and destabilizing third term.

As an enactment of masochistic fantasy, *Suicide in B-Flat* conforms almost uncannily well to the psychoanalytical paradigms. Formally, Shepard not only mobilizes the exemplary masochistic structure, the whodunit, the literary form that most arouses suspense in the reader or spectator, but also finds a way of prolonging that suspense indefinitely. By refusing finally to elucidate the mystery, he leaves the reader or spectator in a state of frustrated and pleasurable unknowing that is by no means incompatible with the play's overriding comic tone (Reik emphasizes that masochistic performance "seldom becomes a matter of 'deadly earnest,'" as sadism often does).[29] Furthermore, Shepard is constantly taunting the reader or spectator, providing, by means of the conflicting explanations of the crime, both a way of solving the case and the proof of its insolubility. And as is so often the case in masochistic practices that depend on ritualistic reiteration, the play's action clearly suggests a ceremony, or more exactly, a series of sacrificial performances in which identities are both ritualistically assumed and cast off. Paullette even labels the performance a "ritual" (221).

Yet it is on the level of subjectivity that *Suicide in B-Flat* most strikingly conforms to the masochistic model. The apparent suicide, Niles, is clearly split in three, into an active and murderous self, a passive and suffering one, and a spectatorial self who observes and meditates upon the scene. Niles's fissured identity is introduced even before his entrance in the two biographies of Niles that Louis and Pablo construct. Both narratives focus on Niles the irascible genius who suffers (like so many other Shepard heroes) from a serious case of *dispossession*. In both fantasies, the jazz musician is radically alienated from his own body. According to Louis, Niles hears his own voice "like it belongs to another body" (196). In Pablo's more melodramatic narrative, Niles's "music was driving him mad," and he began to feel "possessed . . . by his own gift": "His own voracious hunger for sound became like a demon. Another body within him that lashed out without warning. That took hold of him and swept him away. Each time with more and more violence until his weaker side began to collapse" (203). According to Pablo, Niles's "weaker side" was destroyed by another body within, the active, sadistic, demonic part of the self. And late in the play, this process of destruction is enacted literally as Niles takes on two roles, the cowboy and the millionaire (by donning two costumes, "a kid's cowboy outfit" and "black tails"), in order to kill off these two selves (212, 221).

Yet Niles is by no means the only masochistic subject. Pablo and Louis, almost indistinguishable doubles, are themselves bound by a masochistic logic, unwittingly—and ridiculously—obstructing each other's efforts. "I know you've been trying to sabotage this project right from the start," Pablo warns his sidekick. "There's something in you that wants to destroy me" (198). Moreover, the suicidal circumstance that they have come to investigate becomes strangely contagious, or rather (like Reik's masochistic scene) subject to endless repetition and variation. Early in the play Louis "*suddenly*" and inexplicably "*puts the butcher knife up to his own neck as though about to kill himself.*" Then, Dr. Strangelove–like, he "*starts to struggle with one hand against the hand that's holding the knife against his neck*" (203). This contagion points to the virtual interchangeability of victim and detective. When Niles's selves are shot, Louis and Pablo are the ones who feel the pain. "IT MAKES NO DIFFERENCE," Pablo exclaims, "WHETHER OR NOT WE WERE DESTROYED FROM WITHIN OR WITHOUT!" (223). And when Niles finally turns himself in, the relationship between criminal and detective, inside and outside, self and Other, becomes completely, finally, radically destabilized: "Are you inside me or outside me?" Niles asks his doubles. "Am I buzzing away at your membranes? Your brain waves? Driving you berserk? . . . Or am I just like you? Just exactly like you? . . . So exactly that we're not even apart. Not even separate. Not even two things but just one. Only one. Indivisible" (229). When Niles finishes this speech, Pablo and Louis come up on either side of him and handcuff him "*so that all three are locked to each other,*" slave to master, master to slave, indissolubly linked in a logic of interchangeability (229).

In its search for the killer within the self, for doubles that are at once radically different and self-identical, *Suicide in B-Flat* stages the dynamics of masochistic desire *en abîme*, vertiginously rewriting the economy of self and Other. The final image in the play is an image of masochistic desire fulfilled: the one in thrall to the Other, to that upon which it depends for its identity; the criminal bound—emotionally, physically, violently—to the police. This image suggests that the master-slave dialectic is the key to the construction of the categories of self and Other in this play. In so doing it provides what is the master narrative not only of *Suicide in B-Flat* but of so many of Shepard's plays: the self comes to believe that it has lost its true being because the latter has been hijacked by an Other, outside the self. Separated from its inner essence, feeling bereft, it is ineluctably drawn to this Other that, it believes, both contains and is its true being. Desiring to assimilate this being, it shackles itself to its Other. Yet because it is unable to become or reincorporate its Other, it can only in the end reiterate its tragic enslavement ad infinitum (like the eagle and the cat clawing each other to death in the final lines of *Curse of the Starving Class*).[30] Moreover, as *Suicide* demonstrates, within this master-slave dialectic the positions of self and Other are always reversible. For which subject, in the play's final tableau, is really the slave? Are not the police as enslaved to the criminal as the criminal is to the police? Does not the one find its very being through its utter submission to the Other? Yet as *Suicide in B-Flat* makes clear (and as Hegel's master-slave dialectic confirms), this desire for the Other is also the very ground of what is called self-consciousness. As Judith Butler explains, "Self-consciousness seeks a reflection of its own identity through the Other, but finds instead the enslaving and engulfing potential of the Other."[31] Seeking itself, seeking its misplaced identity (remember the face blown off of the victim?), the subject tracks down the Other only to find that it is always already enthralled to the Other, humiliated and consumed by a double that is finally revealed to be sited catastrophically both within and without the self.

The Violence of Desire

I began my analysis of the masculine mystique in Shepard by citing an interview in which he notes that because "humiliation," "inferiority," and "failure" are so "deeply rooted" in the American male, the latter must "invariably" "act out" a "violent" "idea of manhood." In other words, male subjectivity in Shepard is founded on a split between a pas-

sive and humiliated self and an active and violent self. The desire to sub-
mit or be submitted to that links one part to another part of the self,
Niles to the police, the police to Niles, is, I believe, the primary libidinal
mode in Shepard's work and *Iron John* (and in so many recent cultural
productions). Significantly, however, it is usually marked less by eroticism than by *violence,* by a longing to dominate and consume the Other.
For is not the violence that circulates between self and Other the very
mark of disavowed desire, the sign by which desire becomes visible? And
does not this closed system—joining self with Other, humiliation with
exultation, pain with pleasure—precisely describe the masochistic economy of desire?

A glance at *Suicide in B-Flat, The Tooth of Crime, Action,* or *True West*
will reveal that this masochistic logic produces both a distinctively masculinized subject and an unmistakably masculine network of social relations. Shepard's feminist critics have often pointed out that this network ensures that women in his plays almost without exception will
assume peripheral roles: "Men have their showdowns or face the prover-
bial abyss while women are absorbed in simple activities and simplistic
thoughts."[32] Like Bly's writings, and like the plays of David Mamet, John
Patrick Shanley, and many other playwrights, Shepard's works privilege
the male bond as a kind of transcendental connection, while the writer
himself observes in one interview, "It always seemed to me that there
was more mystery to relationships between men."[33] Almost all of his
plays attest to a level of intensity and "mystery" in male bonding that is
rarely evident in relations between men and women. This intensity
leads Florence Falk, with some justification, to note that Shepard's masculine world is "essentially homoerotic," a claim contested by Alan
Shepard, who, noting how accusations of homosexuality function in
Shepard's plays, asserts that, on the contrary, "Shepard's territory is not
principally homoerotic but homophobic."[34]

Amending both Falk and Alan Shepard, I want to argue that Sam
Shepard's writing produces a brotherhood that—like the culture of
which it is a part—is *both* homoerotic *and* homophobic (and this too
brings Shepard's masculinism perilously close to that of Bly and the
men's movement). As Eve Kosofsky Sedgwick has pointed out, within a
homophobic, patriarchal culture the range of male bonds is far less continuous than the range of female bonds. A clear demarcation between

homosociality and homosexuality is rigorously policed so as to insure that "'men-promoting-the-interests-of-men'" will not be confused with "'men-loving-men.'"[35] Within a patriarchal culture, the more intense male homosocial relations become, the more intensely male homosexual desire becomes stigmatized and proscribed. As Sedgwick notes, the vigilant policing of the male bond ensures that desire between men will rarely be directly expressed in (what passes for heterosexual) discourse.

One effect of this policing is the constant displacement of homoeroticism throughout Shepard's work (and this feature has been crucial, I believe, in producing Shepard as *the* emblematic American playwright of his generation). On the one hand, as I have argued, there is an extraordinary overvaluation of and overinvestment in the male bond. On the other, this bond is also relentlessly subject to the brutal injunction against homosexual desire that organizes both Shepard's playwriting and, more generally, post–World War II American culture (the 1960s counterculture in which Shepard was a player no less than the domestic revival before it).[36] As a result, the male bond is always the site of intense anxiety, and the homoeroticism that perpetually threatens it is being constantly dislocated, abstracted, or (more ominously) translated into violence between men. In *The Tooth of Crime,* it figures in the deadly game of rivalry that Hoss and Crow play out, a dance of death and desire that ends with Crow's appropriation of Hoss's life, title, and girlfriend. (Crow twice humiliates Hoss by accusing him of being a "fag" and by forcing him down to his knees in a state of abjection and sexual slavery: "Just get down on my thing boy!")[37] In *Suicide in B-Flat,* on the other hand, because male desire is reconfigured as a fiercely competitive rivalry among all the men, its erotic dimension is almost entirely silenced and suppressed. Two of the more puzzling and obscure transactions in the play, however, unmistakably bear its imprint: Petrone's inexplicable decision to sit on Pablo's lap, followed by Pablo's inexplicable decision to sit on Louis's lap (200, 208).

The volatility of male desires in Shepard and the extraordinary level of anxiety they evoke guarantee that the masochistic scenario will be routinely heterosexualized, which is to say, submitted to the binary logic of gender. For as Freud's analysis suggests, the logic of masochism is gendered, and within a patriarchal culture, the active/passive binarism tends to be reinscribed within a masculine/feminine one. As a result of this reinscription, masculine desire in Shepard habitually produces violence against women or against another part of the male self that is obligatorily feminized. In a 1992 interview, Shepard specifies the connections among violence, gender, and the divided self: "You know, in yourself, that the female part of one's self as a man is, for the most part, battered and beaten up and kicked to shit just like some women in relationships. That men themselves batter their own female part to their own detriment."[38] In *Suicide,* the two parts of Niles that are "battered" and killed off, the cowboy and the millionaire, are infantilized and feminized respectively in relation to the cool jazz musician (212, 221). And while there is no explicit brutalizing of women in this play (as there is in *A Lie of the Mind*), the violence of desire still leaves its traces in the recurrent scream of a woman that punctuates the play. Listening in the dead silence, Pablo and Louis (mistakenly) think they hear the sound of "a woman screaming," "like a woman being tortured" (199). Shortly thereafter, the *"high shrill scream of a woman"* inexplicably sounds, which, Shepard indicates, *"should be delivered like a musical note,"* which is to say, aestheticized, made into an object to be consumed (200).

Freud called the particular mode of battering the feminine part of the self reflexive sadomasochism and described it as mediating between sadism and masochism proper. In "Instincts and Their Vicissitudes," he observes that "a primary masochism . . . seems not to be met with," and he argues instead that masochism represents a "reversal" of sadism (and the transformation of an active into a passive aim: "sadism turned round upon the subject's own ego"). But because this turning round is a "process," it includes an intermediate (or reflexive) stage in which the "object" of sadistic violence "is given up and replaced," not by an "extraneous person" but "by the subject's self." Unlike sadism or masochism proper, reflexive sadomasochism has the effect of splitting the subject's ego between a sadistic (or masculinized) half and a masochistic (or feminized) half. So the reflexive sadomasochist, rather than humiliate and master others, turns this impulse back upon him- or herself: "The desire to torture has turned into self-torture and self-punishment."[39] And it is reflexive sadomasochism, I believe, that forms the "structuring action" of what I would call the new white male fantasmatic, producing the man whose violent instincts are turned not only against others but also against the self.[40] This is the figure who became ubiquitous in U.S. culture during the 1980s, whose likenesses populate the militia movement, and who has come to dominate both mass and elite cultural representations (although, as *Suicide* suggests, it appears much more obliquely and esoterically in what remains of elite culture).

Suicide in B-Flat, as an exercise in the production of a seditious Other within the self to be punished and subjugated, represents a virtual textbook case of reflexive sadomasochism. And what of Shepard's other plays of the 1970s, *The Tooth of Crime, Action,* and *True West?* Are they not as well beholden to the logic of reflexive sadomasochism? Consider another fatal narrative, Shooter's story in *Action* about "a guy" who "began to fear his own body" until he was finally killed by it: "One day it just had enough and killed him." And then there's Jeep's self-torture in the play's final speech, as he describes his entrapment, his "stalking [him]self" in a "*cell*" that he both remembers and creates anew as he speaks his lines: "I'd just crash against the wall. I'd just smash my head in."[41] (In both cases, the subject of the enunciation is serendipitously masculinized at the expense of the subject of the utterance, who is figured as a fragile and feminized body.) Theodor Reik provides an elegant distillation of the brutal (and brutalizing) logic of reflexive sadomasochism: "*As I do to you, so do I to me.*"[42]

In so many of Shepard's plays, reflexive sadomasochism functions as a kind of fantasmatic engine that relentlessly reproduces a tough male subject who proves his orneriness by subjugating and battering his (feminized) Other. Kaja Silverman emphasizes that "because it does not demand the renunciation of activity," reflexive sadomasochism "is ideally suited for negotiating the contradictions inherent in masculinity. The male subject can indulge his appetite for pain without at the same time calling into question . . . his virility."[43] Niles, Crow, Shooter, Jeep, and Austin prove their masculinity (and their ability to contain a mutinous self) by staging a battle with an Other who is simultaneously figured as a part of the self. If Niles's masochism is the most flamboyant and fully dramatized of the five, perhaps that is the result of his being an artist, a jazz musician, the one most acutely in danger of being feminized, the one most insecure about his masculinity. Reflexive sadomasochism allows Niles (as it did so many jazz-loving White Negroes of the 1950s) not only to subjugate but also and more importantly to disavow the tainted, artistic, feminized parts of the self by killing them off.

It permits each of these Shepard protagonists to prove his manhood, to verify his strength and courage, to prove that he has the right stuff by kicking his Other "to shit."

Backlash

Reflexive sadomasochism is, I believe, far more than an idiosyncratic libidinal logic that Shepard happened upon in the late 1970s. Rather, it seems to me to be the linchpin to a new American masculinity that has been produced in response to five historical events: the reemergence of the feminist movement; the rise of the lesbian and gay movements; the loss of the Vietnam War; the end of the post–World War II economic boom and a resultant and steady decline in the income of white working- and lower-middle-class men; and the success of the civil rights movement in effecting a partial redress of gross historical inequities through affirmative action legislation.

Although much has been written about all of these events, I would like to focus on the last, which I find particularly decisive for the production of this new masculinity. As has been well documented, civil rights legislation of the 1960s did enable some African Americans to make significant gains economically and socially. But legislation alone was unable to transmute the long and violent history of racism in the United States, and by the end of the 1960s the income of African Americans was still only 61 percent that of white Americans.[44]

During the 1970s, the remarkable and continuing prosperity of white men relative to women and African Americans by no means prevented the former from identifying themselves as the victims of the slender and precarious gains made by the latter groups. As the economy contracted during the mid-1970s and unemployment rates rose for both whites and blacks, the white response to the progress of black Americans began to shift.[45] The landmark case was the lawsuit that Allan Bakke, an ex-Marine and Vietnam veteran, brought in 1974 against the University of California for twice denying him admission to its medical school at Davis. Insisting that the university's quota system for racial minorities violated his constitutional rights, Bakke styled himself a victim of discrimination. Four years later the Supreme Court supported his claim, striking down quotas while upholding the principle of affirmative action. Liberals decried the decision. In his dissent, Thurgood Marshall pointed to an ignominious history of oppression, insisting that the "experience of Negroes in America is not merely the history of slavery alone, but also that [of] a whole people [who] were marked inferior by the law. And that mark has endured."[46] Jesse Jackson called the decision a "devastating blow to our civil rights struggle" and saw it—prophetically—as "consistent with the country's shift to the right, a shift in mood from redemption to punishment."[47]

Yet the *Bakke* decision was so widely debated and publicized in part because it served as a sign of the emergence of a backlash against civil rights and affirmative action during a period of economic retrenchment, a sign of the desire for the "punishment" of African Americans for purportedly compromising the white standard of living. Conservatives applauded the blow to what they—in an audacious attempt to equate the grievances of white males with the legacies of slavery—called "reverse racism," which, Robert Allen points out, "attempts to make racial minorities scapegoats for the problems that have been fostered by the inherent social irresponsibility of the corporations and banks that dominate" the U.S. economy.[48] Turning a blind eye to history (and anticipating the total amnesia that would characterize conservative discourse of the 1980s), one irate correspondent speciously blamed "minority fetishism" for a decline in American competitiveness and "law enforcement," for the decay of American cities, and for the deterioration of the public school system.[49] Yet as Allen emphasizes, these accusations end up blaming those who historically have been the victims of racist violence and ignore the "institutional racism" that is maintained by the "'normal' operation of the institutional and capitalist market mechanisms."[50]

The severe recession of the mid-1970s and the end of the post–World War II economic boom had dire consequences for the United States. Not only did they stall the move toward social justice, but they also produced a backlash against feminism, affirmative action, and lesbian and gay civil rights. Moreover, they became imbricated with a sense of profound anxiety over the loss of the Vietnam War, and more generally over the United States' role as an imperial power. These signal changes, I am arguing, eventually produced a wholesale and complex reconfiguration of white American masculinity. Just as the Vietnam War divided the country, so did it initially produce two competing versions of masculinity. During the late 1960s, normative masculine identity continued to be organized around occupational stability and fatherhood, and the real man was supposed to be independent, adventurous, and morally upright. Yet among those young enough to protest the Vietnam War, "macho," as the writers of the *Newsweek* review of *The Right Stuff* point out, became virtually "a dirty word." It was precisely among this group, generally identified with the counterculture, that a new concept of masculinity began to take hold. For the Sam Shepard of *Suicide in B-Flat* and *The Right Stuff,* for the Robert Bly in search of "the deep masculine," the heroics of John Wayne were embarrassingly out of place. In reacting against this clamorous, confident virility, Shepard and his generation reimagined the white male subject as if to solve the following problems: How can masculinity authenticate itself in a world grown increasingly suspicious of direct military intervention and the violent subjugation of native populations? How can it respond to the demands of feminism without forfeiting its male prerogative? How can it adjust to irrevocable economic decline?

As the various European empires dissolved, as the older mode of colonial domination by foreign armies was gradually dismantled, a neocolonialism emerged to consolidate the international division of labor (with the Third World serving as the First World's proletariat) along with a "free" market guaranteed to exacerbate the inequitable distribution of wealth both nationally and globally.[51] In the wake of African independence, after the fall of Saigon, as the World Bank and the International Monetary Fund replaced the colonial armies, as hegemony came to substitute for military might, and as subtle coercion supplanted brute force, a new masculinity began to take shape in America that was no longer contingent either upon the production of enemies *out there* or upon nakedly imperialistic forays abroad. Having a new set of cultural conflicts to negotiate, it became more independent, more pliable, more apparently responsive to the demands of local populations and to the challenges posed by various rebellions (like the feminist insurgency). Yet at the same time, as the last vestiges of traditional societies were being penetrated by market forces, as the "older village structures and precapitalist forms of agriculture" in the Third World were being "systematically destroyed," as "nature" was increasingly being sacrificed to "culture," European American men were becoming increasingly domesticated and bureaucratized.[52] For the professional, managerial, and technical sectors of the U.S. labor force had expanded so quickly that by the early 1970s the United States had become "the only country to employ more people in services than in the production of tangible goods."[53] Under these circumstances, it became all the more urgent that the masculine fantasmatic be reconstructed to bear the unmistakable traces of a robust, independent, and entrepreneurial masculinity. The new fantasmatic of the 1970s, therefore, features not the gallant commander leading his regiment to glory but the lone guerrilla (like Rambo) making his way through the dark jungle, picking off enemy soldiers, on a dangerous and mysterious mission; or the test pilot described by Tom Wolfe, fascinatedly peering into the abyss:

> The idea here . . . seemed to be that a man should have the ability to go up in a hurtling piece of machinery and put his hide on the line and then have the moxie, the reflexes, the experience, the coolness, to pull it back in the last yawning moment—and then go up again *the next day*, and the next day, and every next day, even if the series should prove infinite. [54]

Not only does reflexive sadomasochism provide the ideal mechanism to turn this new hero's pain into pleasure, but it also allows him to adjust to the exigencies of living in a (post)feminist and post-*Bakke* culture. It authorizes him to be both wild and domestic, to cultivate a "feminine" part of the self (or at least to endure his feminized flesh) and at the same time to subjugate it violently, and to take on the roles simultaneously of aggressor and of casualty of feminism and affirmative action. It allows him to play the part of victim and yet be a man.

And this is where the men's movement comes in again. For what is perhaps most remarkable about Robert Bly's discourse of "deep" masculinity is its stress on a primordial and untouchable inwardness, its ability to produce a pure—and fantasmatic—virility that will accord with polite social norms while leaving unsullied the "Wild Man" within. Moreover, Bly seems oblivious to the deeply racist cast of his theory of masculinity. For despite the participation of a few African American men in the men's movement, Bly's "mythopoetics" remains a "white mythology," firmly rooted in imperialist fantasies.[55] One of the most revealing moments in *Iron John* is his recounting of what he claims to be an African initiation ritual in which a boy, after having fasted for three days, sits in a circle with a group of older men: "One of the older men takes up a knife, opens a vein in his own arm, and lets a little of his blood flow into a gourd or bowl." And so on around the circle. "When the bowl arrives at the young man, he is invited to take" a drink. Bly comments that in this way, not only does the boy learn to take "nourishment" from men, but "he also learns that the knife can be used for many purposes besides wounding others" (15). In other words, he learns that the knife can always be turned against the self and that the act of self-mutilation is the purest expression of virility. And all the better that this lesson should be taught the white American male by African bodies, by black bodies who, in Bly's imperialist fantasmatic, approximate "the deep masculine" far more effectively than the Western subject, marooned as he is in a feminized culture. And yet, does not the *desire to be the Other*, to appropriate his cultural apparatus, at the same time betray a barely concealed *terror of the Other*? Does not this narrative, and the masochistic logic that drives it, represent the last stand of the embattled European American male, now grown enraged and paranoid at seeing his economic power diminished, now blaming this diminution not only on women but also on those dark-skinned Others, whether in the Third World or America's inner cities?

In conclusion, I want to observe that although this new masculinity takes a peculiar detour indeed to its pleasure and power, it has been extraordinarily successful in helping maintain the economic and political dominion of white men in America. One 1993 survey compared the racial and sexual composition of senior corporate executives between 1979 and 1989. It found that in those ten years the proportion of African Americans had increased from .2 to .6 percent of the total, Latinos from .1 to .4 percent, and women from .5 to 3 percent.[56] Yet many white American men still consider themselves an oppressed group, the victims of discrimination, intolerance, and "reverse racism." "The white male," one whines, "is the most persecuted person in the United States."[57] But as one African American man is quoted as saying, "European males have always had the propensity to say 'I feel threatened' while holding a gun to somebody else's head."[58]

American cultural productions since the mid-1970s have insistently reenacted this contradictory spectacle of white men proclaiming themselves victims while simultaneously menacing—or blowing away—somebody else. *Iron John* and the plays of Sam Shepard are filled with images of self-torture used to consolidate the sense that the white American male truly knows how to take it like a man. Like Sam Shepard as Chuck Yeager in *The Right Stuff,* the russian-roulette-addicted Nick (Christopher Walken) in *The Deer Hunter,* the self-tortured John J. Rambo of Sylvester Stallone's *Rambo* trilogy, or Michael Douglas in virtually any of his roles from the late 1980s and 1990s, these heroes remonstrate against a culture made uneasy by traditional machismo by proclaiming themselves victims, by turning violence upon themselves and so demonstrating their implacable toughness, their ability to savor their self-inflicted wounds. As is apparent from the conduct of each of these heroes, this process does not rule out the possibility of turning violence against others, especially women or feminized and racialized Others (like Asian men) who happen to get in the way. In all these instances, reflexive sadomasochism operates, I believe, as the primary libidinal logic that produces what passes for masculinity. Yet at the same time, and most tellingly, this logic remains stunningly unacknowledged in American culture. Concealed under a veneer of willfulness, resilience, grief, anger, or guilt—and desperately disavowed by the male subject—reflexive sadomasochism has become the unconscious of the new white masculinity. And in that sense, to the degree that it remains hidden and yet decisive, undeclared and yet constitutive of male subjectivity, it may be said to occupy a *closet*, a site of repression, a private space that is at the same time pivotal for the production of public practices and subjects. Kosmo is hardly the only Shepard hero with "a sadomasochist hid in his closet." Perhaps it's time now to "out" these other heroes; to "out" Robert Bly, Sam Shepard, and the culture they instantiate; and to admit that what white men *really* want, what gives them the greatest thrill, is pain.

Chapter Six

A Different Kind of Closet Drama

or, the melancholy heterosexuality of jane bowles

A great admirer of the writing of his friend Jane Bowles, Tennessee Williams observed that her only play, *In the Summer House* (1953), with its "acute admixture of humor and pathos" and "profound sensibility," "stands quite superbly alone among works for the American theatre." Yet as is so often the case with unique works of art, its solitary splendor provoked a "bewildered" response from critics.[1] Although the actors received glowing notices in the New York press and the text itself some respectful nods, all the reviewers admitted to being somewhat baffled by the play's characters and plot. Understandably intimidated by such a discomfiting Broadway play, they recognized that there is more to it than first meets the eye (or ear), even if they weren't sure exactly what that was. They also understood that, in a Broadway season dominated by middlebrow entertainments, *In the Summer House* stakes a claim for a kind of highbrow art by furnishing theatergoers with "one of those rare evenings rich with provocative food for thought and conversation."[2] For although this drama employs the conventions of postwar realism, it does so in a far more idiosyncratic and unpredictable way than even the most adventurous of Williams's own plays. Bowles's combination of formal, characterological, and thematic eccentricities inspired irreconcilable opinions. William Hawkins, for example, castigates Bowles for ignoring "the surface of characters" at the expense of a fully illuminated "inside essence."[3] Walter Kerr, in contrast, criticizes Bowles for precisely the opposite flaw, her alleged "reluctance to pry beneath a painstakingly accurate surface."[4]

Perhaps most striking about the New York reviews of *In the Summer House,* however, is the flood of pathologizing adjectives and nouns. For Robert Coleman, in particular, this "macabre" play, teeming with "maladjusted people," represents a "bitter study in abnormality," the product of an unnatural intercourse between "William Saroyan and Kraft-Ebing [*sic*]."[5] The other reviews, meanwhile, note that the play's "overwrought," "impenetrable," "morbid," "very badly adjusted," "mentally deranged," and "lunatic" characters suffer variously from "neurotic egotism," "dementia," and other assorted "psychic difficulties."[6] In case the (misspelled) name Krafft-Ebing were not a dead giveaway, these labels—so reminiscent of the damning critical appraisals of Tennessee Williams's works during the 1950s—were the incriminatory euphemisms (during the zenith of McCarthyism, the Cold War, and American Freudianism) used to describe those who in less polite company might have been called sickos, perverts, and homos. And although none of the reviewers explicitly accuses the characters of sexual aberrations, all suffer a serious unease with a play whose author, producer (Oliver Smith), star (Judith Anderson), composer (Paul Bowles), and director (José Quintero) could have been branded perverts.

Those historians and other arbiters of culture who properly judge the 1950s the most sexually and politically repressive decade of the twentieth century also usually consider the very end of the century a period in which sexual dissidence was widely, if reluctantly, sanctioned. The fin de siècle destigmatization of homosexuality was accompanied, moreover, by the appearance of numerous books and articles that consider the relationship between homosexuals and the performing art in which they have most flourished, theater. And while many of these texts counter the dismal history of oppression with a celebration of visibility (which has itself been the subject of some well-taken critiques), there is no consensus as to how a homosexual looks (or sounds) on stage.[7] In an era dominated by social constructionists, almost all critics acknowledge the historical contingency and variability of both normative and dissident sexual identities. As Jill Dolan cautiously and correctly notes, the rise of antihomophobic scholarship and theater practices has by no means resolved the difficulty of denominating sexual subjectivity: "As lesbian work is brought out of its marginalized context and traded as critical currency in heterosexual academic and theater venues, the question of the performance's 'readability' becomes complicated."[8]

Like so many pre-Stonewall studies in abnormality, *In the Summer House* does not have a single character who can be read as being unequivocally lesbian or gay. Moreover, the longstanding, unstable, and unpredictable relationship between identities and desires by no means simplifies the problem of sexual desire in the play. Martha Vicinus's observation about historical texts is equally applicable to dramatic texts like this one: "Lesbian desire is everywhere, even as it may be nowhere. Put bluntly, we lack any general agreement about what constitutes a lesbian."[9] The absence of a character generally agreed upon as lesbian perhaps explains the curious nonappearance of both Jane Bowles and her play in the most comprehensive studies of homosexuality and theater (by Kaier Curtin and Alan Sinfield).[10] That absence is also the sign, I believe, of what is most bewildering and important about *In the Summer House,* a play that both reaffirms and contests the pathologizing logic of postwar homophobia. Like the early "closet dramas" of Tennessee Williams, Bowles's text is able to safeguard homosexual identities and facilitate an almost wild proliferation of queer desires only by keeping the homosexual perpetually out of sight, invisible, elsewhere. As in so much postwar American drama, however, the absent homosexual has left traces throughout the text that point the way to its own erasure. But Bowles's play adopts fundamentally different strategies than the coded texts of Williams and Inge. For *In the Summer House* most clearly and subtly dramatizes the structure not of homosexuality but of that which passes for heterosexuality. Indeed, no other American play of this period illuminates the structure of heterosexuality with the disconcerting clarity of *In the Summer House.* No play is more shot through with the melancholy that results (in a heterosexual regime) from foreclosing a homosexual cathexis and refusing even to grieve that incalculable loss. In its melancholy desperation—it is an almost unimaginably sad text—it does indeed, as Williams declared, stand "superbly alone," a different kind of closet drama, one in which invisibility refers both to the disappearance of the pervert and to the play's own regrettable exclusion (alas!) from the canon of queer theater.

In the Summer House has many of the features of the postwar closet drama—intense and overwrought desires that deconstruct the opposition between the homosocial and the homosexual, powerful cross-gender identifications on the part of leading characters, a withheld guilty secret, and the relentless (and sometimes inexplicable) circulation of shameful feelings. Add to those a series of narcissistic doubles and loveless marriages. Because of these features, the play might be read as a kind of theatrical echo of a novel like Nella Larsen's *Passing* (1929), in which homoeroticism is everywhere yet homosexuality per se is nowhere. For there is no question that the play (like Larsen's novel) fixates upon relations between women that are far more volatile, ambivalent, and compelling than any heterosocial interactions.

In the Summer House centers on three mother/daughter pairs (Gertrude and Molly, Mrs. Constable and Vivian, Mrs. Lopez and Frederica), each bond cemented by a terrible confluence of passionate love and hatred. Each pair, moreover, is as asymmetrical as it is emotionally violent. Gertrude, Vivian, and Mrs. Lopez exert such tremendous power over their partners that they are able to intimidate, shame, and nearly silence them. Gertrude's ability to hold her daughter "*spellbound*" serves as a kind of template for the other relationships.[11] For in each of them, one is domineering, extroverted, and verbally excessive; the other passive, laconic, and secretive.

What is perhaps most striking about the three dyads, however, is their unremitting triangulation. The play's action centers on two erotic triangles, in both of which the desiring subjects are young women, Molly and Vivian. Indeed, desire is only discernible in this play as a product of a jealous triangulation in which two women copy each other's desires by vying for a third party. Thus, Molly and Vivian are locked in a violent competition for Gertrude, whom Vivian studies "*with adoration*" while Molly watches her, "*a beam of hate in her eye*" (229). The visual incitement for desire, moreover, is a constant in this play. "The day you came I was standing on the porch watching you," Molly says to Vivian.

You put your arm around my mother, and told her she had beautiful hair, then you saw my summer house and you told her how much you loved it. You went and sat in it and you yelled, Come out, Molly. I'm in your little house. You've tried in every way since you came to push me out. She hates you. (238)

The merest glance of one woman at another is enough to produce desire, which here means the desire to copy the desire of the other, to replace her, to *be* the other. In this unmistakable—and single-sex—revision of the Oedipal triangle, Vivian attempts to supplant Molly in her mother's affection by taking her place, entering the dark, silent, womblike space of Gertrude's love. Yet if Molly is to be believed, this attempt to appropriate the desire of the other ends up precisely translating love into hatred, or rather, leading Molly to ventriloquize her loathing of her rival through the contested object of desire.[12] The participation of Molly and Vivian in a second erotic triangle simply reinforces the primacy of this same-sex relationship despite the fact that this second one features a more legitimate (because male) object of desire: Lionel. After Gertrude leaves the three young people on the beach, Molly *"crosses wistfully back to her former place next to Lionel, but Vivian—eager to cut her out whenever she can—rushes to Lionel's side, and crouches on her heels exactly where Molly was sitting before"* (230). Even more clearly than in the preceding example, Vivian scrupulously copies her rival and in doing so betrays the fact that her link to Molly is far more powerful and emotionally fraught than her link to Lionel. Providing a female analogue to the erotic triangles that Eve Kosofsky Sedgwick maps in *Between Men*—the triangles that men fashion to disavow the primacy of their own same-sex relations—those in *In the Summer House* are symptomatic of desires so intense and unstable that they undermine the distinctions between the homosocial and homosexual.[13] They also undermine the distinction between love and hatred insofar as this undecidable passion is the clearest evidence that Vivian's mysterious death is the result not of a terrible accident but of foul play.

Even after Vivian's death, desire remains strictly triangulated. Gertrude's sudden return following her disastrous marriage to Mr. Solares merely shifts the configuration by placing Molly in the center of the triangle, as Gertrude forces her to choose between Lionel and herself. Yet even here Lionel is shunted aside, rendered nearly invisible and psychologically opaque. Unable to play the role of desiring subject, he is as completely and *"hopeless[ly]"* *"overpowered"* by Gertrude as Molly is (292). Vivian's desires, meanwhile, are kept in circulation by her mother, who, in one of the play's more outrageous proposals, imagines a Mexican version of her white, bourgeois self in an erotic triangle with Molly's mother: "If I were a man, I'd marry Mrs. Lopez. She'd be my type. We should both have been men. Two Spanish men, married to Mrs. Lopez" (277). Undermining the distinctions between female and male, heterosexual and homosexual, Mrs. Constable's drunken, transgendered fantasy yet again establishes the primacy of the erotic triangle and in so doing provides the play's only fantasy of a marriage that could be imagined as anything other than a disaster.

Mrs. Constable's transgendered reverie is also symptomatic of the profound identification that women in the play feel with men. This identification is clearest in the case of Gertrude, who, through the operation of the negative Oedipus complex—another source for and sign of homosexuality—identifies completely with her opposite-sexed parent and desires her same-sexed parent. The words she speaks in her first nearly interminable monologue, while *"lost in a dream"* (the first six words are later repeated as the very last words of the play), clearly establish the primacy of cross-sex identification: "When I was a little girl I made up my mind that I was going to be just like him [her father]. He was my model, my ideal" (212). And later she reflects: "I take after my father. [. . .] We were exactly alike" (280). Yet as is so often the case in plays about "very badly adjusted" people, her identification is so extreme that it becomes almost indistinguishable from her desire for the same parent, whom she also "worshipped" and for whom she fancied herself a "true love" (212). The impossibility of clearly separating identification from desire turns out to be yet another symptom of triangulation and of the contradictory make-up of these "impenetrable" characters. For does not the passion between Molly and Vivian challenge the distinction between the two in a similar way? Does each want *to be* or *to have* the other? To assimilate or to destroy? In Gertrude's case, however, the third party turns out not to be her mother—a figure whom the play completely suppresses—but her sister Ellen (clearly a stand-in for her mother), the "frail and delicate" one whom her father "spoiled" and "pitied," the one around whom he "used to put his arms" and with whom "he went away" for "two whole weeks" (for what licit or illicit purpose we can only guess), leaving a dejected Gertrude behind (212). For Gertrude's desperate assertion inadvertently betrays her own self-delusion and her refusal to admit that she was never, in fact, the object of his love. She thereby enacts precisely the point that Judith Butler makes about the scandal of negative Oedipus: "The [same-sexed] parent is not only prohibited as an object of love, but is internalized as a . . . withholding object of love."[14] Thus Gertrude recalls: "I was his true love. He never showed it . . . He was so frightened Ellen would guess. He didn't want her to be jealous, by I knew the truth . . . He didn't have to show it" (212; ellipses in the original). And Gertrude is not alone in trying to internalize the father. Mrs. Constable believes that Vivian and her late husband "belonged to each other," while Gertrude imagines that Molly's mockery of her is a "trait of yours you inherit from your father" (263, 213).

The complex patterns of identification and desire in *In the Summer House* transform desire into a female prerogative while suggesting that this license is clearly the result of women's strong—yet prohibited—identification with men, specifically their fathers. In this play-world ruled by the laws of the negative Oedipus complex, women learn how to desire (other women) by becoming their fathers. This process of cross-gender subject formation thereby places women in what a heterosexual regime would understand to be a deceitful relationship with themselves. They not only turn themselves into what they should not be but also disavow what they know (precisely because that knowledge is unbearable). They torment the women they desire, and, unlike men, they "scheme" (235). They are, in short, irreducibly double. And the purest symptom of their doubleness, and their obligation to disavow, is their compulsive heterosexuality, their inability to recognize that there might in fact be something altogether more fascinating and powerful going on between and among them.

All of the features denominated earlier work to position *In the Summer House* as a paradigmatic closet drama, a text that, because it is unable to speak its desires, displaces, disavows, and triangulates them. Yet unlike any other closet drama, the play inadvertently reveals the operation of that psychic mechanism that, in the service of heterosexuality, demands the renunciation of homosexual possibilities. For as Judith Butler points out, heterosexuality is founded on the repudiation of homosexual cathexes, a loss that compulsory heterosexuality absolutely forbids the subject to acknowledge or mourn. And this proscription induces the condition that Freud, in his essay "Mourning and Melancholia," describes as melancholia, "a profoundly painful dejection, . . . loss of the capacity to love, [and] inhibition of all activity."[15] Since the leading characters in *In the Summer House*—heterosexuals all—are unable to mourn the loss of desire, they must endure the distress associated with "the melancholic denial/preservation of homosexuality."[16] As Freud notes, "the loss of the object"—in this case, the same-sexed parent whom one is forbidden to desire and, later, substitutes for that parent—leads to an internalization of that sense of loss that renders the subject permanently and inconsolably bereft.[17] The repression of homosexual desires in all the characters thus suffuses the play with a sense of gloom, injury, and despair. For if these desires are never avowed, they can never be mourned and eventually discharged. (Heterosexualization induces melancholy because the subject is usually unconscious of what he or she has had to forsake, unlike homosexualization, in which the subject is usually all too conscious of what he or she has rejected and, as a result, is able to mourn for the repudiated desires.) Because the consolidation of a heterosexual identity is thus always accompanied by melancholia, one can begin to understand the meaning of one of the most remarkable and revealing passages in the play, remarkable precisely because it is both deeply evocative and puzzling. At the beginning of the last act—a crucial point in so many modern dramas for a coded revelation of what is really going on—Molly and Lionel meditate on the past:

> LIONEL: Molly, when you close your eyes and picture the world do you see it dark? (*Molly doesn't answer right away*) Do you, Molly? Do you see it dark behind your eyes?
> MOLLY: I . . . I don't know . . . I see parts of it dark.
> LIONEL: Like what?
> MOLLY: Like woods . . . like pine-tree woods.
> LIONEL: I see it dark, but beautiful like the ocean is right now. And like I saw it once when I was a child . . . just before a total eclipse. Did you ever see a total eclipse?
> MOLLY: I never saw any kind of eclipse.
> LIONEL: I saw one with my brother. There was a shadow over the whole earth. I was afraid then, but it stayed in my memory like

something that was beautiful. It made me afraid but I knew it was
beautiful.

[...]

LIONEL: (*Tentative*) Did you ever worry about running far away
from sad things when you were young, and then later getting older
and not being able to find your way back to them ever again, even
when you wanted to?

MOLLY: You would never want to find your way back to sad things.

LIONEL: But you might have lost wonderful things, too, mixed in
with the sad ones. (260–61; unbracketed ellipses in the original)

Steeped in melancholy, meditating on loss, Lionel remembers what
he has forsaken as being frightening, "beautiful," and finally—because it
has utterly vanished—irretrievable. He begins by constructing a kind of
mirror image of the world, a "dark, but beautiful" world just moments
before a total eclipse, when the darkness itself is luminous, miraculous,
sublime. His memory of this darkness-that-is-the-light takes him back
to his childhood, to the moment when he became no longer one, when
he gazed upon the eclipse not alone, but with his brother, a brother who
is his own mirror image, his shadow self, the embodiment of his own
lost childhood, the loved one whom he has lost, the phantom lover he
never had. For it is precisely the radical possibilities that he glimpsed at
that brilliantly dark moment that made him so "afraid," despite (or perhaps because of) its overwhelming beauty. Compelled to run "far away"
from these "sad" but "wonderful" things, he suddenly and irreversibly
became a subject, little knowing that he might not ever, "even when [he]
wanted to," "find [his] way back to them again."

This extraordinary passage functions virtually as an allegorization of
melancholic subject formation, of the process that demands that one
flee and forget the same-sexed lover whom one dares not love. Even the
language that Bowles uses uncannily echoes Freud's explanation of how
the abandoned love object is unwittingly internalized and set up as a
critical agency within the subject's ego: "Thus the shadow of the object
fell upon the ego, so that the latter could henceforth be criticized by a
special mental faculty . . . like the forsaken object."[18] For the never quite
glimpsed lost object of love has no more substance than a shadow, the
shadow that Lionel seems to miss so frightfully: the nonheterosexual

possibilities that have been foreclosed by his marriage to Molly, the only one to whom he can explain/not explain his grief. Because fixed sexual and gendered identities are, as Butler argues, "the consequence of loss, gender identification is a kind of melancholia in which the sex of the prohibited object is internalized as a prohibition," as the lost possibility, the shadow, the brother whose loss Lionel can never recognize or grieve. And it is little wonder that it is Lionel, the character with the most secure gender identity, who can tell the story of this loss. For as Butler notes, "the stricter and more stable the gender affinity, the less resolved the original loss"—and the more melancholic the subject.[19] Because Molly, like all the female characters, has a more unstable and problematic sexual identity, she cannot grasp the situation that Lionel describes with quite the same acuity. The one shadowed person whom Molly is able to imagine, however, should hardly come as a surprise: her mother. "It used to come and pass over her whole life," she says, "and make it dark" (261). And even Lionel is able to see this darkness when he confronts Gertrude upon her return after the "terrible mistake" of her marriage to Mr. Solares (278): "You're like a wall around Molly, some kind of shadow between us" (284).

The shadow that comes between Molly and Lionel is, however, far more than the invidious determination of a possessive mother. For the relationship between Molly and Gertrude is more complex and ambivalent than would be possible if the play were simply an illustration of the dangerous "Momism" of McCarthyite fantasies—the overzealous mother who smothers and perverts her children with her suffocating tenacity.[20] *In the Summer House* instead suggests a different model for female relations that is even more scandalous than Momism vis-à-vis the sexual norms of the postwar domestic revival.

There may not be a lesbian in the text, but there is unquestionably a model proffered for lesbian relationships and identities. I am referring to the mother-daughter model, which here supplants the most public and mythologized lesbian paradigm of the 1950s: butch-femme. Butch-femme is usually theorized as a lesbian couple's redeployment of the masculine/feminine hierarchy, a redeployment that has long been controversial both within and without lesbian communities. Does it merely reinscribe heterosexual relations at their most oppressive (as so many 1970s lesbian-feminists believed), or is it a subversive reimagining and implicit critique of heterosexuality (as Judith Butler argues)? One thing is certain, however: butch-femme relationships are as varied as the self-identifications of the two women involved. For there is no fixed meaning for either term, each of which is defined relationally and by visual cues and styles.[21] Trying to reclaim butch-femme, Butler insists that the butch-femme couple "is not a simple assimilation of lesbianism back into the terms of heterosexuality. As one lesbian femme explained, she likes her boys to be girls, meaning that 'being a girl' contextualizes and resignifies 'masculinity' in a butch identity."[22] Butch-femme, in other words, is not a fraudulent copy of heterosexuality. Rather, it reveals (for Butler at least) the always already imitative nature of heterosexualized identities. But the so-called sex wars of the 1980s (the struggles between lesbian-feminists and sex-positive feminists like Judith Butler and Gayle Rubin) long postdate the butch-femme model contemporaneous with *In The Summer House*. Psychologists of the period during which Jane Bowles was writing, unlike Butler, hardly regarded butch-femme as an emancipatory figuration. On the contrary, they understood it to be a relationship between the authentic—that is, mannish—lesbian (the butch) and what Havelock Ellis would have labeled a situational lesbian, a woman seduced by a butch for the lack of a real—that is, male—alternative.[23] Thus one 1950s Freudian believed that the butch "enters into competition with men and often compensates for her sense of inferiority by imitating the dress and mannerisms of men."[24] Although the butch may have been labeled a pathological figure, the femme was—and remains, in some quarters—virtually impossible to theorize. But for postwar psychologists, butch-femme represented lesbianism as it truly was—a pathetic counterfeit.

In the Summer House neither engages with nor draws upon the butch-femme model. Yes, Gertrude, Vivian, and Mrs. Lopez are powerful and aggressive women in relation to their relatively passive opposite numbers. But in none of these mother-daughter relationships is the more aggressive one clearly masculinized. In fact, each, despite her forcefulness, plays traditionally feminine roles: impulsive mother and bride, vivacious and uninhibited young woman, and bountiful mother. Their dress and mien, moreover, are not butch in the least (this is especially important given the importance of visual signs in designating the butch). Gertrude is described as a "*beautiful middle-aged woman with . . . a good carriage and bright red hair"* (207). Vivian is a *"painfully thin" "young girl of fifteen"* whose *"eyes appear to pop out of her head with excitement"* (223). And Mrs. Lopez is a *"fat and middle-aged"* woman wearing a *"hat decorated with flowers"* (214). These are scarcely the hardened butch dykes of postwar fantasy. On the other hand, the emotional violence in the play, especially between Gertrude and Molly, suggests that there is a certain sadomasochistic dynamic playing itself out: Gertrude berates and torments her daughter, who seems to need (and perhaps enjoy) such treatment. But it would be a mistake, I believe, both historically and psychically, simply to equate the sadist with masculinity or sadomasochism with butch-femme.

If one were to try to guess the nature of the connection between Gertrude and Molly—not knowing they were blood relations—one would almost certainly think they were lovers. As Gayle Austin notes, "Men have no power to intervene in this mother-daughter dyad."[25] And there are several moments in the play when Bowles seems to be almost daring the audience to read the two as lovers.[26] This is particularly true in the climactic nuptial scene of act 1, in which Bowles puts on display two women in bridal gowns with not a husband in sight. As Austin observes, "The absence of the grooms until the leave-taking at the very end of the scene leaves the visual impression that the two brides have just married each other." (This spectacle of an apparent same-sex wedding is echoed provocatively in a mass-cultural text from the same year, *Gentlemen Prefer Blondes,* at the end of which Marilyn Monroe and Jane Russell, about to be married, wearing matching outfits, look lovingly into each other's eyes.)[27] And Austin is certainly correct to note that this stage picture dramatizes "the oedipal scene Freud could not envision: the daughter's desire to marry her first love object, her mother."[28] For the scene represents the fulfillment of the negative Oedipus complex—it is as if Oedipus were coupled off with Laios rather than Jocasta. During the wedding sequence Molly implores her mother to stay and tries to give her her own wedding bouquet in a scene that would seem, if one did not know the play, to portray the desperate appeal of a spurned lover:

MOLLY: I picked them for you! [. . .] They're flowers for you! [. . .] I love you. I love you. Don't leave me. I love you. Don't go away!

GERTRUDE: (*Shocked and white*) Molly, stop. You can't go on like this!

MOLLY: I love you. You can't go!

GERTRUDE: I didn't think you cared this much. If you really feel this way, why have you tormented me so . . .

MOLLY: I never have. I never have.

GERTRUDE: You have. You have in a thousand different ways. What about the summer house? [. . .] What about the vine, and the ocean, what about that? If you cared this much why have you tormented me so about the water . . . when you knew how ashamed I was . . . Crazy, unnatural fear . . . why didn't you try to overcome it, if you love me so much? Answer that!

(*Molly, in a frenzy of despair, starts clawing at her dress, pulling it open.*)

MOLLY: I will. I will. I'll overcome it. I'm sorry. I'll go in the water right away. I'm going now. I'm going . . .

(*Molly rips off her veil and throws it on the wedding table and makes a break for the gate to the ocean. Gertrude in horror grabs Molly's arm and drags her back into the garden.*)

GERTRUDE: Stop it! Come back here at once. Are you insane? Button your dress. They'll see you . . . they'll find you this way and think you're insane . . .

MOLLY: I was going in the water . . .

GERTRUDE: Button your dress. Are you insane! This is what I meant. I've always known it was there, this violence. I've told you again and again that I was frightened. I wasn't sure what I meant . . . I didn't want to be sure. But I was right, there's something heavy and dangerous inside you, like some terrible rock that's ready to explode . . . And it's been getting worse all the time. I can't bear it any more. I've got to get away, out of this garden. That's why I married. That's why I'm going away. (252–53; unbracketed ellipses in the original)

This scene between Gertrude and Molly is the clearest demonstration of the play's insistence on always having it both ways, on setting forth an almost endless circulation of same-sex desires and in the same gesture disavowing them completely. It is driven by the possessive love that each has for the other—a love that dare not speak its name or show its face. It is filled with lines ("I love you!" "Don't go away!" "I didn't think you cared this much") that unmistakably mimic the conventional verbal formulas associated with a showdown between two impassioned lovers, or alternatively (depending on one's point of view) that unmistakably expose those formulas for the stereotypes they are. But even more striking than these outcries is the pivotal position of the summer house in Gertrude's peroration, the summer house that the play uses to construct and secure the oppositions between outside and inside, known and unknown, visible and invisible, the secreted and the revealed, and that it employs as the very figure of interiority. Indeed, Bowles herself underscores the metaphorical status of this architectural curiosity: "The people in my play are all covering up something about themselves. Each of them has her summer house."[29] The image of the summer house as withheld secret is juxtaposed scenically against Molly's attempt to tear off her bridal gown, an action that dramatizes simultaneously the revelation of what lies beneath the flight from marriage, and the even more scandalous notion (in this mother-daughter tête-à-tête) of a sexual invitation. The summer house, moreover, is set off against the ocean and Molly's "crazy, unnatural fear" of water, a fear whose basis is never elucidated. Both Gertrude's accusations and the visual details of this scene thereby dramatize the desublimation of violence, the pathologization of deviance, and the insane fears that are linked to the revelation of sexual and "psychic difficulties" during the most repressive decade of the twentieth century. Even more important, they shine a spotlight on concealment itself only to find it impossible to illuminate. The summer house thus becomes the site of unknowing, darkness, torment, and "crazy, unnatural fear" as well as (in Bowles's words) a "haven" from those very terrors.[30] The wedding scene then has the effect of at once reinforcing the impermeability of the closet and revealing the closet for what it is—that is, the socially constructed site that heterosexuality requires both to contain sexual perversions and to mark itself as normative.

Bowles's insistent habit of disavowal (perhaps even from herself) distinguishes the play from the other postwar closet dramas and insures that it remains, in Williams's words, "quite superbly alone among works for the American theatre." For unlike the plays of Williams or Inge, *In the*

Summer House seems oblivious to what it implies. Certainly, in no other play of the period are familial relationships used to guarantee the preposterousness of an all-too-obvious homoeroticism. Because the latter is rendered impossible before the fact, lesbian desires are able both to proliferate unchecked and to remain invisible. For the act of foreclosure has the paradoxical effect of unleashing all the possibilities that it attempts to close down. It is then hardly a coincidence that Gertrude uses the same strategy in her interpersonal relationships that Bowles uses in the play: she denies what is happening before her eyes precisely because she knows it to be unalterably true. Much like Gertrude, Bowles uses repeated disavowals and erotic triangulations to reassure an obsessively heterosexualized culture that her characters may be "maladjusted," but they're not perverts. Bowles accomplishes this, however, by producing a play—on Broadway, no less!—in which homosexual desires are simultaneously everywhere and nowhere. It is little wonder then that the critics suspected there was something a little queer about the play. But for once, the symptoms of perversion that they may have correctly intuited disappeared whenever they tried to identify them. What they failed to recognize is that the pathology the play uncovers happens to be none other than heterosexuality itself. By so boldly and presumptuously exposing the perverse structure of heterosexuality, the play succeeds brilliantly, some thirty years after Stonewall, in hoodwinking even the most shrewd analyst of queer theater (like Alan Sinfield). By both speaking and refusing to speak the unutterable, by both staging and refusing to stage what cannot be seen, *In the Summer House* reveals itself the symptom of a melancholy heterosexuality, a heterosexuality so infinitely sad because it can never admit to itself that it will always be in mourning.

Chapter Seven

Eat Me

Unable to utter the two words that comprise the impudent title of this chapter, a white slave whispers something else to his black master: "You know what you have to do now?" And the master knows. He silently picks up his slave's fragile body, places it "on a clean-swept table," and devours it. In "twenty-four hours the splintered bones" were licked "clean."[1]

"Desire and the Black Masseur," published in the 1948 volume *One Arm,* is Tennessee Williams's most notorious text. It was doubtlessly the story's brazen representation of homosexuality, cross-race desire, sado-masochism, and cannibalism that led a reviewer in *Time* magazine to note—quite memorably I think—that "this collection of short stories wears the scent of human garbage as if it were the latest Parisian perfume."[2] Deftly linking haute couture with shit, the anonymous critic is eager to assure the reader that he or she, unlike Williams, knows the difference between them. Yet even to draw this link, the critic suggests that he or she has unwittingly been drawn into a certain, let's say, sado-masochistic logic so often in play in and around Williams's most scandalous texts. For despite the claims of political and cultural conservatives, sadomasochistic subjectivities and practices are far more widespread and far more difficult to contain than is often believed. Freud judged them "the most common and the most significant of all the perversions," while Theodor Reik, in a boldly universalizing move, insisted that "traces" of what Freud called moral masochism (in which the connection with sexuality is "loosened") "will be found in the tendencies and behavior of every one of us."[3] Following a different line of argumentation, Kaja Silverman, meanwhile, asserts that masochism is crucial to understanding the articulation of the modern subject because "conventional subjectivity . . . closely adjoins moral masochism."[4] And indeed, it is far more than coincidental that the emergence during the early modern period of masochism (or erotic flagellation) as a distinctive and perverse sexual practice corresponds precisely with the decline of the corporal punishment of children and the rise of the self-disciplining subject. To this extent, it seems to me that masochism is by no means a perversion or form of false consciousness but rather the very ground of subjectivity itself. What could be more masochistic than the dutiful bourgeois subject who is forced to subjugate his or her desires, on the one hand, to the cruel exigencies of the superego and, on the other, to the circulation of capital? But that's another story.

The story I want to tell here concerns the relationship between cannibalism and sadomasochism in Williams's work of the 1940s and 1950s. Why, I am asking, during the height of McCarthyism and the post–World War II boom, are these tropes always conjoined with male homosexuality? What do these linkages tell us not only about Williams's fantasies but, more important, about the culture of which he was a part? What is the power that transmutes pain into pleasure? Why, when an anonymous critic thinks of shit, should Parisian perfume fill the air?

The two texts of Williams that most explicitly foreground cannibalism are "Desire and the Black Masseur," finished in 1946, and *Suddenly Last Summer,* first performed in 1958. Each focuses on the self-destruction of a white man: the one, Anthony Burns, a timid, anonymous, clerk; the other, Sebastian Venable, a poet, aesthete, and ugly American. Each relies on suspense and a shocking and climactic revelation of cannibalism. Each is avowedly allegorical, mixing the literal with the figurative and imagining the death of the protagonist as a sacrificial act, a kind of martyrdom. Each carefully and vividly juxtaposes blinding whiteness against red roses, the red of scarlet fire engines, and the red of blood. Each chooses as agents of death dusky objects of desire who take revenge for real or imagined wrongs. Rather than divide this brief essay between these two texts, I will concentrate on "Desire and the Black Masseur" because it more explicitly dramatizes both the linkages I am interested in pursuing and the sadomasochistic logic that, I believe, unconsciously structures so many of Williams's most troublingly erotic texts.

Employing an omniscient narrator, "Desire and the Black Masseur" tells the story of the self-immolation of Anthony Burns. His submissive temperament is established in the very first sentence, in the narrator's note that "from his very beginning" he "had betrayed an instinct for being included in things that swallowed him up." A man who never felt "secure," he did, however, feel more "secure at the movies than anywhere else": "The darkness absorbed him gently so that he was like a particle of food dissolving in a big hot mouth" (216). One day Burns happens into a Turkish bathhouse employing Negro masseurs who "alone" seem possessed of "authority" (218). Assigned a masseur who "raised up his black palm and brought it down with a terrific whack on the middle of Burns' soft belly," the little man experiences the blow not as pain but as "a feeling of pleasure." As the blows "increased in violence . . . the little man grew more and more fiercely hot with his true satisfaction, until all at once a knot came loose in his loins and released a warm flow" (220). Instantly addicted to the pleasurable pain, Burns returns "time and again," suffering broken ribs and a leg until finally he and the masseur are ejected from the bathhouse ("perverted . . . monster[s]," mumbles the manager), taking refuge in "a room in the town's Negro section." "For a week the passion between them continued," until the narrative culminates in the passage I quoted at the beginning of this chapter. "You know what you have to do now?" Burns asks. And the masseur knows. He silently picks up his slave's fragile body, places it "on a clean-swept table," and devours it. His victim destroyed, the masseur moves "to another city" to await another martyr (221, 223).

In many respects, this story documents what could be called a textbook case of male masochism. Burns's sexual tastes are clearly those that Freud associates with the so-called feminine masochist, whose character Freud—intriguingly—is able to discern only in men because, as Silverman notes, it is "an accepted—indeed a requisite—element of 'normal' female subjectivity."[5] According to Freud, the feminine masochist gets pleasure from "being pinioned, bound, beaten painfully, whipped, . . . forced to obey unconditionally, defiled, degraded," which is to say, from being "placed in a situation characteristic of womanhood, *i.e.,* . . . castrated."[6] Moreover, the narrator's observation that Burns "unconsciously" elects to surrender himself "to violent treatment by others with the idea of thereby clearing [him]self of his guilt" (217) neatly corresponds to Freud's explanation that "a feeling of guilt comes to expression" because it is "assumed that the subject has committed some crime . . . which is to be expiated by his undergoing the pain and torture."[7] Burns is feminized and castrated in relation to the masseur— by his timidity, his small physical stature, his "womanish feet," his status as a petty bourgeois, his taste for pain, and, perhaps most of all, his whiteness (219). The masseur, in contrast, is masculinized and phallicized by his air of "force and resolution," his physical strength, his giantlike stature, his violence, and, most of all, his blackness. I argue in *Communists, Cowboys, and Queers* that throughout Williams's work, as in so many cultural productions of his period (and ours, for that matter), African American men and, more generally, men of color or even dark-complexioned men are insistently produced as hypermasculinized and eroticized figures, which is to say, objects of both desire and fear.[8] With Burns and the masseur placed in a gendered opposition to each other, their relationship, like most S/M scenarios, revises and reconfigures the binarisms that tend to circulate in a heterosexual fantasmatic. But with a difference. For in this scenario, as in so many Williams texts, the feminized one is the one granted the position of desiring subject. He is the one with a history, the one who comes from an identifiably bourgeois world, the one who will most likely be the reader's primary point of identification. And he is white. The masculinized masseur, on the other hand, is produced as an object of desire, the one without a name, the silent one, the consumer, the one whose history remains unknown. He is a tantalizing mystery, a dangerous enigma, an agent of a cruel and violent god: the black man as Other.

In its rush toward immolation, the relationship between Burns and the masseur seems a definitive playing out of masochistic fantasy, which, according to Reik, always produces a highly ritualized and symbolic "scene" that "corresponds . . . to the staging of a drama."[9] It is little wonder, then, that this intensely theatricalized scene would appeal to a playwright. For S/M practitioners are always playwrights, compulsively and carefully staging their minidramas in such a way that pain will be neatly transmuted into pleasure. Yet one of the most striking features of Williams's story is the virtual absence of motivation for this minidrama. The fantasies that would seem to be animating the characters are never spelled out. There is almost no dialogue. Rather, images and actions come almost cinematically to substitute for narrativization. The omniscient narrator is turned into a voyeur, a silent spectator (not unlike Burns himself at the movies), and the intensely privatized passions of the masochist are made fodder for the narrative spectacle.

In some respects, the highly spectacularized realm that the little clerk and his masseur inhabit is starkly black and white. Yet for Burns and the world in which he passes, whiteness is ideological, the sign of both fullness and emptiness, aceticism and luxury, the sacred and the profane. In the bathhouse the "white-collar clerk" is stripped of his bourgeois accessories and draped in "white fabric," walks "barefooted along the moist white tiles," and passes through the "white curtains" to lie on a "bare white table" (218–20). At the end of the story the only things that remain of him are his "bare white bones." The masseur, meanwhile, is insistently blackened and mystified. He seems "very dark" against the white fabric, a "black giant" who, the narrator notes, "hated white-skinned bodies because they abused his pride" (218–20). While this last observation recalls perhaps the antiracist stance that Williams often adopted in interviews, it puts the emphasis more on privatized emotions than on the social institutions that produce racism. It suggests that racism (and the opposition to racism) is more a personal—and sexual—project than a political one (which of course it was for many Americans before *Brown v. Board of Education* and the birth of the modern civil rights movement). The characterization of the masseur also comes perilously close to evoking the fantasy of the vengeful black male rapist that has been used so successfully as a justification for lynching and other forms of racist violence.

I want to shift for a moment to a psychoanalytical register in part because I want to analyze how whiteness and blackness function as erotic placeholders within the narrative. Whiteness for Williams is associated with the restless and contradictory nature of desire, and blackness with what Lacan calls *objet a,* that which stands in for the object of satisfaction. Like the imperial and imperious whiteness that is its sign, the little clerk's desire is marked by an insistent narrative tumescence; it is "so much too big for him that it swallowed him up" (217). An erotic analogy for whiteness—the mixture of every color of light—it is a swelling immensity, an exorbitance that crushes and overwhelms the subject. Blackness, in contrast, is associated with satiety, with the "dark picture house" in which Anthony Burns finds satisfaction and with the masseur (216). It is dangerous and ultimately fatal. Both white and black, in other words, are imagined in this text as being in essence erotic categories. "Desire and the Black Masseur" thus attempts finally—and troublingly—to depoliticize and metaphysicalize race. This move becomes particularly clear in the final paragraph, in which the narrative turns precipitously from the drama of the masseur to that of "the earth's whole population," which "twisted and writhed beneath the manipulation of night's black fingers and the white ones of day with skeletons splintered and flesh reduced to pulp." In the end, black and white are allegorized as the world is reimagined in terms of an unresolved opposition between white masochism and black sadism, out of which "the answer, perfection, was slowly evolved through torture" (223). At the same time that the narrative produces a black and white allegory, it is unable to expunge a third term, a trace of red running through the text: the "red neon sign" of the bathhouse, the red of "the Rose of the World as He bled on the cross," the red of the flames of a burning house, the "scarlet" fire engines, and of course the red of the blaze inscribed in Anthony Burns's very name (217, 222). Disrupting the play of binary oppositions, red is rendered sacred, marking the violence of sacrifice, death, consumption, dismemberment, cannibalism.

The ending of the story attempts both to universalize the blaze of saintly Anthony Burns and, by means of a reference to Christ's passion, to present it as part of a sacred process. For the room to which the masseur has moved his charge stands opposite a black church from "whose open windows spilled out the mounting exhortations of a preacher." Since the season happens to be the end of Lent, Burns and the masseur hear retold the sacrifice of him who "was nailed on a cross for the sins of the world" (222). Williams thus explicitly draws a parallel between his hapless white-collar clerk and a more celebrated sacrificial lamb. As a result of this comparison, the devouring of Burns's body is figured as a kind of eucharist. (Williams's emphasis on the theological and ritualistic aspects of the narrative represents perhaps his attempt to position this story as a quasi-sacred, highbrow text whose elevated position in the cultural hierarchy will excuse, and even justify, such hyperbolic sexual perversity.) Yet the cannibalization of Burns also represents the culmination of the masochistic narrative. For as Freud explains, "The erotogenic type of masochism passes through all of the developmental stages of the libido," the oral, anal, phallic, and genital.[10] In the first stage, the oral, it is manifest in "the fear of being devoured by the totem-animal (father)," a fear that, like all fears, cloaks desire. Expanding on Freud, Reik documents a number of cannibalistic fantasies among his masochistic subjects and notes that they "sometimes appear more unconcealed with men" than with women.[11] I would like to suggest here that cannibalism functions not as a break with the rest of the narrative but rather as the oral manifestation and end of this sado-masochistic logic. It simultaneously represents the dissolution of the subject and the fulfillment of Burns's desires, which, as I noted earlier, have from the beginning been conceptualized in oral terms: he delights most, after all, in being swallowed up (216).

What is perhaps most remarkable about Williams's retelling of this masochistic fantasy in his cool, lean, gothic prose is the mutual imbrication of desire and horror. This imbrication certainly connects the narrative to the Burkean concept of the sublime that Robert Gross so compellingly details in his analysis of *Suddenly Last Summer.*[12] I would like, however, to take issue with Gross's emphasis, following Deleuze's theory of masochism, on the mother-son relationship. For it seems to me that both Williams texts come much closer to supporting the Freudian model of male masochism, which privileges the father-son relationship and understands masochism as a reactivation of the Oedipus complex. In "Desire and the Black Masseur" the masseur is figured simultaneously as a cruel and loving father who must be appeased by the infantilized Burns and as a stand-in and delegate for a violent god. In *Suddenly Last Summer* Sebastian similarly imagines a relationship with a violent father:

> CATHARINE: completing—a sort of!—*image!*—he had of himself as
>   a sort of!—*sacrifice* to a!—*terrible* sort of a—
> DOCTOR: —God?[13]

In both texts the masochistic proclivities of the protagonists lead the subject, as Freud notes, to create "a temptation to 'sinful acts' which must then be expiated by . . . the chastisement from the great parental authority of Fate. In order to provoke punishment from the parent-substitute the masochist must do something inexpedient, . . . ruin the prospects which the real world offers him, and possibly destroy his own existence in the world of reality."[14] Both Anthony Burns and Sebastian

Venable are sacrificed to terrible fathers, dismembered and consumed to expiate their imagined sins.

Yet what, you may be wondering, are their sins? On the one hand, Burns, by virtue of being transformed into a sacrificial victim, is universalized into an exemplar of "the earth's whole population" (223), while Sebastian is on a frantic search "for God" (17). And the very names of both characters evoke widely venerated saints: Anthony a hallucination-prone mystic and Sebastian, with his luminous body pierced by arrows (in so many Italian Renaissance paintings at least), the very model of a Christian martyr and a homoerotic icon. On the other hand, both characters may be seen simultaneously to be minoritized by their sexual desires and practices. And here I am thinking less of their penchant for pain than of their desire for persons of the same sex. The intense homophobia of the domestic revival of the late 1940s and 1950s, which violently pathologized and criminalized lesbians and gay men, has been well documented, and I will not rehearse it here. But I would like to emphasize the profound psychic toll of this pathologization on all those who happen to be homosexual and yet who, efficiently interpellated into culture, imagine homosexual persons—like themselves—to be depraved. During the heyday of McCathyism, queers were (and still are to some extent) produced as abjected beings, those, in Judith Butler's estimation, "who are not yet 'subjects,' but who form the constitutive outside to the domain of the subject." Taking up "those 'unlivable' and 'uninhabitable' zones of social life," they suffered (and still suffer) socially, politically, and psychically.[15] Yet what is perhaps most striking to me about both of these Williams texts is the curious way that abjection is ghosted by a sense of bliss, or, in the extraordinary words of Mrs. Venable, the way that "the shadow was almost as luminous as the light" (21). It is precisely this undecidability between light and darkness, between black and white, between abjection and bliss, that is incessantly played out in what I am tempted to call the queer white male fantasmatic of the 1940s and 1950s, one that swings unpredictably between intense pain and pleasure, yet in which the two positions are finally revealed to be virtually interchangeable.

Consider Williams next to two other writers with whom he is rarely associated: William Burroughs and Allen Ginsberg. Are not *Naked Lunch* and "Howl" as deeply committed to enacting this undecidability as these two texts of Williams? Think, for example, of the orgasmic hanging sequences in *Naked Lunch* or of Ginsberg's notorious lines: "I saw the best minds of my generation . . . / let themselves be fucked in the ass by saintly motorcyclists, and screamed with joy."[16] How else is one to understand the ecstasy in all these texts, which proceeds from and, indeed, is predicated upon abasement? This is by no means to suggest that sadomasochism and homosexuality are synonymous or that one causes the other. But it is to acknowledge the fact that during this period, in a wide variety of cultural productions, especially in elite or avant-gardist cultures, homosexual desires and subjectivities more often than not play themselves out through gorgeously sadomasochistic fantasies.

There is, finally, one more ingredient I want to toss into this stew of homosexuality, sadomasochism, and cannibalism. For in evaluating the relationship between and among these figurations, one must consider a relative novelty of the late 1940s and 1950s: the consumerism that fueled the postwar economic boom. As David Harvey observes, "Postwar Fordism has to be seen . . . less as a mere system of mass production and more as a total way of life. Mass production meant standardization of product as well as mass consumption."[17] With the giddy institutionalization of commodity culture after the war, one sees a shift in emphasis in a great many cultural texts from relations of production to those of consumption. And it seems to me that this new focus on the consumer, and indeed on the very act of consumption, is played out in a rather original and startling way in these two Williams texts. Catharine Holly is thus quite correct when she insists that her "tale" of Sebastian's death is no mere fiction but "a true story of our time and the world we live in" (47). The terrible truth that both texts reveal is that within consumer culture it is the consumer him- or herself who is finally consumed by the very act of consumption. As Marx famously observes about what he calls the fetishism of commodities, "It is nothing but the definite social relation between men themselves which assumes [in the commodity] . . . the fantastic form of a relation between things."[18] Within consumer culture, production, like Anthony Burns himself, is swallowed up by consumption, the producer by the things that he or she produces. The one comes to substitute for the other, in the same way that (for one critic at least) Parisian perfume comes to substitute for shit.

The violent reciprocity that exists between these two spheres brings to mind another extravagant artifact of the postwar boom, this time Roger Corman's 1960 film, *The Little Shop of Horrors*. In the film, an eager young amateur botanist develops a man-eating plant named Audrey who, astonishingly, also has the capacity for speech. The two words it utters are the complement to the two words that comprise the title of this essay: "Feed me." A nightmare version of the vagina dentata, Audrey consumes human beings in order to live. She thereby dramatizes the fears and desires that the consumer might have wanted to whisper lovingly to the commodity: feed me, don't eat me; nourish me, don't consume me. For animating Audrey's fervid flesh are the same fantasies that underwrite both "Desire and the Black Masseur" and *Suddenly Last Summer,* the same terror of being consumed by the very commodities that we so desperately and compulsively desire. "Nourish me, feed me," the hungry postwar subject pleads. To which the commodity responds: "The more of me you consume, the more fully I will possess you. Eat me . . . at your peril."

Chapter Eight

In and Out

The year 1997 could well be remembered as the one in which Hollywood came out. After the success of dozens of independent gay and lesbian films, the major studios finally awoke to the fact that not everyone in America is straight. And TV, somewhat uncharacteristically, led the way. The fictional Ellen Morgan wrestled with her sexuality on prime time while the real Ellen DeGeneres (usually with then-girlfriend Anne Heche in tow) toured the talk-show circuit, posed with President Clinton, and was named *Entertainment Weekly*'s Entertainer of the Year. Riding its initial high and rallying liberal supporters, *Ellen* proved for one short year that coming out can actually improve a TV show.

But gay men, both in feature films and on TV, were strangely elusive in those antediluvian days when *Will and Grace* was just a twinkle in a producer's eye. We may be everywhere, as the saying goes, but in Hollywood, both onscreen and off, we remained far more retiring—and closeted—than our proud sisters. During the fall season, however, when Hollywood's most prestigious films are released, our images multiplied unexpectedly on the screens at the local multiplex. In the wake of *The Birdcage*'s success, three major-studio releases featured gay male characters in leading roles. *In and Out, Midnight in the Garden of Good and Evil,* and *As Good as It Gets* present gay men as, if not exactly ordinary people, then at least colorful and ubiquitous players on the contemporary American scene. And while all three films clearly show gay sexual identities to be incontestably different from a heterosexual norm, all implicitly or explicitly urge tolerance and a healthy respect for diversity. All thereby attest to what Hollywood likes to consider its liberalism, open-heartedness, and embrace of difference. A mere thirty-six years after the demise of the Motion Picture Production Code, the movies, it would seem, finally discovered that gay men are neither psychopaths nor box-office poison.

In fact, however, these three films are, I believe, far more ambivalent representations than Hollywood and most of its critics would like to think. Take, for example, *In and Out,* arguably the canniest of the three and the only one to foreground not only the social and personal traumas connected with coming out but also the very codes that film and television have used to represent gay men. As written by Paul Rudnick, one of the few openly gay screenwriters, the film centers on Howard Brackett (Kevin Kline) coming to terms with his sexual identity after being outed by a former student at the Academy Awards ceremony. Subjected to the relentless scrutiny of the media, his townsfolk, and his family, the chaste Howard initially denies the opprobrious charge but ends up coming out in the most public way imaginable, at his wedding (much to the chagrin, it hardly need be said, of his long-suffering fiancée). Although summarily fired from his teaching job, he is finally reinstated when, at high-school graduation, all the townsfolk, led by an appreciative student, confess one by one that they too are gay. This final (and, it must be said, rather sentimental, if moving) scene, coupled with the wedding reception that Howard's mother engineers for herself, signals the utopian acceptance of Howard's now-benign sexual difference by his community and, by implication, the traditional, small-town America his community so clearly emblematizes. Countering the long-held assumption that homosexuality belongs behind locked doors, and standing up to the religious right's attacks on the allegedly corrupting influence of homosexually predatory teachers, the film suggests that gay men, as upstanding citizens and exemplary educators, can be at home in the public sphere.

In its challenge to the distinction between public and private, *In and Out* deftly performs the oscillation signified by its title. But, like *As Good as It Gets,* it does so at a considerable price—by completely desexualizing gay men. Howard comes out not because he experiences desire for another man (sexual desire and passion, both films assure us, are always already the prerogatives of heterosexuals) but by confronting his unquenchable thirst for disco, Broadway musicals, and Barbra Streisand—

that is, the cultural markers stereotypically associated with gay men. And while the film trades rather ingeniously on these markers, its only homosexual act, the agonizingly long kiss that Peter (Tom Selleck, of all people) plants on a squirming, resistant Howard, is a comic tour de force, not a sign of eros. The gay man, then, that the film manages finally to embrace and proudly universalize is an unmistakably scrubbed, middle-class, virginal, white professional—in short, an exemplary citizen whom even the Pope could love.

Yet the invisibility of homosexual desire in *In and Out* and *As Good as It Gets* does not mean that it was absent from the silver screen. *Midnight in the Garden of Good and Evil,* adapted from John Berendt's best-selling chronicle, manages rather neatly to produce sexualized gay men in the persons of Jim Williams (Kevin Spacey, who loudly and relentlessly proclaims his presumed heterosexuality in the popular press), the rich, reckless, and closeted Southern gentleman; his tough, working-class hustler beau, who seems to have wandered in from a Genet novel; and the strange and seductive Lady Chablis (as played by herself), an extravagant black drag queen, virtually the only kind of gay African American male who doesn't fly below Hollywood's radar. These variously pathological, criminal, and exotic creatures are set in opposition against a safely heterosexualized version of the book's narrator and his flirtatious girlfriend. The film, in other words, manages to portray gay men as desiring subjects only by reaching back into a mythologized past, into the gothic elegance and mystery of aristocratic Southern culture—in short, by resuscitating the closet drama (think *Suddenly Last Summer*). Mobilizing all the conventions of the form, it revels in evasions, furtive cravings, innuendoes, withheld secrets, and homocidal passions. And its plot, propelled by the machinations of a closeted gay man, ends in a literal or symbolic death understood to be both the inevitable cost of desire and the wages of sin.

Yet *Midnight* was by no means the only film of the fall to resurrect this by no means dead formula. In fact, two rather more critically acclaimed movies also made use of the conventions of the closet drama. *L.A. Confidential,* honored as best picture of the year by numerous critics' circles, is an elegantly brutal film noir. And film noir, as Richard Dyer and other critics have argued, is a form long associated with both femmes fatales and dangerous men coded either implicitly or explicitly as gay (think

Strangers on a Train). Although centered around a heterosexual love affair, *L.A. Confidential* is filled with men who have sex—or are suspected
of having sex—with other men, from the corrupt district attorney, to the
struggling young actor he murders, to the African American hoods
framed by the LAPD. One of the film's heroes, Jack (Kevin Spacey again),
seen with only one woman (dubbed an "ingenue dyke"), seems unusually
knowledgeable about L.A.'s hidden gay subculture, is clearly marked by
the personal mannerisms that film noir uses to code gay men, and is conveniently dispatched before the end of the film. Even the two protagonists
are locked in a homophobic/homoerotic struggle over the femme fatale
so obvious to her that she must reassure one before bedding him: "Fucking me and fucking Bud aren't the same thing." And true to stereotype,
the source of contamination in the end turns out to be the closeted,
homicidal D.A.

Yet as closet dramas go, *L.A. Confidential* pales next to a film whose
flagrantly queer subtext was noted by not a single critic. Set in the not-
too-distant future, *Gattaca* imagines a dystopian world in which the ge-
netically engineered majority keep their inferiors as menials. The im-
perfect Vincent (Ethan Hawke), however, rebels against this order and
plots to trade identities with a wheelchair-bound former star swimmer,
Jerome (Jude Law), so that he can qualify for an expedition to Titan, Sat-
urn's largest moon. Taking up a new identity, Vincent becomes the im-
perfect replica of the perfect Jerome in a relationship that unmistakably
echoes Vincent's envious and competitive rapport with his own geneti-
cally engineered brother. Trading places, becoming narcissistic doubles
of each other (much like Dorian Gray and his picture), the two outsiders
make a great couple: "You look so right together!" Moreover, the film
makes it clear that the swimmer has fallen for the astronaut, a suspicion
that is confirmed at the end when Jerome immolates himself as his twin
blasts off for Titan. And while Uma Thurman gives an incandescent performance as Vincent's romantic interest, she remains, as one critic put it,
strangely superfluous to what is unmistakably a tragic love story between two men.

What makes *Gattaca* so interesting and novel as a closet drama,
though, are its fantasies about science. For the film's obsessions intersect
almost too neatly with the well-publicized debates during the late 1990s
over the supposed existence of a "gay gene." Moreover, the methods of

genetic surveillance clearly position this film as a post-AIDS fantasy. The Gattaca Corporation constantly monitors the bodily refuse and fluids of its employees: hair, dandruff, blood, and urine. And much of the film's considerable dramatic tension results from anxiety over the proper exchange of bodily fluids between the two men, which must be done in precisely the right way lest disaster ensue. Imagining a world in which a misplaced drop of blood or one stray eyelash is enough to produce personal catastrophe or death, *Gattaca* redefines and updates the conventions of the closet drama. Moreover, its use of these conventions is underscored by the fact that this very stylish film is set in a kind of retro-future, a future that reads as a technologized version of the 1950s (the era, not coincidentally, of the most celebrated closet dramas and films noirs). And the choice of Gore Vidal to play the film's villain serves to remind us that he is the author of a seminal 1946 work with its own pair of narcissistic doubles, *The City and the Pillar,* which both codified the conventions of the postwar homosexual novel and spelled out the allure and danger of the closet.

So what are we to make of 1997 being the year in which gay men in Hollywood both came out of the closet and beat a panicked retreat back in? How to reconcile *Gattaca* with *In and Out*? Like our lesbian sisters before us, gay men are becoming increasingly visible not only in Hollywood but also in the public sphere. *In and Out* (and later *Will and Grace*) provide proof that gay men have now joined the list of benign social deviants who can provide the fodder for farcical comedies. *As Good as It Gets,* meanwhile, demonstrates in the person of Simon (Greg Kinnear) that gay men are cute, passive, long-suffering creatures just waiting to be inspired and redeemed by the affection—and aestheticized flesh—of a good woman. Despite these compromised representations, this new visibility could be a gauge of real social progress. And since films do far more than mechanically reflect the social order, these two must also be seen as potentially powerful ways of promulgating antihomophobic attitudes, of convincing the good people of Anytown, USA, that gay men and lesbians make good citizens. Of course, in order to pass as good citizens we must be compliant and forego our pleasures. We may not desire. We dare not have sex. And it helps if we happen to be middle-class, white, and male. Under these conditions, we will be invited to take our seats at America's multicultural smorgasbord. We will be invited to share in the delights that await us at the resplendent table, the delights whose consumption confirms our identity as good citizens, which is to say, good consumers.

Those of us who choose not to follow in the footsteps of Howard and Simon can expect to end up like the victims of films noirs and other closet dramas. For if nothing else, this nostalgia for the dramas and tragedies of the closet, coming as it did hot on the heels of Ellen's outing, testifies to the dogged persistence of homophobic fears even as antidiscrimination laws continued to be passed and the Supreme Court struck down Colorado's attempt to nullify civil rights protection for homosexuals. This nostalgia, like Hollywood's mid-1990s fascination with killer lesbians (vide *Basic Instinct, Single White Female, Heavenly Creatures,* and *Bound*), testifies to the fact that the homophobic tropes and stereotypes of fifty years ago are very much alive in our national fantasies today, that gay men and lesbians, especially those whose perversions are believed to threaten the social and economic order, are routinely pathologized and killed off. The resuscitation of the closet drama represents, then, the other side of the new visibility of gay men and is a sign of the wish that we queers would just go away, that we would retire again to the closet and play out our tragic dramas in the privacy of our own homes. Yet at the same time, we must recall that this resuscitation also represents a distinctive cinematic strategy that, in a Hollywood overrun by increasingly banal and formulaic product, allows for the construction of a drama haunted by the past, a symbolic drama, above all a drama with highbrow pretensions. As such, it is a sign of nostalgia for Hollywood's days of glory, before the 1960s and the demise of the studio system. For the closeted gay man, like the femme fatale (now renovated in the person of the killer lesbian), is a slightly antiquated figure whose very presence lends a touch of mystery, art, and class and is a mark of a filmmaker's serious ambitions. He is fashioned the emblem of the natural and the artificial, the masculine and the feminine, the normal and the inexplicable, the revealed and the hidden—in short, of art itself.

Yet life has a curious way of copying art. And 1997's closet dramas were eerily replicated by those narratives and images involving criminalized gay men that were splashed across the pages of the media: Andrew Cunanan's killing spree, assumed initially (and wrongly) to be the result of his supposed seropositivity; the Heaven's Gate mass suicide, blamed on the repressed homosexuality of the cult's leader, Marshall Applewhite; and the sensationalized and alarmist coverage given the news that some gay men are barebacking (having sex without condoms). As if they had been scripted by the writers of *L.A. Confidential* or *Gattaca*, these events were packaged so as to capitalize on the fear that gay men are sex-crazed sociopaths who can barely control their homicidal and suicidal impulses and can be treated (like Applewhite) only by castration. Given the pervasiveness of this fear, it is little wonder that Howard and Simon can be redeemed only by being desexualized, which is to say, castrated. Yet the narrative of *As Good as It Gets* proves, perhaps inadvertently, that even the desexualized gay man may fall prey to violence, may become the victim of the sex-crazed sociopath who represents his out-of-control double. This relationship was tacitly acknowledged in those media accounts during the summer of 1997 that constructed the murdered Gianni Versace as the "good," monogamous homosexual struck down by his "bad," promiscuous Other. This narrative thereby dramatizes a deconstruction of the opposition between the real and the fictional. For Cunanan's real-life crime spree (whose reportage was so clearly modelled on pre-Stonewall fictions) has become the fodder for even more cinematic fictions that masquerade as truth. A&E released an hour-long documentary on Cunanan in 1999, while Cinemax scheduled a second one for its Reel Life series in 2001. Real life or reel life, indeed! And after that, who knows? Maybe Paul Rudnick will pen a little post-closet drama entitled *Down and Out,* in which Howard Brackett moves to San Francisco, trades in his Barbra Streisand records for nipple clamps, but never learns (to borrow that old homophobic adage) to cover his ass.

Chapter Nine

Paula Vogel as Male Impersonator

If, as an impressionable young woman, Paula Vogel had not discovered John Waters's movies and his greatest star, Divine, she might have had to invent them. For Paula has long been fascinated by drag in all its many guises. This fascination is a result of her belief that gender is a kind of floating signifier that can attach itself to bodies and texts in unpredictable ways. Her belief in gender's transferability, moreover, is linked to her understanding of the very being of performance, which she knows is more likely to destabilize than fix identities, and of drama, which she knows to be the most dialogical of all literary forms. Her belief, however, does not in any way deny the tyranny of gendered norms. On the contrary. Paula will be the first to admit the crushing authority of convention. "Every time a male character walks on the stage," she notes, "whether it's a bit role or it's [a] David Mamet [character], he is trailing the mantle of Hamlet." On the other hand, "when a woman character walks on stage, she's trailing Gertrude or Ophelia or Lady Macbeth."[1] Yet this situation is by no means immutable. Because people must learn to be readers and spectators (and playwrights, for that matter), and because all conventions are historically produced and thus changeable, both people and conventions can be transformed. After all, "all subjects," as Paula insists, "are impeachable. That's the great thing about drama." Drama by its nature has the power to de-essentialize:

"There is no 'there' there. There's no authenticity. There's no absolute truth, it's who's in the room."[2]

The first room that Paula and I shared in which we had the delicious opportunity to watch Divine cavort in a playpen with a mountain of dead fish was at Cornell University more than a quarter-century ago. Paula took me to see *Pink Flamingos* and *Female Trouble,* two films that would forever change my life. (Paula has regularly been my teacher, both during and after Cornell.) Our excursion to the movies occurred just a few weeks after we two first-year graduate students had shyly come out to each other and had begun trying to live the gay life in Ithaca. Although Paula was certainly not the first lesbian I had met, she was the first to initiate me in the mysteries and wonders of feminism, drag, and gay liberation—all three of which came together in the most stunning way in John Waters's early masterpieces. From the moment that Divine heaved her parents into the Christmas tree, I knew that we would long share a deep, abiding passion for the most fierce drag queen of all time. But while we could agree on John Waters, our opinions sometimes clashed over playwrights, chief among them Bertolt Brecht. I would passionately defend Brecht, the writer who introduced me to Marxism and theories of cultural politics, while Paula remained ambivalent. She more often than not expressed her appreciation for Brecht's theories of epic theater but found his antifeminist attitudes and practices somewhat distasteful.

Some twenty-five years later, Paula still loves Divine and still maintains "a love/hate relationship" with Brecht. Although she admires his critique of the canons of realism and his theory of estrangement (*Verfremdung*), she is rightfully indignant at his unashamed theft of the concept from Viktor Shklovsky. And she has some serious reservations about his attempts to distantiate and estrange historical events and characters. She, in contrast, favors a more empathic approach (which she obviously did not learn from John Waters), preferring to lead audiences to sympathize with figures, both historical and otherwise, they might otherwise find abhorrent.[3] She is most intent on reeducating spectators. Her deeply conflicted response to Brecht—who had precisely the same goal—is, I believe, far more than a quirk of personal taste. It is in fact quite revealing of Paula's own strategies as a playwright. Even the phrase she uses to describe that response—"love-hate relationship"—betrays a kind of doubleness, a sense of playing both sides at the same time, that,

I believe, leaves its mark in virtually all of her plays. Like Brecht's epic theater, her work is rooted in a tradition of theatrical realism that she works assiduously to critique and undermine. Like Brecht, she is insistent on revealing the historicity and the ideological predispositions of those things that most members of the theatergoing class take for granted. Like Brecht, she relishes the political potential in the formalist concept of defamiliarization.

Where Paula differs most provocatively from her illustrious predecessor is in her production of gendered differences, in her position vis-à-vis a long tradition of what might be called patriarchal playwriting, and—related to these—in the mode of address she uses as a writer. Unlike Brecht, she is an avowed feminist, and all her plays are centered around female characters who trail "Gertrude or Ophelia or Lady Macbeth" behind them. But beyond this rather generalized observation, she is as difficult to pin down as her writing. This is in part because of her penchant for multiple points of identification and her fondness for (if you'll pardon the contradiction) a kind of dialectical polemicism. She delights in using different dramatic styles, even within a single play. From the deconstructionist personal narrative of *How I Learned to Drive* to the farce of *The Mineola Twins,* from the lyrical realism of *The Oldest Profession* to the surrealism of *Hot 'n' Throbbing,* Paula has experimented restlessly with dramatic forms and conventions. And like so many of Brecht's mature plays, most of her own make use of a narrative voice: Anna in *The Baltimore Waltz,* Li'l Bit in *How I Learned to Drive,* Myra and Myrna in *The Mineola Twins,* and the several bodied and disembodied narrators in *Hot 'n' Throbbing.* Yet this catalog suggests that Paula's narrative voices, unlike Brecht's, are both multiple and predominantly female. Although one can't miss the multiple narrators in the last two plays, *The Baltimore Waltz,* too, represents a performance of doubleness and surrogacy. Anna, at some distance from herself and her desires, "stand[s] in" and ventriloquizes for both herself and Carl in much the same way that these two fictional siblings stand in and ventriloquize for Paula and her late brother Carl.[4] In *Drive,* Li'l Bit is explicitly split into different selves, her several younger and older selves and, most crucially, the innocent self who once "lived in [her] body" and the older, objectified self who, after being touched by her Uncle Peck, "retreated above the neck."[5] And as in most plays with multiple selves and points of view, one can never be certain who is speaking. In *Drive*, the members of the Greek Chorus impersonate a number of different characters, while in *Hot 'n' Throbbing*, the Voice-Over both speaks and does not—cannot—speak for Charlene. The production of multiple selves will always problematize and undermine the autonomy of the subject.

If the doubled characters in Paula's plays are both questioning and assertive, reckless and judicious, seductive and suspicious of erotic pleasure, they are oddly reminiscent of the most distinctive of Brecht's own split characters: Shen Te and Shui Ta in *The Good Person of Setzuan*. In this parable, Brecht uses the split subject (as authored by Shen Te herself) to dramatize the schizophrenia that capitalism inevitably produces: because one cannot prosper in a market economy and remain good, one is involuntarily split into a bad half that exploits others and a good half that embodies Brecht's—and Marx's—notion of innate human benevolence. The good self manufactures her bad twin initially in an act of desperate improvisation. But she soon realizes that she cannot do without the practical part of the self and in the end is literally held hostage by her entrepreneurial double, not unlike a Dr. Frankenstein (in another myth about the production of the modern subject) who becomes the casualty of the very monster he has fabricated. This tragic separation between Shen Te and Shui Ta, between pleasure and survival, is itself an echo of a divided self in an earlier Brecht play, *The Seven Deadly Sins*, whose doubled protagonist is split between the rational, practical Anna I and the passionate, hedonistic Anna II. Much like the Mineola twins (identical "except in the chestal area"), with their very different attitudes toward pleasure, the two Annas dramatize the necessarily self-defeating subject produced by those puritanical moral systems that, preferring the hoarding of *jouissance* to its expense, have historically been linked to capitalist modes of accumulation.[6]

Despite the obvious kinship between *The Seven Deadly Sins* and *The Mineola Twins* (including both plays' resemblance to a psychomachia), I want to return to a consideration of *The Good Person* because of the way it links human labor, morality, and gender. Unlike the other two plays, with their female protagonists, *The Good Person* underlines the fact that good and bad correspond to a gendered opposition in capitalist—and patriarchal—societies. The feminine (almost collapsed here into the maternal) is routinely regarded as altruistic, nurturing, and self-sacrificing.

The masculine, on the other hand, is imagined as acquisitive, aggressive, and selfish. Men accomplish things; women represent accomplishments. Men (like Shui Ta) assert themselves in prose; women (like Shen Te) prefer a kind of poetic indirection. Despite its seeming inflexibility, even this rather stereotypical polarization is problematized insofar as the play reveals that Shui Ta is authored by a woman who is authored by a man. *The Good Person* thereby ends up, I believe, exposing the construction and social function of gendered norms. It demonstrates both the error and the efficacy of this bipolarity, or, if one prefers, its historicity.

I would like to argue here that Paula, as a playwright, uses a strategy uncannily similar to Shen Te's. Dissatisfied with the limitations imposed upon her by a patriarchal society, dramaturgical tradition, and institutional structure, she has predicated her own feminist practices on a kind of male impersonation. Recognizing the power and pervasiveness of a masculine mystique, especially in theatrical circles, she has learned how, as a feminist, to write *like* a man. And in emphasizing this metaphorical link, I want to insist that this relation is not one of copy to original but one of copy to a copy that masquerades as original. For there is nothing essentially and unchangingly masculine in writing styles associated with Sophocles, Shakespeare, or Shaw. When I argue that she writes like a man, I mean to say that she imitates—with a difference—the strategies that male playwrights have long used. In some cases, as with *Desdemona*, *Meg*, and *And Baby Makes Seven*, she deliberately appropriates and re-imagines major patriarchal texts: *Othello*, *A Man for All Seasons*, and *Who's Afraid of Virginia Woolf?*, respectively. *Hot 'n' Throbbing*, meanwhile, represents a damning appraisal of the paradigmatically masculinist character of literary modernism (from D. H. Lawrence to Henry Miller, James Joyce to Vladimir Nabakov), as well as a critique of those playwrights, like John Patrick Shanley and David Mamet, whose work romanticizes violence against women. And Charlene herself practices a kind of male impersonation. In a play that is so clearly about the material effects of writing, it is no accident that her pornography represents a parodic redeployment of a genre on which men have long held a monopoly, much as Paula's own playwriting represents a revision and repossession of a highly masculinized textual practice.

It is no secret that playwriting has been dominated more completely by men than the composition of any other performing art—with the possible exception of what has regrettably been christened classical music. In most traditional theater histories (at least the ones Paula and I studied in graduate school), Aphra Behn is the only woman playwright before the twentieth century usually judged a major figure. Lynda Hart rightly describes the difficulty that women playwrights have had historically entering the public sphere: "The theatre is the sphere most removed from the confines of domesticity, thus the woman who ventures to be heard in this space takes a greater risk than the woman poet or novelist."[7] The place for women in the theater before the twentieth century was on stage—once they were given leave to perform, that is. From Ophelia to Hedda Gabler, Antigone to Mother Courage, women have been the spectacularized, suffering heroines in many canonical playtexts. Paula herself explains the difference: "I knew I wanted to be in the theater. But it never occurred to me that I'd write plays. Girls just didn't think in those terms. The assumption was if you were interested in drama, then clearly you wanted to be an actress."[8] And as Hart notes, the history of theater and even the etymology of the word have long rendered the woman playwright an oxymoron. "The *theatron*, the place of viewing," has made her at best "anomalistic," or at worst, "when visible," "deviant."[9]

Writing at the end of the 1980s, Hart prescribes subversion as the remedy for the marginalization of the woman playwright. She reacts against the attempts of many 1970s cultural feminists (and lesbian-feminists, in particular) to produce a uniquely woman-centered theater by recognizing that the celebration of formerly reviled characteristics simply inverts and thereby perpetuates patriarchal hierarchical structures. Inversion does not in itself fundamentally alter oppressive formations. Like many of her comrades in arms reared on Derrida and the French feminists, she urges the writer not to seize a stage that was never hers in the first place but "to analyze . . . and disrupt . . . the ideological codes embedded in the inherited structures of dramatic representation." By doing so, women playwrights have the opportunity of "canceling and deforming the structures that have held women framed, stilled, embedded, [and] revoking the forms that have misrepresented women." Like many of her contemporaries (most notably, Sue-Ellen Case, Elin Diamond, and Jill Dolan), Hart considers theatrical realism particularly insidious for its tendency to reinforce and reify sexual subjugation. The power to deform must therefore come from offstage, from the wingspace: "When the understudies seize the stage, when the stagehands come out from the wings and address the audience, Reality is exposed as illusionism and the woman playwright can begin to be heard."[10] According to the tenets of late 1980s/early 1990s feminism, the excluded ones are uniquely well suited to expose mimesis, realism, and reality for the oppressive fictions they are.

Those plays of Paula's with early drafts that date from the mid-1970s, *Meg* and *Desdemona,* tend to use dramatic strategies much like those outlined by Hart. Both center around female characters (Sir Thomas More's daughter, Meg, and Shakespeare's strangled heroine) who are marginalized in the approved—that is, masculinist—narratives that are the subject of Paula's critique. Her dramatic strategy is to give each a more articulate voice, if less political and social power, then her male antagonists. But unlike more orthodox 1970s cultural feminists, Paula does not invert Shakespeare's misogynist fable and celebrate a virginal martyr. On the contrary, she makes Desdemona much more the high-class whore than the bumptious Othello could ever imagine. By so fiercely parroting both the violent class distinctions and the misogyny of the original (while avoiding Shakespearean vocabulary and syntax), Paula does not so much invert as expose (to ridicule?) the systems of domination that Shakespeare takes for granted.

Paula's later plays, however, modify the patterns established in these early works and offer a model for playwriting rather different from the one outlined by Lynda Hart and other 1980s feminists. For it is in these later works (with first drafts that postdate 1980) that Paula becomes less concerned with letting the understudies seize the stage than with developing a complex, subtle, and deconstructionist mode of male impersonation (one that was not to the taste of many 1980s feminists). This textual strategy, which was then quite risky, clearly emblematizes—and anticipates!—the subversive gender performances over which Judith Butler waxed so admiring in the late 1980s. This strategy may also serve to remind readers that Paula is a contemporary not of Jane Chambers but of Holly Hughes, Cherríe Moraga, Peggy Shaw, and Lois Weaver. (It is also one reason why it took so long for Paula to become an established and successful playwright: she was ahead of her time. *And Baby Makes Seven,* for example, a play that infuriated some lesbian-feminists during the 1980s, took more than ten years to receive an off-Broadway production.) Paula's work is clearly linked to the reaction against lesbian-feminism and to the rise of a deconstructionist feminism that takes the split subject for granted and explicitly problematizes (and often critiques) the ontologies of theater and performance. At the same time, it looks back to an earlier theorization of cross-gender performance that has too often (and regrettably) been overlooked in theater studies.

When Paula first drew my attention to Esther Newton's groundbreaking study of pre-Stonewall female impersonators, *Mother Camp*, first published in 1972, I little suspected how thoroughly she had absorbed its lessons. Quite gloriously alone among anthropologists of that period, Newton regards the homosexual drag queen as a subject who illuminates the relation between gender deviance and sexual deviance. Although both forms were widely denounced (and pathologized), female impersonators represent a special case for Newton. They are multiply censured, living as they do at the "illegitimate junction of the homosexual and show business subcultures," in neither of which are they fully accepted. They thus remain the unnatural offspring of two subcultures long themselves considered unnatural. Yet this multiple stigmatization ironically affords the female impersonator both a measure of group identification and a sense of belonging. For Newton suggests (in a gesture that twenty-five years later was to become commonplace among feminists like Judith Butler) that the female impersonator turns private shame into a kind of public celebration, that he embraces a kind of gay pride *avant la lettre* (Newton always uses masculine pronouns to designate the female impersonator). Using the vocabulary of sex roles so popular in postwar social science, she emphasizes that "membership in the homosexual community *socializes*" an "underlying psychological conflict in sex role identification . . . by providing it with a form and an audience":

In fact *the* distinguishing characteristic of drag, as opposed to heterosexual transvestism, is its group character; *all* drag, whether formal, informal, or professional, has a theatrical structure and style. There is no drag without an actor and his audience, and there is no drag without drama (or theatricality). . . . The drag queen looks in the mirror of the audience and sees his female image reflected back approvingly.[11]

Because Newton understands female impersonation as being virtually synonymous with theater, the multiply marginalized impersonator finds himself ironically the very emblem of theatricality itself (which, in this context, could be seen to denote the spectacularization of deviance). He also discovers himself an utterly split subject—much like Shen Te/Shui Ta. But unlike the latter, who is always ashamed at having to confront her/his other and correct her/his errors of judgment, the female impersonator is delighted to (mis)recognize his female self staring back at him in the mirror.

In grasping the implications of *Mother Camp,* Paula both turns Newton's assertions inside out and labors to elevate drag in the cultural hierarchy. Hers is a theater that says that there is no drama without drag. For like Newton, she adopts an expansive concept of drag, recognizing that it has "a broader referent: any clothing that signifies a social role."[12] Thus for Esther Newton and Paula, every social role or sex role represents a kind of masquerade. The actor playing Jim in *The Mineola Twins* may be the only one in Paula's plays who is called upon literally to cross-dress. But all of her plays play with the idea of drag. And drag here denotes a woman making and taking up a masculine identification. By that I mean not that Paula's female characters are really men in drag or that they even want to be men but that, more often than not, they sustain a powerful psychic identification with men—and with the social and sexual power that men are able to wield (think Shui Ta). And identification, for Freud at least, is "not simply one psychical mechanism among others, but the operation itself whereby the human subject is constituted."[13] It represents "not simple imitation but *assimilation.*"[14] To that extent, cross-sex identification, as in *In the Summer House* (a play Paula loves deeply and to which she introduced me), is symptomatic of the workings of the negative Oedipus complex. Paula's women characters use a "'just-as-if'" model to fashion themselves *like* men.[15] Consider *And Baby Makes Seven*, which reverses the (negative) Oedipal generational arrangement by using two lesbians to impersonate their own imaginary boy children, at least one of whom, Henri, masquerades as the incestuous, gay female nephew of his "Uncle Peter." "I want to have your baby!!" he cries out.[16] Or *Baltimore Waltz*, which regenders the so-called first-generation, gay AIDS play as a heterosexual drama by allowing Anna, fucking her way across Europe, to take the place of her furtive brother, the casualty of negative Oedipus, who used to play "with [his] sister's dolls until [his] parents found out."[17]

Perhaps the most subtle and complex example in Paula's work of male impersonation (and of the split subjectivity to which it is linked) is her Pulitzer Prize–winning play, *How I Learned to Drive*. At first glance, the play appears to be—or rather, to play off—the idea of a rather conventionalized, heterosexual, May-December romance. The crucial difference, however, revealed at the end of the first scene, is that the two lovers are in fact uncle and niece. But several scenes into the play, it becomes clear that it aims to produce far more than an Oprah-style confessional narrative or even a (psycho)analysis of pedophilia or incest. *Drive* represents instead, among other things, a dramatization of the mirror stage—the move from the Imaginary to the Symbolic, from the infant (the primordial self unable to differentiate itself from its mother) to the split ego that, gazing at itself in the mirror, develops "an internalized psychic . . . sensory image of the self and the objects of the world."[18] For it is the mirror stage that, according to Lacan, projects "the individual into history" and compels him or her to assume "the armour of an alienating identity."[19]

How I Learned to Drive both metaphorizes and spatializes the formation of the split subject by splitting the heroine, Li'l Bit, into two selves: into a nonsubject (like *The Seven Deadly Sins*'s Anna II) still wrapped in the Imaginary, who has yet to experience differentiation; and a subjected subject (like Anna I), the one "very old, very cynical of the world," who long before became an object to herself (and others).[20] This splitting of the self is dramatized in part by a perceptual transformation. At the beginning of the play, Li'l Bit is lost in memories of the suburban Maryland of her youth, completely absorbed in the touch, smell, and taste of a "warm summer evening" (7). This perceptivity conjoins her with the past, with the land, and with the body (both the maternal body and her own), as she imagines herself miraculously whole again through the power of memory. But as Li'l Bit knows all too well—and as anyone who has become a subject can tell you—this primordial wholeness cannot last, and the remainder of the play shows her being taken for a ride that will lead—or rather, has led—her into another realm. (My inability to decide which tense to use is a symptom of the difficulty of even describing the mirror stage, a difficulty that seems to motivate the play's double time scheme.) For that traumatic moment called the mirror stage, which is here represented as that instant when for the first time *"Peck puts his hands on Li'l Bit's breasts,"* absolutely obliterates the Imaginary, turning the Symbolic into something that has always already happened (90). It is thus hardly a coincidence that throughout the play Li'l Bit's breasts—"these alien life forces, these two mounds of flesh"—function as the sign of "the armour of an alienating identity" (57). The Symbolic order they emblematize is dominated, unlike the Imaginary, by sight and hearing. For if touch, smell, and taste are the signs of intimacy and wholeness, then sight and hearing are undeniably the most objectifying of the senses; they introduce a radical breach between subject and object. It is thus no accident that the very center of the play is a photo shoot, for it is in this scene that Li'l Bit most graphically—and theatrically—becomes an object for her Uncle Peck and, more ominously, for herself as well. For the Symbolic is conceptualized as a kind of theater. And theater, after all, is an art that depends most on sight and hearing. Like the photo shoot, it will always produce figures who are subjected to the scrutiny of voyeuristic spectators. By dramatizing her entrance into the Symbolic, in other words, the play discovers that Li'l Bit has become an actor in a drama. (It is thus a canny choice on Paula's part to call the supporting players the Greek Chorus, thereby evoking the origins of the Western theatrical tradition.)

If *How I Learned to Drive* is indeed a dramatization of the production of the theater of the self, it obliges Li'l Bit to be constructed through an act of identification, "the operation," after all, "whereby the human subject is constituted." And Li'l Bit is in several respects fashioned *like* a man. According to the logic of sexual difference, the Phallus (which represents not the penis but that transcendental signifier that defies representation) is that "around which both men and women define themselves as complementary."[21] For according to Lacan, the Phallus is "the privileged signifier of that mark in which the role of the logos is joined with the advent of desire," or in other words, that sign of a sign in which language and desire are mutually constituted.[22] Men are said to "have" the Phallus, while women are said to "be" the Phallus. (Both of these are of course impossible relations to a nonobject, hence the scare quotes.) This arrangement means that women, insofar as they "are" the Phallus, cannot "have" it. And as a result, they are positioned on the side of lack. But Li'l Bit defies this patriarchal logic in a most original and startling way. According to the narrative the Chorus tells about Li'l Bit's birth, after the nurse's cries of "'It's a girl!,'" "we whipped your diapers down and parted your chubby little legs—and right between your legs there was— . . . Just a little bit" (13–14). Li'l Bit, in other words, has a "bit" between her legs that entitles her to a different relationship to the Phallus than that of the two female Greek Chorus members. (Since the Phallus most emphatically is not "the organ . . . that it symbolizes," the scale of Li'l Bit's "bit" is immaterial. What matters is that she lacks lack.)[23] And while this relationship does not exactly make her a man, it does fashion her *like* a man.

Li'l Bit's masculine identification is, moreover, more than anatomical. It is, after all, the Female Greek Chorus (as Mother, the one who raised her) who advises her to "stay away from *ladies'* drinks" and to "drink, instead, like a man" (24). And it is her Uncle Peck (the one whose name would suggest that he has at the least a privileged relationship to the Phallus) who teaches her how to be a desiring subject. For her sexual initiation is inextricably linked to her learning how to drive, how to master that unmistakably feminized machine with which, she notes, a "boy" typically "falls in love," that "thing that bears his weight with speed" (46). Indeed, the play hinges on a clever contradiction—that by learning to drive, Li'l Bit both (mis)recognizes her self-as-object and discovers another "'she'" over which she has complete control (51). Even Peck seems aware of this incongruity, as he caresses her and confesses to her:

> You're the nearest to a son I'll ever have—and I want to give you something. . . .
>
> There's something about driving—when you're in control of the car, just you and the machine and the road—that nobody can take from you. A power. I feel more myself in my car than anywhere else. And that's what I want to give to you. . . .
>
> I want to teach you to drive like a man. . . .
>
> Men are taught to drive with confidence—with aggression. The road belongs to them. (50)

Peck thus labors to produce Li'l Bit as a niece who is also a son, a woman who is also a man (because Li'l Bit's unnamed father is absent from the text, Peck functions in part as his stand-in). An old-fashioned gentleman to the end, he teaches Li'l Bit to "treat her [the car, that is] with respect," speaking of that seductive machine so reminiscent of that "someone who responds to your touch—someone who performs just for you and gives you what you ask for." At that crucial moment in her education, Li'l Bit chooses to identify with her uncle (the one whose appellation undermines the difference between "having" and "being"?) and accept his gendered *Weltanschauung:* "I closed my eyes—and decided not to change the gender" (51). She decides, in other words, that she will drive like a man, that she will "have" the Phallus that Peck offers her.

In choosing to play the man, Li'l Bit clearly takes up a masculine subject position vis-à-vis "the thing that bears his weight with speed." But the consequences of her male impersonation are even more complex than Peck could ever imagine. For in learning how to drive, Li'l Bit learns to be both desiring subject and desired object, both molester and violated one, both initiator and disciple, both taker and giver. She also learns how to write and to teach, or rather, that driving, sex, playwriting, and teaching are dramaturgical practices. For to excel in any of them, one must both provoke and anticipate others' responses, one must "learn to think what the other guy is going to do before he does it" (50). It is then hardly by chance that Li'l Bit describes her seduction of a high-school senior, and the lesson she offers him, as a drama, from its "slightly comical 'first act,'" to its "extremely capable and forceful and *sustained* second act," right down to its "post-play discussion" (41). The foregrounding of sex as both lesson and drama serves as a reminder that it is the theater, after all, that gives Li'l Bit the time and the place to comprehend and remake the theater of the self. By putting herself in the driver's seat, she learns, in other words, how to teach and how to write.

By linking driving, teaching, playwriting, and phallic authority, *How I Learned to Drive* provides the most nuanced example of male impersonation in Paula's work. It also suggests the difficulty, for a culture that has long confused gender identity with sexual identity, of distinguishing between drag and homosexuality. "After all," Eve Kosofsky Sedgwick notes teasingly, "'everyone already knows' that cross-dressing usually at least alludes to homosexuality."[24] For Li'l Bit's taking up a masculine role serves, if not exactly to turn her into a lesbian, then at the least to eroti-cize her relationship with one feminine object—the automobile. On the one hand, Li'l Bit's narrative emphasizes her willing or unwilling partici-pation in heterosexual liaisons—with Peck, the high-school student, and her lascivious schoolmates. And the play is filled with heterosexual se-duction, taunting, and swagger, despite the fact that all the heterosexual relationships—between Peck and Li'l Bit, Peck and his wife, Grandma and Big Papa, Mother and her ex-husband—are laughable, gruesome fail-ures. *How I Learned to Drive* then, like so many post– World War II plays, focuses almost exclusively on cross-sex relationships while documenting the miscarriage of heterosexuality (isn't this what upper-middlebrow American drama is supposed to do?). On the other hand, Li'l Bit makes no attempt to conceal the rumor that while in college she was "kicked out of that fancy school" because she "fooled around with a rich man's daughter" (21). And when she tries to stave off her uncle's advances, she confesses, "well, yes, I am seeing other—," carefully avoiding specifying the sex of her admirer(s) (80). The high-school student she seduces, moreover, does happen to attend Walt Whitman High.

The absence of homosexual cathexes in *How I Learned to Drive* (or, for that matter, in any of Paula's plays except *And Baby Makes Seven* and *The Mineola Twins*) does not, however, mean that these are not lesbian texts. But to consider *How I Learned to Drive* a lesbian play is to assume an equivalence between sexual dissidence and gender dissidence, a not unlikely assumption (and one that Esther Newton makes). Moreover, there is a long history (which goes back at least to Freud) of linking a "masculinity complex" in women with homosexuality. Diane Hamer elaborates on this link in suggestive ways for thinking about Paula's pose as a writer:

> Lesbianism is less a claim to phallic possession . . . than it is a refusal of the meanings attached to castration. As such it is a refusal of any easy or straightforward allocation of masculine and feminine positions around the phallus. Instead it suggests a much more fluid and flexible relationship to the positions around which desire is organized.[25]

Because Paula's work (like that of Virginia Woolf, Gertrude Stein, Djuna Barnes, and Jane Bowles) evinces a "fluid and flexible relationship" to desire and to gendered positions, it exemplifies, I believe, a mode of writing that could be characterized as a lesbian modernism that destabilizes and unsettles sexual identities and desires. (This is in contradistinction to the much more unambiguously lesbian writing of Radclyffe Hall or Audre Lorde, which is so intent on anchoring desire in an essentialized female body.) One might in fact argue that Paula, like Jane Bowles before her, has reinvented the closet drama, that form and tradition that Sedgwick describes as being "so inexhaustibly and gorgeously productive."[26] For *How I Learned to Drive* admits to an act of concealment in Li'l Bit's very first line: "Sometimes to tell a secret, you first have to teach a lesson" (7). And the text never makes it absolutely clear what the secret is. The incest and pedophilia are revealed at the top. Perhaps the secret is not that *How I Learned to Drive* is a lesbian play with a lesbian protagonist, but that, like *The Glass Menagerie,* it is about the production of a future pervert, one who remains, strictly speaking, absent from the text. For like Williams's play, it is intent on speeding its narrator off into a gloriously undefined futurity—or, in Williams's words, a "world . . . lit by lightning!"—that at once leaves the past behind and recognizes the impossibility of that project.[27]

A key to Paula's reimagination of the closet drama in *How I Learned to Drive* is contained in a throwaway speech given by Uncle Peck—throwaway because its content seems arbitrary and irrelevant to the play's action. While liquoring up Li'l Bit on the Eastern Shore, he recites the history of the town they're in:

> When the British sailed up this very river in the dead of night . . . they were going to bombard the heck out of this town. But the town fathers were ready for them. They crept up all the trees with lanterns so that the British would think they saw the town lights and they aimed their cannons too high. (22)

Peck's story is one of trickery, of an illusion carefully staged to forfend catastrophe. If this narrative is, as I am arguing, a revelation of Paula's methods as a playwright, it suggests that *How I Learned to Drive* is, like the scene by the river, a spectacle of one thing being taken for another. In the case of a play that was easily assimilated to what one writer then called "the current, confessional climate," awarded a Pulitzer Prize, and produced more widely in the United States than any other play during the 1998–99 season, Paula (in imitation of "the town fathers") has managed to smuggle in a drag show that seems anything but, a feminist play with a hero who molests little girls, and a lesbian play filled to overflowing with dysfunctional heterosexuals.[28]

How I Learned to Drive's penchant for deception also guarantees that it will not threaten male theater critics and the patriarchal theater establishment too severely, despite the fact that it is centered around a woman in psychic drag. For it does not, after all, excoriate masculinity or phallic authority per se. Yet at the same time, it became the first Pulitzer Prize–winning play by a woman that neither recycled antifeminist clichés nor resuscitated the already moribund conventions of a domestic realism long associated with scribbling women. Its fragmentation of narrative and subjectivity guarantees that it will work very differently from the plays of the three women who won the Pulitzer Prize for drama during the 1980s, Beth Henley, Marsha Norman, and Wendy Wasserstein. Most of their works—so popular during that decade and so determinedly censured by many feminist critics—do what Alisa Solomon aptly describes (in an extraordinarily pithy review of *The Heidi Chronicles*) as representing "intelligent, educated women, and assur[ing] us that they are funny for the same, traditional reasons women have always been funny: they hate their bodies, can't find a man, and don't believe in themselves."[29] Not all the plays by Henley, Norman, and Wasserstein from this period focus on the affluent and cultured, but most recycle these misogynist clichés and stereotypes in a surprisingly uncritical way. *How I Learned to Drive,* in contrast, seems almost as if it were written to answer Solomon's objections by analyzing precisely the etiology of these clichés and stereotypes. "Here's why women learn to hate their bodies," the play seems to say. "Here's why they don't believe in themselves, and here's a woman who is learning that she doesn't need to find a man."

The success of *How I Learned to Drive* seems to me to be the result of many different factors—besides the fact that it happens to be a fine play. It was a well-timed contribution to the culture of confession; a complex and nonpolemical feminist intervention that successfully appeals to the overwhelmingly liberal theatergoing audience; a canny amalgam of a distinctively American empathic realism with a kind of Brechtian epic theater; and a vigorous blending of the conventions of popular comedy with the seriousness and sophistication that theatergoers prize in elite culture. Paula's dramaturgical method may be deconstructionist, but it relies more heavily on empathy, meticulously deliberate plotting, a teleological structure, careful attention to the stuff of history, and a somewhat more literary style than the work of many of her contemporaries. It represents, in short, Paula's successful assimilation—and critique—of a style of playwriting that has historically been coded as masculine. If nothing else, there is a sense of assurance in the way in which the play addresses its audience that is more reminiscent of *Glengarry Glen Ross* than *The Heidi Chronicles*. Yet Paula's theatrical cross-dressing, like Divine's (at least in Michael Moon's estimation), endeavors neither to lull her audience into complacency nor to "conceal or disavow what a dangerous act drag can be, onstage and off."[30] For like the cross-gender performance of her fellow Baltimore native, Paula's represents a way of defiantly taking the stage.

If Paula's work can be seen as a critique of the one playwright with whom she most clearly has a "love/hate relationship," it would have to be read both as reiterating the brutally gendered binarism that *The Good Person of Setzuan* dramatizes and as interrogating that division of labor. For her work, like so much recent feminist writing, does not deny the different material and ideological effects produced by the opposition between masculine and feminine. It does, however, question the finality of this division, not by offering a radically different vision of society but by insinuating an alternative model of subjectivity. Where Brecht requires two opposing characters (Shen Te/Shui Ta, Anna I/Anna II) to dramatize the schizophrenia that capitalism produces, Paula usually requires only one self-contradictory subject who encloses within her or him both this debilitating division and a remedy for that division, much like the maniacal Dr. Todesrocheln, who, with his Dr. Strangelovean, out-of-control left hand, gleefully offers up both death and a cure for death. For if Brecht's plays characteristically end in a state of impasse and paralysis, Paula's more often than not gesture toward a future that is utterly different, a fantastic, utopian future in which lovers can be forever reunited and self-division healed. This is not to say that they duplicitously offer up the impossible as the real, but that they coax into being, if only in the imagination, an intimation of an absolute Other. This Other, however, functions like a speck of sand in an oyster, both as an irritant and as the basis for a sublime transformation. Sited both within and without the self, this irksome Other leads the subject to struggle against herself, much like *The Baltimore Waltz*'s Anna and her dexterous extremities, Mr. Left and Mr. Right, those mischievously phallic actors whose sole function seems to be to turn Anna into a Scheherazade ("I would make up stories about my hands").[31] Paula's work relentlessly associates the production of narrative with the struggle for a kind of phallic authority. The intractability of this struggle, however, makes it impossible to know exactly who is spinning the narrative—Mr. Left or Mr. Right, Myra or Myrna, Ruth or Henri, Anna or Carl, Paula the writer or Paula the critic, Paula the feminist or Paula the male impersonator. And if I have spun a narrative for Paula in this chapter, perhaps that is because she has, from time to time, spun one for me.

Notes

Preface

1. Jill Dolan, *Geographies of Learning: Theory and Practice, Activism and Performance* (Middletown, Conn.: Wesleyan University Press, 2001), 45–46.
2. See Bertolt Brecht, "The Modern Theatre Is the Epic Theatre," in *Brecht on Theatre: The Development of an Aesthetic,* ed. and trans. John Willett (New York: Hill and Wang, 1964), 33–42.
3. Pierre Bourdieu, "The Market of Symbolic Goods," in *The Field of Cultural Production: Essays on Art and Literature,* ed. Randal Johnson (New York: Columbia University Press, 1993), 131.
4. Karl Marx, *Capital,* in *The Marx-Engels Reader,* ed. Robert C. Tucker (New York: W. W. Norton, 1972), 215.

Chapter One

1. Michael Kammen, *American Culture, American Tastes: Social Change and the Twentieth Century* (New York: Knopf, 1999), 74. See also Lawrence W. Levine, *Highbrow/Lowbrow: The Emergence of Cultural Hierarchy in America* (Cambridge: Harvard University Press, 1988), 221–22.
2. Janice Radway, "Scandal of the Middlebrow: The Book-of-the-Month Club, Class Fracture, and Critical Authority," *South Atlantic Quarterly* 89, no. 4 (1990): 707.
3. Kammen, *American Culture, American Tastes,* 95–96.
4. Russell Lynes, "Highbrow, Lowbrow, Middlebrow," in *The Tastemakers* (New York: Harper and Brothers, 1954), 320.
5. Andrew Ross, *No Respect: Intellectuals and Popular Culture* (New York: Routledge, 1989), 42–43, 47.
6. Dwight Macdonald, "Masscult and Midcult," *Partisan Review* 27, no. 2 (1960): 220.
7. Lynes, "Highbrow, Lowbrow, Middlebrow," 311.
8. Randal Johnson, introduction to *The Field of Cultural Production: Essays on Art and Literature,* by Pierre Bourdieu (New York: Columbia University Press, 1993), 15.

9. Joan Shelley Rubin, *The Making of Middlebrow Culture* (Chapel Hill: University of North Carolina Press, 1992), 11.

10. Ross, *No Respect*, 62, 59.

11. John Seabrook, *Nobrow* (New York: Knopf, 2000), 27.

12. Lynes, "Highbrow, Lowbrow, Middlebrow," 318, 313.

13. Clement Greenberg, quoted in Lynes, "Highbrow, Lowbrow, Middlebrow," 313–14.

14. Janice Radway, "On the Gender of the Middlebrow Consumer and the Threat of the Culturally Fraudulent Female," *South Atlantic Quarterly* 93, no. 4 (1994): 883, 872, 874, 880.

15. Quoted in Radway, "Scandal of the Middlebrow," 707.

16. Radway, "On the Gender of the Middlebrow Consumer," 887.

17. Lawrence S. Wittner, *Cold War America: From Hiroshima to Watergate* (New York: Praeger, 1974), 47.

18. Lynes, "Highbrow, Lowbrow, Middlebrow," 331–32.

19. Macdonald, "Masscult and Midcult," 215, 210.

20. Dwight Macdonald, "Masscult and Midcult: II," *Partisan Review* 27, no. 4 (1960): 592.

21. Macdonald, "Masscult and Midcult," 226.

22. Elaine Tyler May, *Homeward Bound: American Families in the Cold War Era* (New York: Basic Books, 1988), 97, 95.

23. Macdonald, "Masscult and Midcult: II," 592.

24. Macdonald, "Masscult and Midcult: II," 605.

25. Quoted in Elaine Tyler May, *Homeward Bound*, 95.

26. Donald W. Goodwin, *Anxiety* (New York: Oxford University Press, 1986), 3.

27. Goodwin, *Anxiety*, 41; Rollo May, *The Meaning of Anxiety*, cited in Goodwin, *Anxiety*, 4.

28. Goodwin, *Anxiety*, 5.

29. Sigmund Freud, *Three Essays on the Theory of Sexuality*, trans. and ed. James Strachey (New York: Basic Books, 1962), 11.

30. Ross, *No Respect*, 60–61.

31. Rollo May, *The Meaning of Anxiety*, cited in Goodwin, *Anxiety*, 42.

32. Kammen, *American Culture, American Tastes*, 14.

33. Seabrook, *Nobrow*, 162.

34. Quoted in Rick Poynor, "Branded Journalism," *Metropolis*, October 2000, 115.

35. Seabrook, *Nobrow*, 101.

36. Seabrook, *Nobrow*, 28.

37. Robert W. McChesney, "The New Global Media," *The Nation*, November 29, 1999, 11; Robert W. McChesney, "Media Globalopoly," *The Nation*, November 29, 1999, 3.

38. Seabrook, *Nobrow*, 171.

39. Seabrook, *Nobrow*, 66.

40. Reproduced in Kammen, *American Culture, American Tastes*, 98–99.

41. Macdonald, "Masscult and Midcult: II," 594.

42. Macdonald, "Masscult and Midcult: II," 616.

43. Pierre Bourdieu, "The Field of Cultural Production," in *The Field of Cultural Production: Essays on Art and Literature,* ed. Randal Johnson (New York: Columbia University Press, 1993), 39.

44. Pierre Bourdieu, *Distinction: A Social Critique of the Judgement of Taste,* trans. Richard Nice (Cambridge: Harvard University Press, 1984), 54.

45. Marianne Conroy, "Acting Out: Method Acting, the National Culture, and the Middlebrow Disposition in Cold War America," *Criticism* 35, no. 2 (spring 1993): 241.

46. See Philip Auslander, *Liveness: Performance in a Mediatized Culture* (London: Routledge, 1999).

47. Jack Poggi, *Theater in America: The Impact of Economic Forces, 1870–1967* (Ithaca: Cornell University Press, 1968), 85.

48. Paul DiMaggio, "Cultural Boundaries and Structural Change: The Extension of the High Culture Model to Theater, Opera, and Dance, 1900–1940," in *Cultivating Differences: Symbolic Boundaries and the Making of Inequality,* ed. Michèle Lamong and Marcel Fournier (Chicago: University of Chicago Press, 1992), 22.

49. Quoted in DiMaggio, "Cultural Boundaries and Structural Change," 35.

50. Poggi, *Theater in America,* 99; DiMaggio, "Cultural Boundaries and Structural Change," 25, 27.

51. Quoted in Poggi, *Theater in America,* 106.

52. DiMaggio, "Cultural Boundaries and Structural Change," 25.

53. DiMaggio, "Cultural Boundaries and Structural Change," 30.

54. DiMaggio, "Cultural Boundaries and Structural Change," 22.

55. DiMaggio, "Cultural Boundaries and Structural Change," 28.

56. Poggi, *Theater in America,* 88.

57. See Poggi, *Theater in America,* 99–148.

58. Poggi, *Theater in America,* 88.

59. David Nasaw, *Going Out: The Rise and Fall of Public Amusements* (Cambridge: Harvard University Press, 1999), 49.

60. Poggi, *Theater in America,* 30.

61. DiMaggio, "Cultural Boundaries and Structural Change," 29; Poggi, *Theater in America,* 80.

62. See Poggi, *Theater in America,* 41–45, 89.

63. Poggi, *Theater in America,* 42.

64. Poggi, *Theater in America,* 39–40.

65. Poggi, *Theater in America,* 77.

66. Conroy, "Acting Out," 240.

67. Poggi, *Theater in America,* 42.

68. C. D. Throsby and G. A. Withers, *The Economics of the Performing Arts* (Aldershot, Eng.: Gregg Revivals, 1993), 96.

69. See Harold L. Vogel, *Entertainment Industry Economics: A Guide for Financial Analysis* (Cambridge: Cambridge University Press, 1998), 281.

70. Vogel, *Entertainment Industry Economics,* 282.

71. Vogel, *Entertainment Industry Economics,* 285.

72. See Throsby and Withers, *The Economics of the Performing Arts,* 29.

73. William J. Baumol and William G. Bowen, *Performing Arts: The Economic Dilemma* (New York: Twentieth Century Fund, 1966), 162, 164.

74. See Poggi, *Theater in America,* 65–71.

75. Baumol and Bowen, *Performing Arts,* 163.

76. Poggi, *Theater in America,* 85.

77. Quoted in Poggi, *Theater in America,* 255.

78. Throsby and Withers, *The Economics of the Performing Arts,* 54.

79. John Hohenberg, *The Pulitzer Prizes: A History of the Awards in Books, Drama, Music, and Journalism, Based on the Private Files over Six Decades* (New York: Columbia University Press, 1974), 19.

80. Hohenberg, *The Pulitzer Prizes,* 102; Alexander Woollcott, quoted in Hohenberg, *The Pulitzer Prizes,* 45.

81. Hohenberg, *The Pulitzer Prizes,* 95.

82. See Hohenberg, *The Pulitzer Prizes,* 266–69.

83. Thomas P. Adler, *Mirror on the Stage: The Pulitzer Plays as an Approach to American Drama* (West Lafayette, Ind.: Purdue University Press, 1987), x–xi.

84. Hohenberg, *The Pulitzer Prizes,* 269.

85. John L. Toohey, *A History of the Pulitzer Prize Plays* (New York: Citadel Press, 1967), 99.

86. Quoted in Toohey, *A History of the Pulitzer Prize Plays,* 102.

87. Geoffrey Block, "The Broadway Canon from *Show Boat* to *West Side Story* and the European Operatic Ideal," *Journal of Musicology* 11, no. 4 (1993): 529.

88. Gerald Mast, *Can't Help Singin': The American Musical on Stage and Screen* (Woodstock, N.Y.: Overlook Press, 1987), 1.

89. Stanley Green, *The World of Musical Comedy* (New York: Da Capo, 1980), 216.

90. Toohey, *A History of the Pulitzer Prize Plays,* 237.

91. Andrea Most, "'You've Got to Be Carefully Taught': The Politics of Race in Rodgers and Hammerstein's *South Pacific,*" *Theatre Journal* 52 (May 2000): 311.

92. Brooks Atkinson, "At the Theatre," *New York Times,* April 8, 1949.

93. Howard Barnes, quoted in Toohey, *A History of the Pulitzer Prize Plays,* 236.

94. David Ewen, *Complete Book of the American Musical Theatre* (New York: Henry Holt and Company, 1959), 265; Mark Kirkeby, liner notes to CD reissue of original cast recording of *South Pacific* (Sony SK 60722, 1998), 9.

95. Philip D. Beidler, "*South Pacific* and American Remembering; or, 'Josh, We're Going to Buy This Son of a Bitch!'" *Journal of American Studies* 27 (1993): 213.

96. Beidler, "*South Pacific* and American Remembering," 214–15.

97. Richard Rodgers writes: "If the main love story is serious, the secondary romance is usually employed to provide comic relief—such as Ado Annie and Will Parker in *Oklahoma!* or Carrie Pipperidge and Mr. Snow in *Carousel.* But in

South Pacific we had two serious themes, with the second becoming a tragedy when young Cable is killed during the mission." Richard Rodgers, *Musical Stages: An Autobiography* (New York: Random House, 1975), 259.

98. Ralph P. Locke, "Constructing the Oriental 'Other': Saint-Saëns's *Samson et Dalila,*" *Cambridge Opera Journal* 3, no. 3 (1991): 263.

99. Richard Rodgers, Oscar Hammerstein II, and Joshua Logan, *South Pacific,* in *Six Plays by Rodgers and Hammerstein* (New York: Modern Library, 1959), 303. All further citations will be noted in the text.

100. Beidler, "*South Pacific* and American Remembering," 213–14.

101. Most, "'You've Got to Be Carefully Taught,'" 315.

102. See Most, "'You've Got to Be Carefully Taught,'" 307.

103. Bruce A. McConachie, "The 'Oriental' Musicals of Rodgers and Hammerstein and the U.S. War in Southeast Asia," *Theatre Journal* 46 (October 1994), 392.

104. Rose Subotnik, lecture on Rodgers and Hammerstein's orientalism, spring 1999, Music 134/English 139, Brown University. My reading is heavily indebted to her analysis of Rodgers and Hammerstein's orientalism.

105. Beidler, "*South Pacific* and American Remembering," 219.

106. Gerald Early, "Pulp and Circumstance: The Story of Jazz in High Places," in *The Jazz Cadence of American Culture,* ed. Robert G. O'Meally (New York: Columbia University Press, 1998), 418, 401, 407, 426.

107. Jeffrey Melnick, *A Right to Sing the Blues: African Americans, Jews, and American Popular Song* (Cambridge: Harvard University Press, 1999), 37.

108. Jonathan Larson, *Rent* libretto, CD (Dreamworks DSMD2-50003), 1:23 (1996). Because there are no page numbers, I identify the source of lyrics by citing act and song number. All further citations will be noted in the text.

109. Ben Brantley, review of *Rent, New York Times,* April 30, 1996.

110. Peter Marks, "Looking on Broadway for a Bohemian Home," *New York Times,* February 26, 1996.

111. John Simon, review of *Rent, New York,* May 13, 1996.

112. Jonathan Larson, *Rent,* with interviews and text by Evelyn McDonnell and Katherine Silberger (New York: William Morrow, 1997), 135.

113. Bruce Weber, "Renewing the Lease on the Innocence of Youth," *New York Times,* August 18, 2000.

114. Marks, "Looking on Broadway for a Bohemian Home."

115. Howard Kissel, "*Rent* Comes Due on Broadway," *Daily News,* April 30, 1996.

116. Quoted in Larson, *Rent,* with interviews and text by McDonnell and Silberger, 29.

117. Quoted in Larson, *Rent,* with interviews and text by McDonnell and Silberger, 157.

118. Weber, "Renewing the Lease on the Innocence of Youth."

119. Peter Bürger, *Theory of the Avant-Garde,* trans. Michael Shaw (Minneapolis: University of Minnesota Press, 1984), 22.

120. Seabrook, *Nobrow,* 69.

121. Michael Yearby and Jim Nicola, quoted in Larson, *Rent,* with interviews and text by McDonnell and Silberger, 40, 23.

122. Quoted in Larson, *Rent,* with interviews and text by McDonnell and Silberger, 25.

123. Quoted in Larson, *Rent,* with interviews and text by McDonnell and Silberger, 26.

124. Kissel, "*Rent* Comes Due on Broadway."

125. Larson, *Rent,* with interviews and text by McDonnell and Silberger, 35.

126. Larson, *Rent,* with interviews and text by McDonnell and Silberger, 35, 26.

127. Weber, "Renewing the Lease on the Innocence of Youth."

128. Although transgender was becoming an increasingly important identity (and site of subversion) during the mid-1990s, the play and the production team unequivocally imagine Angel as a gay man and transvestite. See Larson, *Rent,* with interviews and text by McDonnell and Silberger, 21.

129. Larson, *Rent,* with interviews and text by McDonnell and Silberger, 25.

130. Kissel, "*Rent* Comes Due on Broadway."

131. Simon, review of *Rent.*

132. Ben Brantley, "Theater Review: Enter Singing: Young, Hopeful, and Taking On the Big Time," *New York Times,* April 30, 1996, C13.

133. Advertisement, "There's a Room for Rent," *Rent* Web site, 1999.

134. Jeremy Gerard, review of *Rent,* May 6, 1996, *National Theatre Critics' Reviews* 56, no. 2 (1996): 250.

135. Tom Frank, "Hip Is Dead," *The Nation,* April 1, 1996, 18.

136. Larson, *Rent,* with interviews and text by McDonnell and Silberger, 133.

137. Larson, *Rent,* with interviews and text by McDonnell and Silberger, 59.

138. Quoted in Larson, *Rent,* with interviews and text by McDonnell and Silberger, 59.

139. Naomi Klein, *No Logo: Taking Aim at the Brand Bullies* (New York: Picador USA, 1999), 21.

140. Klein, *No Logo,* 28.

141. See Peter Lunenfeld, "Hipbrow." Available at <http://www.db.heise.de/tp/english/inhalt/kino/3147/1.html>.

142. Walter Benjamin, "The Work of Art in the Age of Mechanical Reproduction," in *Illuminations,* ed. Hannah Arendt, trans. Harry Zohn (New York: Schocken, 1969), 221.

143. Ben Brantley, "Broadway Doesn't Live There Anymore," *New York Times,* November 7, 1999.

144. Quoted in Stephanie Coen, with Stephen C. Forman and Ben Cameron, "The Field and Its Challenges," *American Theatre,* January 2000, 101.

145. Brantley, "Broadway Doesn't Live There Anymore."

146. Coen, with Forman and Cameron, "The Field and Its Challenges," 101.

147. Edward W. Said, *Representations of the Intellectual* (New York: Vintage, 1994), 28.

148. Rubin, *The Making of Middlebrow Culture,* 13.

149. Gerald Bordman, *The Oxford Companion to American Theatre* (New York: Oxford University Press, 1992), 42; Martin Banham, *The Cambridge Guide to Theatre* (Cambridge: Cambridge University Press, 1995), 56.

150. Banham, *The Cambridge Guide to Theatre,* 56; Brooks Atkinson and Albert Hirschfeld, *The Lively Years: 1920–1973* (New York: Association Press, 1973), 5.

151. Atkinson and Hirschfeld, *The Lively Years,* 5.

152. Atkinson and Hirschfeld, *The Lively Years,* 6.

153. Bordman, *The Oxford Companion to American Theatre,* 576; Banham, *The Cambridge Guide to Theatre,* 920.

154. Frank Rich, "East Village Story," *New York Times,* March 2, 1996.

155. Ben Brantley, Vincent Canby, Peter Marks, and Andrea Stevens, "London–New York: A One-Way Street?" *New York Times,* February 21, 1999.

156. Bruce Weber, "The Last Meow: A Fence Sitter Sums Up," *New York Times,* September 1, 2000.

157. Zannie Giraud Voss and Glenn B. Voss, with Judith Cooper Guido and Christopher Shuff, "Theatre Facts 1998," in *American Theatre,* July/August 1999, 9.

158. Coen, with Forman and Cameron, "The Field and Its Challenges," 103, 100.

159. Jesse McKinley, "Stalking Tony Award, a Revue Is Moving," *New York Times,* April 5, 1999.

160. Todd Haimes, quoted in Robin Pogrebin, "Nary a Drama on Broadway," *New York Times,* December 28, 1999.

161. Coen, with Foreman and Cameron, "The Field and Its Challenges," 100.

162. Quoted in Barry Singer, "Youngsters Reach Broadway Bearing Gifts: Musical Scores," *New York Times,* August 27, 2000.

Chapter Two

1. Eve Kosofsky Sedgwick, *Tendencies* (Durham: Duke University Press, 1993), 8–9.

2. See, for example, Maria Maggenti, "Women as Queer Nationals," *Out/look* (winter 1991): 20–23; and Guy Trebay, "In Your Face," *Village Voice,* August 14, 1990, 37–39.

3. Jill Dolan, "Building a Theatrical Vernacular: Responsibility, Community, Ambivalence, and Queer Theatre," *Modern Drama* 39, no. 1 (1996): 2.

4. Wendy Brown, "Wounded Attachments: Late Modern Oppositional Political Formations," in *The Identity in Question,* ed. John Rajchman (New York: Routledge, 1995), 207.

5. Alan Sinfield, *Out on Stage: Lesbian and Gay Theatre in the Twentieth Century* (New Haven: Yale University Press, 1999), 6. Although frequently more descriptive than analytical in its approach, *Out on Stage* remains the best history of lesbian and gay theater.

6. George Chauncey, *Gay New York: Gender, Urban Culture, and the Making of the Gay Male World, 1890–1940* (New York: Basic Books, 1994), 301–2, 191.

7. Quoted in Sinfield, *Out on Stage,* 8.

8. Stacy Wolf, *A Problem Like Maria: Gender, Sexuality, and American Musicals* (Ann Arbor: University of Michigan Press, 2002), 20.

9. See D. A. Miller, *Place for Us: [Essay on the Broadway Musical]* (Cambridge: Harvard University Press, 1998).

10. Wolf, *A Problem Like Maria,* 16–17.

11. See, for example, Barbara Janowitz, "Theatre Facts 93," insert in *American Theatre,* April 1994, 4–5.

12. For a much more detailed critique of *Angels in America,* see chapter 4.

13. Review of *One Arm,* by Tennessee Williams, *Time,* January 3, 1955, 76.

14. Howard Taubman, "Not What It Seems: Homosexual Motif Gets Heterosexual Guise," *New York Times,* November 5, 1961.

15. Stanley Kauffmann, "Homosexual Drama and Its Disguises," *New York Times,* January 23, 1966.

16. Kauffmann, "Homosexual Drama and Its Disguises."

17. See, for example, Elaine Tyler May, *Homeward Bound.*

18. Taubman, "Not What It Seems"; Kauffmann, "Homosexual Drama and Its Disguises."

19. Terrence McNally, *Love! Valour! Compassion! and A Perfect Ganesh: Two Plays* (New York: Plume, 1995), 69.

20. Monique Wittig, *The Straight Mind and Other Essays* (Boston: Beacon Press, 1992), 61.

21. My thanks to Marvin Carlson for pointing this out to me.

22. Holly Hughes, *Clit Notes: A Sapphic Sampler* (New York: Grove, 1996), 171.

23. Hughes, *Clit Notes,* 2–3.

24. Transcript, "Reading and Writing Out," Center for Lesbian and Gay Studies (CLAGS) Queer Theatre Conference, City University of New York, April 28, 1995. All subsequent quotations by these playwrights are taken from the transcript.

25. Christian Metz, *The Imaginary Signifier: Psychoanalysis and the Cinema,* trans. Celia Britton, Annwyl Williams, Ben Brewster, and Alfred Guzzetti (Bloomington: Indiana University Press, 1982), 43. All further citations will be noted in the text.

26. See, for example, Laura Mulvey, *Visual and Other Pleasures* (Bloomington: Indiana University Press, 1989).

27. I am using *identification* here in the sense defined by Laplanche and Pontalis as a "psychological process whereby the subject assimilates an aspect, property or attribute of the other and is transformed, wholly or partially, after the model the other provides. It is by means of a series of identifications that the personality is constituted and specified." J. Laplanche and J.-B. Pontalis, *The Language of Psycho-Analysis,* trans. Donald Nicholson-Smith (New York: W. W. Norton, 1974), 205.

28. André Bazin, "Theater and Cinema: Part Two," in *What is Cinema?* trans. Hugh Gray (Berkeley: University of California Press, 1967), 102, 99.

29. Bazin, "Theater and Cinema," 101, 106.

30. Bazin, "Theater and Cinema," 99.

31. Judith Butler, "Imitation and Gender Insubordination," in *The Lesbian and Gay Studies Reader,* ed. Henry Abelove, Michèle Aina Barale, and David M. Halperin (New York: Routledge, 1993), 313.

32. Judith Butler, *Gender Trouble: Feminism and the Subversion of Identity* (New York: Routledge, 1990), 62.

33. Butler, "Imitation and Gender Insubordination," 310.

34. Judith Butler, *Bodies That Matter: On the Discursive Limits of "Sex"* (New York: Routledge, 1993), 113.

35. David Harvey, *Spaces of Hope* (Berkeley: University of California Press, 2000), 189.

36. Butler, "Imitation and Gender Insubordination," 308.

37. Metz, *The Imaginary Signifier,* 64.

38. Dennis Lim, "Queer and Present Danger," *The Village Voice,* June 6, 2000, 142.

39. Brown, "Wounded Attachments," 206.

40. Interview with Terrence McNally, in *The Playwright's Voice: American Dramatists on Memory, Writing, and the Politics of Culture,* by David Savran (New York: Theatre Communications Group, 1999), 136.

41. The other two nominees were Sam Shepard's *True West* (an old play) and Arthur Miller's *The Ride Down Mt. Morgan* (one of his weaker plays).

42. Dolan, "Building a Theatrical Vernacular," 9–10.

Chapter Three

This essay is dedicated to Marvin Carlson.

1. "Transcript of President Bush's Address on the State of the Union," *New York Times,* January 29, 1992, A16.

2. "Transcript of Bush's State of the Union Message to the Nation," *New York Times,* February 1, 1990, D22; "Transcript of Bush's State of the Union Message to the Nation," *New York Times,* January 30, 1991, A12; "Transcript of President Bush's Address on the State of the Union," *New York Times,* January 29, 1992, A16.

3. James Taranto, quoted in Thomas Frank, "The Rise of Market Populism: America's New Secular Religion," *The Nation,* October 30, 2000, 19.

4. "Transcript of Bush's State of the Union Message to the Nation," *New York Times,* January 30, 1991, A12.

5. Samir Amin, *Capitalism in the Age of Globalization: The Management of Contemporary Society* (London: Zed Books, 1997), 122.

6. Karl Marx, *The Eighteenth Brumaire of Louis Bonaparte* (New York: International Publishers, 1963), 15.

7. Rick Lyman, "The Chills! The Thrills! The Profits!" *New York Times,* August 31, 1999, El.

8. Quoted in Noël Carroll, *The Philosophy of Horror, or Paradoxes of the Heart* (New York: Routledge, 1990), 199.

9. Lyman, "The Chills! The Thrills! The Profits!," El.

10. Carroll, *The Philosophy of Horror,* 165.

11. Jacques Derrida, "The Theater of Cruelty and the Closure of Representation," in *Writing and Difference,* trans. Alan Bass (Chicago: University of Chicago Press, 1978), 235.

12. Marvin Carlson, *The Haunted Stage: The Theatre as Memory Machine* (Ann Arbor: University of Michigan Press, 2001), 1.

13. Joseph Roach, *Cities of the Dead: Circum-Atlantic Performance* (New York: Columbia University Press, 1996), 78.

14. Peggy Phelan, *Unmarked: The Politics of Performance* (London: Routledge, 1993), 146.

15. Pierre Nora, "Between Memory and History: *Les Lieux de Mémoire,*" *Representations* 26 (spring 1989): 8.

16. Nora, "Between Memory and History," 8–9.

17. See R. C. Finucane, *Appearances of the Dead: A Cultural History of Ghosts* (Buffalo: Prometheus Books, 1984).

18. See David Savran, *The Playwright's Voice: American Dramatists on Memory, Writing, and the Politics of Culture* (New York: Theatre Communications Group, 1999).

19. Sigmund Freud, "Mourning and Melancholia" (1917), in *Collected Papers,* ed. Joan Riviere (New York: Basic), 4:153.

20. Freud, "Mourning and Melancholia," 155.

21. Butler, *Gender Trouble,* 57, 61.

22. Nora, "Between Memory and History," 9.

23. Derrida, *Specters of Marx,* 54.

24. Derrida, *Specters of Marx,* 6.

25. Derrida, *Specters of Marx,* 7.

26. Derrida, *Specters of Marx,* 65.

27. Fredric Jameson, "Modernism and Imperialism," in *Nationalism, Colonialism, and Literature,* ed. Terry Eagleton, Fredric Jameson, and Edward W. Said (Minneapolis: University of Minnesota Press, 1990), 50–51.

28. Jean Cocteau, *The Wedding on the Eiffel Tower,* trans. Michael Benedikt, in *Modern French Theatre: An Anthology of Plays,* ed. Michael Benedikt and George E. Wellwarth (New York: Dutton, 1966), 109.

29. Eugène Ionesco, *Rhinoceros,* trans. Derek Prouse, in *Nine Plays of the Modern Theater,* ed. Harold Clurman (New York: Grove Weidenfeld, 1981), 499–500.

30. Harvey, *Spaces of Hope,* 63, 68.

31. Johnson, introduction to *The Field of Cultural Production,* 15.

32. Derrida, *Specters of Marx,* 6–7.

Chapter Four

1. Joseph Roach has suggested to me that the closest analogue to *Angels in America* on the American stage is, in fact, *Uncle Tom's Cabin,* with its tremendous popularity before the Civil War, its epic length, and its skill in addressing the most controversial issues of the time in deeply equivocal ways.

2. John Lahr, "The Theatre: Earth Angels," *The New Yorker,* December 13, 1993, 133.

3. Jack Kroll, "Heaven and Earth on Broadway," *Newsweek,* December 6, 1993, 83; Robert Brustein, "Robert Brustein on Theatre: *Angels in America, " The New Republic,* May 24, 1993, 29.

4. John E. Harris, "Miracle on Forty-eighth Street," *Christopher Street,* March 1994, 6.

5. Frank Rich, "Critic's Notebook: The Reaganite Ethos, with Roy Cohn as a Dark Metaphor," *New York Times,* March 5, 1992.

6. John Clum, *Acting Gay: Male Homosexuality in Modern Drama* (New York: Columbia University Press, 1994), 324.

7. Tony Kushner, *Angels in America: A Gay Fantasia on National Themes. Part One: Millennium Approaches* (New York: Theatre Communications Group, 1993), 95. All further citations will be noted in the text.

8. Frank Rich, "Following an Angel for a Healing Vision of Heaven and Earth," *New York Times,* November 24, 1993.

9. Clum, *Acting Gay,* 314.

10. Tony Kushner, *Angels in America: A Gay Fantasia on National Themes. Part Two: Perestroika* (New York: Theatre Communications Group, 1994), 56. All further citations will be noted in the text.

11. See, for example, Andrea Stevens, "Finding a Devil Within to Portray Roy Cohn," *New York Times,* April 18, 1993.

12. Terry Eagleton, *Walter Benjamin; or, Towards a Revolutionary Criticism* (London: Verso, 1981), 177.

13. Walter Benjamin, "Theses on the Philosophy of History," in *Illuminations,* ed. Hannah Arendt, trans. Harry Zohn (New York: Schocken Books, 1969), 253. All further citations will be noted in the text.

14. Tony Kushner explains: "I've written about my friend Kimberly [Flynn] who is a profound influence on me. And she and I were talking about this utopian thing that we share—she's the person who introduced me to that side of Walter Benjamin. . . . She said jokingly that at times she felt such an extraordinary kinship with him that she thought she was Walter Benjamin reincarnated. And so at one point in the conversation, when I was coming up with names for my characters, I said, 'I had to look up something in Benjamin—not you, but the prior Walter.' That's where the name came from. I had been looking for one of those WASP names that nobody gets called anymore." David Savran, "The Theatre of the Fabulous: An Interview with Tony Kushner," in *Speaking on Stage: Interviews with Contemporary American Playwrights,* ed.

Philip C. Kolin and Colby H. Kullman (Tuscaloosa: University of Alabama Press, forthcoming).

15. Jacques Lacan, "The Signification of the Phallus," in *Ecrits: A Selection*, trans. Alan Sheridan (New York: W. W. Norton, 1977), 286.

16. Elisabeth A. Grosz, *Jacques Lacan: A Feminist Introduction* (London: Routledge, 1990), 74, 67.

17. Benjamin maintained a far less condemnatory attitude toward the increasing technologization of culture than many other Western Marxists. In "The Work of Art in the Age of Mechanical Reproduction," for example, he writes of his qualified approval of the destruction of the aura associated with modern technologies. He explains that because "mechanical reproduction emancipates the work of art from its parasitical dependence on ritual, . . . the total function of art" can "be based on another practice—politics," which for him is clearly preferable. Walter Benjamin, "The Work of Art in the Age of Mechanical Reproduction," 224.

18. Although one could cite a myriad of sources, this quotation is extracted from Friedman, "Once Again."

19. Krishan Kumar, "The End of Socialism? The End of Utopia? The End of History?" in *Utopias and the Millennium,* ed. Krishan Kumar and Stephen Bann (London: Reaktion Books, 1993), 61; Francis Fukuyama, *The End of History and the Last Man,* quoted in Kumar, "The End of Socialism?" 78.

20. Friedman, "Once Again."

21. Ahmad, *In Theory,* 69. Ahmad is summarizing this position as part of his critique of poststructuralism.

22. David Richards, "'Angels' Finds a Poignant Note of Hope," *New York Times,* November 28, 1993.

23. Benedict Anderson, *Imagined Communities: Reflections on the Origin and Spread of Nationalism* (London: Verso, 1991), 6.

24. See Lawrence Kohl, *The Politics of Individualism: Parties and the American Character in the Jacksonian Era* (New York: Oxford University Press, 1989).

25. Klaus J. Hansen, *Mormonism and the American Experience* (Chicago: University of Chicago Press, 1981), 49–50.

26. See Ernest R. Sandeen, *The Roots of Fundamentalism: British and American Millenarianism, 1800–1930* (Chicago: University of Chicago Press, 1970), 42–58.

27. Hansen, *Mormonism and the American Experience,* 52.

28. Joseph Smith, quoted in Hansen, *Mormonism and the American Experience,* 72.

29. See Richard L. Bushman, *Joseph Smith and the Beginnings of Mormonism* (Urbana: University of Illinois Press, 1984), 170.

30. Hansen, *Mormonism and the American Experience,* 119.

31. For a catalog of this violence, see Jan Shipps, *Mormonism: The Story of a New Religious Tradition* (Urbana: University of Illinois Press, 1985), 155–61.

32. Hansen, *Mormonism and the American Experience,* 124–26.

33. Hansen, *Mormonism and the American Experience,* 27, 66.

34. Anderson, *Imagined Communities,* 10–11.

35. Timothy Brennan, "The National Longing for Form," in *Nation and Narration,* ed. Homi K. Bhabha (London: Routledge, 1990), 50.

36. Anderson, *Imagined Communities,* 10–11.

37. Hans Kohn, *Nationalism: Its Meaning and History* (Princeton: Van Nostrand, 1965), 11.

38. Sacvan Bercovitch, "The Problem of Ideology in American Literary History," *Critical Inquiry* 12 (1986): 642–43, 645.

39. Despite the 1994 Republican House and Senate victories (in which the Republicans received the vote of only 20 percent of the electorate) and the grandstanding of Newt Gingrich, the country remains far less conservative on many social issues than the Republicans would like Americans to believe. See Thomas Ferguson, "G.O.P. $$$ Talked; Did Voters Listen?" *The Nation,* December 26, 1994, 792–98.

40. Hazel Carby, "The Multicultural Wars," in *Black Popular Culture,* a project by Michele Wallace, ed. Gina Dent (Seattle: Bay Press, 1992), 197.

41. Bercovitch, "The Problem of Ideology in American Literary History," 649.

42. Lauren Berlant, *The Anatomy of National Fantasy: Hawthorne, Utopia, and Everyday Life* (Chicago: University of Chicago Press, 1991), 31.

43. Barry Brummett, *Contemporary Apocalyptic Rhetoric* (New York: Praeger, 1991), 37–38.

44. Lahr, "The Theatre: Earth Angels," 132.

45. David Román, "November 1, 1992: AIDS/Angels in America," in *Acts of Intervention: Gay Men, U.S. Performance, AIDS* (Bloomington: Indiana University Press, 1998), 213.

46. This is corroborated by Kushner's own statements: "The strain in the American character that I feel the most affection for and that I feel has the most potential for growth is American liberalism, which is incredibly short of what it needs to be and incredibly limited and exclusionary and predicated on all sorts of racist, sexist, homophobic and classist prerogatives. And yet, as Louis asks, why has democracy succeeded in America? And why does it have this potential, as I believe it does? I really believe that there is the potential for radical democracy in this country, one of the few places on earth where I see it as a strong possibility. It doesn't seem to be happening in Russia. There is a tradition of liberalism, a kind of social justice, fair play and tolerance—and each of these things is problematic and can certainly be played upon in the most horrid ways. Reagan kept the most hair-raising anarchist aspects of his agenda hidden and presented himself as a good old-fashioned liberal who kept invoking FDR. It may just be sentimentalism on my part because I am the child of liberal-pinko parents, but I do believe in it—as much as I often find it despicable. It's sort of like the Democratic National Convention every four years: it's horrendous and you can feel it sucking all the energy from progressive movements in this country, with everybody pinning their hopes on this sleazy bunch of guys. But you do have Jesse Jackson getting up and calling the Virgin Mary a single mother, and on an emotional level, and I hope also on a more practical level, I do believe that these are the people in whom to have hope." Savran, "The Theatre of the Fabulous," 24–25.

47. See Tony Kushner, "A Socialism of the Skin," *The Nation,* July 4, 1994, 9–14.

48. Berlant, *The Anatomy of National Fantasy,* 32.

49. Bercovitch, "The Problem of Ideology in American Literary History," 644.

50. Sedgwick used this phrase during the question period that followed a lecture at Brown University, October 1, 1992.

51. Barbara Janowitz, "Theatre Facts 93," *American Theatre,* April 1994, 4–5.

52. Bourdieu, "The Field of Cultural Production," 37–38.

53. Johnson, introduction to *The Field of Cultural Production,* 15.

54. Bennett L. Singer and David Deschamps, eds., *Gay and Lesbian Stats: A Pocket Guide of Facts and Figures* (New York: New Press, 1994), 32.

55. Eve Kosofsky Sedgwick, *Epistemology of the Closet* (Berkeley: University of California Press, 1990), 48–59.

56. It is not the subjects who comprise a bona fide suspect class (like African Americans) that are suspect, but rather the forces of oppression that produce the class. For an analysis of the legal issues around equal protection, see Janet Halley, "The Politics of the Closet: Towards Equal Protection for Gay, Lesbian, and Bisexual Identity," *UCLA Law Review* (June 1989): 915–76.

Chapter Five

1. Michiko Kakutani, "Myths, Dreams, Realities—Sam Shepard's America," *New York Times,* January 29, 1984.

2. For an account of "masculinity therapy," see R. W. Connell, "Drumming Up the Wrong Tree," *Tikkun* 7, no. 1 (1992): 31–32.

3. David Gelman, "Making It All Feel Better," *Newsweek,* November 26, 1990, 67.

4. Sam Shepard, *Mad Dog Blues,* in *The Unseen Hand and Other Plays* (New York: Bantam, 1986), 257.

5. For an excellent critique of *Iron John* and its many errors, see Connell, "Drumming Up the Wrong Tree," 31–36.

6. Robert Bly, *Iron John: A Book About Men* (Reading, MA: Addison-Wesley, 1990), 2. All further citations will be noted in the text.

7. For an analysis of "Momism," see Elaine Tyler May, *Homeward Bound,* 74–75.

8. The most detailed descriptions (and devastating critiques) of the weekend retreats are Doug Stanton's "Inward, Ho!" *Esquire,* October 1991, 113–22; and Jon Tevlin's "Of Hawks and Men: A Weekend Retreat in the Male Wilderness," *Utne Reader,* November/December 1989, 50–59.

9. Susan Faludi, *Backlash: The Undeclared War against American Women* (New York: Crown, 1991), 310.

10. Gordon quoted in Jack Thomas, "The New Man: Finding Another Way to be Male," *Boston Globe,* August 21, 1991, 46.

11. Trip Gabriel, "Call of the Wildmen," *New York Times Magazine,* October 14, 1990, 39; Lance Morrow, "The Child Is Father of the Man," 53.

12. For a fine analysis of gender politics during the height of the Cold War, see Elaine Tyler May, *Homeward Bound,* especially 68–75.

13. Mel Gussow, "Shepard's 'Suicide in B Flat' Presented by Yale Repertory," *New York Times,* October 25, 1976; Martin Tucker, *Sam Shepard* (New York: Continuum, 1992), 108; Don Shewey, *Sam Shepard* (New York: Dell, 1985), 111.

14. Gussow, "Shepard's 'Suicide in B Flat'"; Jack Kroll, "High-Pressure Jazz," *Newsweek,* November 8, 1976, 109.

15. Sam Shepard, *Suicide in B-Flat,* in *Fool for Love and Other Plays* (New York: Bantam, 1984), 216. All further citations will be noted in the text.

16. Sigmund Freud, *Beyond the Pleasure Principle,* trans. and ed. James Strachey (New York: W. W. Norton, 1961), 35.

17. Laplanche and Pontalis, *The Language of Psycho-Analysis,* 97, 102. For an important elaboration of Freud's theory of the death instinct, see Jean Laplanche, *Life and Death in Psychoanalysis,* trans. Jeffrey Mehlman (Baltimore: Johns Hopkins University Press, 1976), 103–24.

18. Sigmund Freud, *Three Essays on the Theory of Sexuality,* trans. and ed. James Strachey (New York: Basic Books, 1962), 25.

19. Sigmund Freud, "The Economic Problem in Masochism," in *General Psychological Theory,* ed. Philip Rieff, trans. James Strachey (New York: Collier, 1963), 194.

20. Laura Mulvey, "Visual Pleasure and Narrative Cinema," *Screen* 16, no. 3 (1975): 14.

21. Theodore Reik, *Masochism in Sex and Society,* trans. Margaret H. Beigel and Gertrud M. Kurth (New York: Grove, 1962), 49.

22. Reik, *Masochism in Sex and Society,* 50.

23. Reik, *Masochism in Sex and Society,* 77.

24. Reik, *Masochism in Sex and Society,* 80.

25. Reik, *Masochism in Sex and Society,* 78.

26. Reik, *Masochism in Sex and Society,* 59.

27. Freud, *Three Essays on the Theory of Sexuality,* 25.

28. See, for example, the case histories in Reik, *Masochism in Sex and Society,* 50–51, 80.

29. Reik, *Masochism in Sex and Society,* 49.

30. Shooter's self-contained narrative (based on a Sufi fable) of the moth and the candle in *Action* is merely a mystical revision of this master narrative. See Sam Shepard, *Action,* in *Fool for Love and Other Plays* (New York: Bantam, 1984), 185.

31. Judith Butler, *Subjects of Desire* (New York: Columbia University Press, 1987), 48.

32. Bonnie Marranca, "Alphabetical Shepard: The Play of Words," in *American Dreams: The Imagination of Sam Shepard,* ed. Bonnie Maranca (New York: Performing Arts Journal Publications, 1981), 30. See also Florence Falk, "Men without Women: The Shepard Landscape," in *American Dreams: The Imagination of Sam Shepard,* ed. Bonnie Maranca (New York: Performing Arts Journal Publications,

1981), 90–103; and Lynda Hart, "Sam Shepard's Pornographic Visions," *Studies in the Literary Imagination* 21, no. 2 (1988): 69–82.

33. Kakutani, "Myths, Dreams, Realities—Sam Shepard's America."

34. Falk, "Men without Women," 97; Alan Shepard, "The Ominous 'Bulgarian' Threat in Sam Shepard's Plays," *Theatre Journal* 44 (March 1992): 60.

35. Eve Kosofsky Sedgwick, *Between Men: English Literature and Male Homosocial Desire* (New York: Columbia University Press, 1985), 3.

36. For a demonstration of homophobia in Shepard's writing, see Alan Shepard, "The Ominous 'Bulgarian' Threat in Sam Shepard's Plays."

37. Sam Shepard, *The Tooth of Crime*, in *Seven Plays* (New York: Bantam, 1981), 241, 236.

38. Carol Rosen, "Silent Tongues: Sam Shepard's Explorations of Emotional Territory," *Village Voice*, August 4, 1992, 36.

39. Sigmund Freud, "Instincts and Their Vicissitudes," in *The Complete Psychological Works of Sigmund Freud*, ed. James Strachey (London: Hogarth Press, 1957), 14:127–28.

40. Laplanche and Pontalis, *The Language of Psycho-Analysis*, 317.

41. Sam Shepard, *Action*, 182, 190.

42. Reik, *Masochism in Sex and Society*, 177.

43. Kaja Silverman, *Male Subjectivity at the Margins* (New York: Routledge, 1992), 326.

44. William H. Chafe, *The Unfinished Journey: America Since World War II* (New York: Oxford, 1986), 438.

45. See James F. Scott, "Brown and Bakke: The Relation between Judicial Decisions and Socioeconomic Conditions," *Phylon* 41, no. 3 (1980): 240–46.

46. "How the Justices Disagreed," *Time*, July 10, 1978, 10.

47. Quoted in "Bakke Wins, Quotas Lose," *Time*, July 10, 1978, 15.

48. Robert L. Allen, "The Bakke Case and Affirmative Action," *The Black Scholar*, September 1977, 9.

49. Kevin P. Phillips, letter to the *Atlantic*, January 1979, 77.

50. Allen, "The Bakke Case and Affirmative Action," 11.

51. For an analysis of this change, see Fredric Jameson, "Periodizing the 60s," in *The Ideologies of Theory: Essays 1971–1986*, vol. 2, *The Syntax of History* (Minneapolis: University of Minnesota Press, 1988), 178–208.

52. Jameson, "Periodizing the 60s," 185.

53. Jerrold M. Starr, "The Peace and Love Generation: Changing Attitudes toward Sex and Violence among College Youth," *Journal of Social Issues* 30, no. 2 (1974): 80.

54. Tom Wolfe, *The Right Stuff* (New York: Farrar, Straus, and Giroux, 1979), 24.

55. See Don Shewey, "Building Bridges at Buffalo Gap," *Common Boundary*, September/October 1992, 23–31.

56. Ellis Cose, "To the Victors, Few Spoils," *Newsweek*, March 29, 1993, 54.

57. Quoted in David Gates, "White Male Paranoia," *Newsweek*, March 29, 1993, 51.

58. Quoted in Gates, "White Male Paranoia," 50.

Chapter Six

My thanks to Susie Schmeiser for her shrewd and nuanced reading of *In the Summer House,* which gave me the impetus to write this essay.

1. Tennessee Williams, *Memoirs* (New York: Bantam, 1976), 201.

2. William Hawkins, "'Summer House' Built to Last," *New York Theatre Critics' Reviews* 14, no. 27 (1953): 169.

3. Hawkins, "'Summer House' Built to Last," 169.

4. Walter F. Kerr, "Theater: 'In the Summer House,'" *New York Theatre Critics' Reviews* 14, no. 27 (1953): 170.

5. Robert Coleman, "'In the Summer House' Opens at Playhouse," *New York Theatre Critics' Reviews* 14, no. 27 (1953): 168.

6. These citations are taken from assorted reviews collected in *New York Theatre Critics' Reviews* 14, no. 27 (1953): 168–71; and Millicent Dillon, *A Little Original Sin: The Life and Work of Jane Bowles* (New York: Holt, Rinehart and Winston, 1981), 227.

7. See especially Phelan, *Unmarked.*

8. Jill Dolan, "'Lesbian' Subjectivity in Realism: Dragging at the Margins of Structure and Ideology," in *Presence and Desire: Essays on Gender, Sexuality, Performance* (Ann Arbor: University of Michigan Press, 1993), 159.

9. Martha Vicinus, "'They Wonder to Which Sex I Belong,'" in *The Lesbian and Gay Studies Reader,* ed. Henry Abelove, Michele Aina Barale, and David M. Halperin (New York: Routledge, 1993), 433.

10. See Kaier Curtin, *"We Can Always Call Them Bulgarians": The Emergence of Lesbians and Gay Men on the American Stage* (Boston: Alyson, 1987); and Sinfield, *Out on Stage.*

11. Jane Bowles, *In the Summer House,* in *My Sister's Hand in Mine: The Collected Works of Jane Bowles* (New York: Noonday Press, 1995), 286. All further citations will be noted in the text.

12. This paradigm is clearly based on René Girard's elaboration of triangular desire in his *Deceit, Desire, and the Novel: Self and Other in Literary Structure,* trans. Yvonne Freccero (Baltimore: Johns Hopkins University Press, 1965).

13. See Sedgwick, *Between Men.*

14. Butler, *Gender Trouble,* 63.

15. Freud, "Mourning and Melancholia," 153.

16. Butler, *Gender Trouble,* 57.

17. Freud, "Mourning and Melancholia," 159.

18. Freud, "Mourning and Melancholia," 159.

19. Butler, *Gender Trouble,* 63.

20. See Elaine Tyler May, *Homeward Bound,* 74–75.

21. See Judith Halberstam, *Female Masculinity* (Durham: Duke University Press, 1998), 118–39.

22. Butler, *Gender Trouble,* 123.

23. See Esther Newton, "The Mythic Mannish Lesbian: Radclyffe Hall and the New Woman," in *Hidden from History: Reclaiming the Gay and Lesbian Past,* ed.

Martin Duberman, Martha Vicinus, and George Chauncey Jr. (New York: Meridian, 1990), 288.

24. Eustace Chesser, quoted in Sinfield, *Out on Stage,* 270.

25. Gayle Austin, *Feminist Theories for Dramatic Criticism* (Ann Arbor: University of Michigan Press, 1990), 70.

26. As Charlotte Goodman notes, this relationship does in fact echo Bowles's relationship with Helvetia Perkins while she was writing the play. Perkins was "a woman approximately her mother's and Gertrude's age, who prodded Jane to choose between herself and Paul Bowles, just as Molly is forced to choose between herself and Lionel." Charlotte Goodman, "Mommy Dearest: Mothers and Daughters in Jane Bowles's *In the Summer House* and Other Plays by Contemporary Women Writers," in *A Tawdry Place of Salvation: The Art of Jane Bowles,* ed. Jennie Skerl (Carbondale: Southern Illinois University Press, 1997), 72.

27. See Alexander Doty, "Everyone's Here for Love: Bisexuality and *Gentlemen Prefer Blondes,*" in *Flaming Classics* (New York: Routledge, 2000), 131–53.

28. Austin, *Feminist Theories for Dramatic Criticism,* 70.

29. Quoted in Goodman, "Mommy Dearest," 71.

30. Quoted in Goodman, "Mommy Dearest," 71.

Chapter Seven

This essay is dedicated to the memory of Linda Dorff, on whose panel at ATHE I first had the opportunity and the pleasure of delivering it.

1. Tennessee Williams, "Desire and the Black Masseur," in *Collected Stories* (New York: Ballantine, 1986), 222. All further citations will be noted in the text.

2. "Mixed Fiction," *Time,* January 3, 1955, 76.

3. Freud, *Three Essays on the Theory of Sexuality,* 23; Freud, "The Economic Problem in Masochism," 196; Reik, *Masochism in Sex and Society,* 9.

4. Silverman, *Male Subjectivity at the Margins,* 192.

5. Silverman, *Male Subjectivity at the Margins,* 189.

6. Freud, "The Economic Problem in Masochism," 193.

7. Freud, "The Economic Problem in Masochism," 193.

8. See David Savran, *Communists, Cowboys, and Queers: The Politics of Masculinity in the Work of Arthur Miller and Tennessee Williams* (Minneapolis: University of Minnesota Press, 1992).

9. Reik, *Masochism in Sex and Society,* 49.

10. Freud, "The Economic Problem in Masochism," 195.

11. Reik, *Masochism in Sex and Society,* 228.

12. See Robert F. Gross, "Consuming Hart: Sublimity and Gay Poetics in *Suddenly Last Summer,*" *Theatre Journal* 47 (May 1995): 229–51.

13. Tennessee Williams, *Suddenly Last Summer,* in *Four Plays* (New York: Signet, 1976), 64. All further citations will be noted in the text.

14. Freud, "The Economic Problem in Masochism," 200.

15. Butler, *Bodies That Matter,* 3.

16. Allen Ginsberg, "Howl," in *Collected Poems, 1947–1980* (New York: Harper and Row, 1984), 127–28.

17. David Harvey, *The Condition of Postmodernity: An Enquiry into the Origins of Cultural Change* (Cambridge, Mass.: Blackwell, 1990), 135.

18. Karl Marx, *Capital: A Critique of Political Economy,* trans. Ben Fowkes (New York: Vintage, 1977), 1:165.

Chapter Nine

I want to thank Malina Brown for asking me to direct an independent study on American drama with her at Brown University, in which I first came up with the idea for this essay.

1. Interview with Paula Vogel, in *The Playwright's Voice: American Dramatists on Memory, Writing, and the Politics of Culture,* by David Savran (New York: Theatre Communications Group, 1999), 273.

2. Interview with Vogel, 280.

3. Interview with Vogel, 275.

4. Ron Vawter, quoted in the epigraph to Paula Vogel, *The Baltimore Waltz,* in *The Baltimore Waltz and Other Plays* (New York: Theatre Communications Group, 1996), 3.

5. Paula Vogel, *How I Learned to Drive,* in *The Mammary Plays: How I Learned to Drive, The Mineola Twins* (New York: Theatre Communications Group, 1998), 90.

6. Paula Vogel, *The Mineola Twins,* in *The Mammary Plays: How I Learned to Drive, The Mineola Twins* (New York: Theatre Communications Group, 1998), 96.

7. Lynda Hart, "Introduction: Performing Feminism," in *Making a Spectacle: Feminist Essays on Contemporary Women's Theatre,* ed. Lynda Hart (Ann Arbor: University of Michigan Press, 1989), 2.

8. Quoted in "Interview—Paula Vogel by Matt Wolf," *The Observer* (London), June 21, 1998.

9. Hart, "Introduction," 2.

10. Hart, "Introduction," 3–4.

11. Esther Newton, *Mother Camp: Female Impersonators in America* (Chicago: University of Chicago Press, 1979), 37.

12. Newton, *Mother Camp,* 3 n.

13. Jean Laplanche and J.-B. Pontalis, *The Language of Psycho-Analysis,* trans. Donald Nicholson-Smith (New York: W. W. Norton, 1974), 206.

14. Freud, cited in Laplanche and Pontalis, *The Language of Psycho-Analysis,* 206.

15. Laplanche and Pontalis, *The Language of Psycho-Analysis,* 205–6.

16. Paula Vogel, *And Baby Makes Seven,* in *The Baltimore Waltz and Other Plays* (New York: Theatre Communications Group, 1996), 66.

17. Vogel, *The Baltimore Waltz,* 34.

18. Grosz, *Jacques Lacan,* 32.

19. Jacques Lacan, "The Mirror Stage," in *Écrits: A Selection,* trans. Alan Sheridan (New York: W. W. Norton, 1977), 4.

20. Vogel, *How I Learned to Drive,* 7. All further citations will be noted in the text.

21. Grosz, *Jacques Lacan,* 116.

22. Lacan, "The Signification of the Phallus," in *Écrits: A Selection,* trans. Alan Sheridan (New York: W. W. Norton, 1977), 287.

23. Lacan, "The Signification of the Phallus," 285.

24. Michael Moon and Eve Kosofsky Sedgwick, "Divinity: A Dossier, A Performance Piece, A Little-Understood Emotion," in *Tendencies,* by Eve Kosofsky Sedgwick (Durham: Duke University Press, 1993), 221.

25. Diane Hamer, quoted in Teresa de Lauretis, *The Practice of Love: Lesbian Sexuality and Perverse Desire* (Bloomington: Indiana University Press, 1994), 31.

26. Sedgwick, *Epistemology of the Closet,* 68.

27. Tennessee Williams, *The Glass Menagerie* (New York: New Directions, 1949), 115.

28. Rebecca Mead, "Drive-By Shooting," *New York,* April 7, 1997, 46.

29. Alisa Solomon, "feminism-something," *Village Voice,* December 29, 1988, 55.

30. Moon and Sedgwick, "Divinity: A Dossier," 220.

31. Vogel, *The Baltimore Waltz,* 52.

Index